SIGN LANGUAGE INTERPRETING FOR THEATRE

SIGN LANGUAGE INTERPRETING FOR THEATRE

A Collaborative Approach

LYNNETTE TAYLOR, STEPHANIE FEYNE,
AND CANDACE BROECKER PENN

Gallaudet University Press
Washington, DC

Gallaudet University Press
gupress.gallaudet.edu

Gallaudet University Press is located on the
traditional territories of Nacotchtank and Piscataway.

Printed in the United States of America
Second printing December 2025

ISBN: 978-1-954622-78-4 (paperback)
ISBN: 978-1-954622-77-7 (ebook)

The Library of Congress Cataloging-in-Publication data for this title
can be found online at http://www.loc.gov.

∞ This paper meets the requirements of ANSI/NISO Z39.48–1992 (Permanence of Paper).

Front cover art: Christine Sun Kim, preparatory drawing for *Bounce Back*, 2023, at the Institute of Contemporary Art, Los Angeles. Courtesy of the artist. Reproduced with permission.

Cover description: Book cover with a black background and all white text. At the top the title is in a serif font in all caps: Sign Language Interpreting for Theatre. Below the title is a drawing by Christine Sun Kim, which features three hands that are palm-up, with two parallel lines that form arches between the hands. Below the drawing is the subtitle in a serif font: A Collaborative Approach. Below the subtitle are the author's names in a serif font in small caps: Lynnette Taylor, Stephanie Feyne, Candace Broecker Penn.

Cover design by Michel Vrana.

To the Deaf communities and the theatres that opened the doors

and

To Alan Champion, who enriched our lives and our work

CONTENTS

NOTE TO READERS

Some of the scripts utilized as examples in this book include references to racism, violence, abortion, and the rise of Nazism in the Weimar Republic. Readers who may be sensitive to these topics, please take note.

PREFACE

The three of us were practicing at the onset of interpreted theatre in the 1970s. Interpreters across the country were starting to step into this venue, often interpreting solo, often without theatre background, and often with no support. These early forays into interpreted theatre drew from our experience as community interpreters. Our work would not have been possible without the warmth and support of the Deaf community—both the greater community that gave us our language and shares its culture with us, and the New York City Deaf community that participates regularly in shaping our work and guiding our path. Our philosophy is rooted in bringing communities together.

New York City, with theatre aplenty, was fertile ground to experiment and support the development of interpreted theatre. Two key organizations, Theatre Development Fund (TDF) and Hands On Sign Interpreted Performances, provided the infrastructure and supports for local interpreted theatre. By the early '90s, recognizing that there was a need for formal training to expand the pool of interpreters for the theatre, TDF received a grant from the National Endowment for the Arts (NEA) to establish a national Interpreting for the Theatre Seminar in partnership with The Juilliard School. The three of us (Candace, Stephanie, and Lynnette) and our colleague Alan Champion developed and co-taught the national weeklong seminar for its entire twelve years. Writing this book would not have been possible without the opportunities offered by Lisa Carling, the director of the Theatre Access Project (TAP) at TDF, and our dear friend and colleague, Beth Prevor, executive director of Hands On.

In the way of things, Candace's and Lynnette's mothers were both named Betty, both single mothers, and both Deaf. They were the first to show us how to travel to and fro between the worlds we came from, and instilled in us a love of the arts and of sign language. Stephanie was raised by her single father, a lyricist, who imbued in her a love of language play. She found her way to theatre interpreting through Lou Fant's "Ameslan" courses at California State University, Northridge (CSUN). She learned American Sign Language (ASL) and traveled between language and culture with us. And however that dance of destiny is choreographed, it brought us together. Over the past forty years, we three have had the good fortune to collectively interpret more than six hundred shows!

Our friend and colleague, Alan Champion, was also raised by a Deaf single mother. Though he is no longer with us, his work lives on in the spirit of this book. He was one of the "greats." Deaf audiences often came to shows to see *him* interpret. From the Phantom to Jean Valjean and Dame Edna, his virtuosity shone through. What Alan brought to every show and to the signing and nonsigning communities was the importance of relationships. He understood that relationships and goodwill form the cornerstone of any endeavor. For him, the theatre was a place to invite more people in, not keep them out. He infused the theatre space with a kind of warmth that made it feel like a small town gathering in a Broadway house. We miss him.

We want to recognize and offer thanks to the National Theatre of the Deaf, which introduced signed language theatre "from New York to New Delhi"[1] for the enjoyment of signing and nonsigning audiences. These artistic endeavors, along with those of other Deaf artists, "bring signed languages into the family of human languages. . . . and accord them the respect they deserve."[2]

This book was written with practitioners in mind. We offer ways to think about the performative nature and complexity of discursive interpretation, with the considerations of designing translations with the live performance and audience in mind. This book covers Deaf involvement, transmodality, artistry, teaming, partnering with the stage, performative elements as part of translatory consideration, interpreting in the virtual space, and building an ecosystem. The collaborative theatre interpreting strategies in this book are informed by the art of theatre, translation theory, and interpreting practice.

This book is based on our practice in New York City, in which a team of three to four interpreters works with a Deaf Director of Interpreters (DOIs) to craft a live interpretation that is performed in a designated place near the stage for a signing audience that is seated near them. For purposes of this book, we will use the term Director of Interpreters rather than other terms in current use. Our examples are drawn from the NYC arts scene. We did not research all the practices across the country. We are cognizant that other theatres may adopt other approaches, such as shadow and zoned interpreting—or even a solo interpreter. These choices will not be addressed in this book. This book also does not address providing tactile or protactile interpretation. Others who have expertise in this specialized area can guide theatres and interpreters in those best practices.

Although others have written on the topic of interpreted theatre, we are focusing on the dialogic or collaborative aspects of the practice. We mention some of the contributors in the field and encourage readers to further research this area. The earliest writings on this subject were from Julie Gebron in 1996 and an entire issue of the Registry of Interpreters for the Deaf (RID) Views in 1998. More recent authors in the United States and the United Kingdom include Michael Richardson, Kaitlyn Mielke, Miriam Ganz Horowitz, Lyndsay Snyder, Danny MacDougall, Peter Llewellyn-Jones, and Siobhán Rocks. There is a link to each of their works in the references section titled "Previous Works on Theatre Interpretation." We look forward to additional conversations, inquiry, and publications on the nature of theatre translation and interpretation.

Recognizing that language is constantly changing in response to the culture, politics, and the social narrative of the time, we have chosen to capitalize the names of linguistic and cultural groups, including "Deaf," with a few intentional exceptions. In addition, when writing about historical events, some of the language used when referring to community identity is the language used by those communities at the time.

This book comes from lived experience and decades spent in conversation with Deaf community members and colleagues about the nature of interpreted theatre. We were still writing during the 2020 Covid pandemic when theatres went dark, a life-altering experience. We acutely felt the loss of these shared cultural and community physical gathering spaces. Corinna Hill describes Ray Oldenburg's concept of "third places"[3] in communities as "crucial for fostering social interactions, creating a sense of belonging, and enhancing overall well-being. Third spaces transcend familial, geographic, generational, and spatial differences as they bring together people."[4]

The importance of these "third spaces" (in our case, the theatre and the rehearsal rooms where we gathered) became even more apparent. We no longer took them for granted but recognized what the loss of these sacred spaces meant in our lives. If anything, it reinforced our thinking about the importance of collective, collaborative, generative interpreted theatre.

What began as the seed idea more than a decade ago has transformed in response to the changing social/political narrative we live in. The United States, and indeed the world, has become more polarized, more intolerant, and more isolated. The idea of community, collaboration, and avenues for conversation across sectors seems even more critical to our survival as a species, to our survival as a compassionate society.

Our wish is that this book will spark further conversations on the nature of interpreted theatre, its importance, and its best practices.

Lynnette, Stephanie, and Candace

Notes

1. "National Theatre of the Deaf History," 2014, ntd.org. 2014, https://old.ntd.org/ntd_history.html.
2. Swarthmore College, "Commencement 2016: Carol Padden," YouTube, May 30, 2016, https://www.youtube.com/watch?v=gJQJDlfs1YI.
3. "Ray Oldenburg," Project for Public Spaces, December 31, 2008, https://www.pps.org/article/roldenburg.
4. Corinna Sara Hill, "Without Our Deaf Clubs, Where Will We Go?" (Paper presented at American Historical Association 138th Annual Meeting, New York City, January 5, 2025).

1

Origins of Interpreted Theatre: Civil Rights and Deaf Artists

It is important to situate the origins of interpreted theatre as part of a larger conversation about social inequity, identity exploration, and artistic exploration, which was happening in the 1970s. Judy Heumann, often referred to as the "mother of the disability movement," captured the zeitgeist of the time with this statement in her memoir: "I simply refused to accept what I was told about who I could be. And I was willing to make a fuss about it."[1]

Of course, interpreted theatre didn't just come out of nowhere. It came about because Deaf people of all cultures, bodies, and classes were leading us there, mapping new terrain in the cultural life of the United States.

The history we share here comes from our lived experience and is one small part of the whole constellation. We hope others will come forward to share stories from the communities of which we were not a part.

Cultural and Social Context

> "If theatre is an exercise in humanity, an exploration in the bounds of it, then it should and must include everyone."
>
> —Levi Holloway, playwright, *Grey House*[2]

When the three of us (Lynnette, Stephanie, Candace) and our colleague Alan Champion were beginning to interpret for the theatre during the vibrant Deaf arts scene of the 1970s and '80s, artists, actors, playwrights, dancers, and musicians were exploring art through a Deaf lens. In many ways, the reason we began interpreting in the theatre was not only from our love of the arts, but it was also because we wanted to go to the theatre with our friends, families, and fellow artists. There had always been pockets of interpreted performances in communities, church activities, and local events or culturally vibrant areas where the Deaf community wanted to partake of the local art scene.

We interpreted as we would in casual, intimate settings with friends and family. We sat next to each other in the audience and offered extemporaneous interpretations of the show. There were no captions at that time and no formalized systems for theatre interpretation. We were participating in what Rachel Kolb and Timothy Y. Loh call "Friendterpreting."[3]

During these moments, our friends, family, or partners would chime in with questions, ask for clarification, provide clarification, or spontaneously revise our interpretation into a version that was more complete, nuanced, and artistic. It was a collaborative interpreting effort.

There were times when an interpretation simply couldn't be called forth. All we could offer was a puzzled brow and a shrug, indicating, "I have no idea how to interpret this!" Nearby hearing audience members showed they weren't always happy with our clandestine interpreting by shushing us or making faces. But we carried on in spite of them, lost in the joy of theatre, in the shared exploration of making meaning.

These early experiences shaped our practice, philosophy, and approach to interpreted theatre. Over time, we began to note when clarification was being asked for, what kind of clarification was being asked for, and when to watch the stage. We were learning what the language and rhythms of the conversation were between the audience, interpreter, and the stage.

These formative conversations became the foundation of our work. As interpreters in an emerging field, we were being guided by community relationships, Deaf community norms, and expectations. Our interpreting developed as a collaborative shared conversation predicated on the understanding that we are part of the Deaf community. As such, our practice was guided by a belief that we had to perform ethically, responsibly, and collaboratively. Our place in this conversation was not only to bring access but also to join in the effort to dismantle discriminatory practices. In this book, we have tried to articulate how these interactions shaped our thinking and approach to interpreted theatre.

SOCIAL ACTIVISM

> "We the people"—the utterance, the chant, the written line—is always missing some group of people it claims to represent.[4]
>
> —Judith Butler, *Notes Toward a Performative Theory of Assembly*

Interpreted theatre came about during a time of major cultural and political changes in United States. During the late 1960s and throughout the '70s, people were taking their issues to the streets, demanding individual and collective rights through the Civil Rights, feminist, gay and lesbian, American Indian Movement, and National Farmworkers Association movements, as well as upheaval over the US involvement in the war in Vietnam. These protests paved the way for disability rights advocates to also take to the streets demanding an end to systems of discrimination. These movements calling for social justice mobilized people to change the landscape of United States.

The Rehabilitation Act of 1973, the first federal civil rights protection for people with disabilities, was based on the language of previous civil rights laws that protected women and minorities.[5] In support of this law, Senator Hubert Humphrey stated, "The time has come to firmly establish the right of disabled Americans to dignity and self-respect as equal and contributing members of society and to end the virtual isolation of millions of children and adults."[6]

While its passage gave the appearance of a positive step, four years later, the teeth of the law—the 504 regulations[7]—still had not been signed and implemented. When Health, Education, and Welfare (HEW) Secretary Joseph Califano failed to sign the regulations by the deadline of April 5, 1977, the Deaf community joined with disability activists in sit-ins and other political actions around the country. Deaf activist Frank Bowe, director of the American Coalition of Citizens with Disabilities (ACCD), led a number of protests throughout the United States.[8]

After a dramatic twenty-eight-day sit-in in San Francisco (the longest nonviolent occupation of a federal building in US history), Secretary Califano capitulated, and Section 504 was finally signed on April 28, 1977.[9] This law served as the basis for the later Americans with Disabilities Act (ADA).

While the 2020 documentary by Nicole Newnham and James LeBrecht, *Crip Camp*,[10] had fantastic footage of many of the Camp Jened alumni involved in the movement, what was not seen as clearly were the Deaf activists who were also present and engaged in the sit-in and the movement. Bay Area Deaf individuals who occupied the building were Dale Dahl, Olin Fortney, and Steve McClelland, putting their lives and careers in jeopardy by occupying the federal building along with their hearing counterparts. Other supporters from the Deaf community went in and out of the building, including Dr. Frank Hochman (the first American Deaf physician), Ken Mikos, Eddie and Joanne Jauregui, and Marlon and Linda Kuntze, among others. Deaf leaders such as Bob Davila and Fred Schrieber participated in strategic meetings and media sessions. When the phone lines were cut, the Deaf activists inside the building became the front line of communication and would sign through the windows to those outside, maintaining communication with colleagues and supporters beyond the walls.

While interpreters Joe Quinn, Jadine Murello, and Lynnette Taylor were mainstays in the building, others came in at different times, as the strategic meetings and public hearings were ongoing. Don Hester and Don Renzulli were some of the other Bay Area interpreters who volunteered their time. Unfortunately, there are no records of all the interpreters. A small delegation from the building (including Jadine Murello, Lynnette Taylor, Olin Fortney, and Steve McClelland) went to confront Secretary Califano and President Carter in Washington, DC.

The Longmore Institute's Virtual Tour of the 504 Sit-in states, "On April 28, 1977, Joseph Califano, Secretary of HEW, signed the Section 504 regulations. Protesters in San Francisco stayed for two more days to clean up and say good-byes. Everyone was energized by this huge accomplishment; there would be no turning back."[11] The "Victory" photo from the *San Francisco Examiner* features Deaf activists Olin Fortney and Steve McClelland holding the Victory banner, along with activist Al Walla on the right, and captures the excitement of the day (figure 1.1).

Figure 1.1. Occupiers and their supporters in San Francisco's Civic Center Plaza celebrate the signing of the Section 504 regulations. Fang family *San Francisco Examiner* photograph archive, © The Regents of the University of California, The Bancroft Library, University of California, Berkeley. This work is made available under a Creative Commons Attribution 4.0 license.

Lynnette recalls,

> It was pure serendipity that I walked into the 504 building. I was at the San Francisco Catholic Charities Deaf Services when a call came through with an emergency request for an interpreter. While I was a heritage signer, I did not have a lot of experience interpreting at the time. Eddie Jauregui, the agency coordinator, handed me the phone and Scott Leubking introduced himself as a disabled activist, and asked if I would be willing to come down and interpret for a protest that was underway in front of the San Francisco Federal Building, home to the Department of Health Education and Welfare. "What kind of demonstration?" I asked, and he said, "We're fighting for the passage of the 504 regulations, a civil rights act for disabled people." Those three words, "civil rights act," changed my life. I had never thought of access as a right. Suddenly I understood my whole history in a different way. My family's lack of access was a denial of rights and of systemic exclusion. Of course, I said yes to what I thought would last a few hours. I ended up spending twenty-eight days occupying the HEW building.
>
> It was during my time in the building that I learned to interpret. My language moved from being the language of my mother, my home language, to a language of my own. It was now being shaped by peer-to-peer interactions and informed by a whole community of political activists. I am forever grateful to all those who were patient and took their time teaching me the craft of and love for interpreting, Deaf and non-Deaf alike.
>
> It was in this building, where a new kind of community was forming (people across all genders, identities, socioeconomic statuses, races, ethnicities, disabilities, etc.), that I began to understand there are many ways to live a life. Anything can happen when you bring a

> community together to envision, then enact change, and, in Judith Butler's words, lay "claim to a public sphere by which one has been abandoned."[12]

Alliances across such a diverse constituency weren't always easily formed. Many meetings went late into the night discussing the pros and cons of some of the provisions in the regulations and its impact on individual communities.[13] The Deaf representatives had concerns about the conflation of physical access with communication access—that language rights were being subsumed under the banner of disability rights and felt that was a precarious political alliance.

Given the broad constituency and diverse communities, each with different interests and needs, this was the first time there were cross-disability conversations. Overcoming the differences and the fears of inequities within the coalition, the coming together is what led to the success of this movement.

Lynnette continues,

> I began to realize that nothing is static—access is not static and/or monolithic—but rather dynamic and responsive to individuals, communities, structures, and social narratives. It is only by sharing proximate and intimate spaces together that we can step out of the constraints of exclusion. For the 504 Sit-In Twentieth Anniversary celebration, Ken Stein, lifelong disability advocate/activist/historian, called it "one of the greatest and most successful 'people's movements' of the twentieth century."[14]

The struggle for civil rights and the experiences of oppression resonated with the Deaf community's experience. In 1975, Tom Humphries coined the term "audism"[15] to define and frame the historical and cultural oppression that Deaf people face in education and mainstream society. In 2012, his definition was published in the *Merriam-Webster Dictionary.*[16]

A Whole New World

With the signing of Section 504 of the Rehabilitation Act came a whole new world of access for the Deaf community. The early linguistic research that recognized American Sign Language (ASL) as a language and, by extension, the Deaf community as a cultural body, ushered in a powerful presence of the signing body in the everyday world. Deaf people's entry into these new venues led the interpreting community into these new arenas. This, in turn, meant a whole new world for sign language interpreters.

Up to this point in time, sign language interpreters primarily worked in the community, service industry, or education. The field of interpreting was nascent and the pool of working interpreters quite small. Historically, interpreters had come from within the Deaf community and learned their skills through shared social and community interactions. With the passage of the 504 Regulations and Public Law 94-142 (the Education of All Handicapped Children Act, later the Individuals with Disabilities Education Act), the demand for interpreters grew overnight. Suddenly, the demand surpassed the supply, and the first interpreter programs, with teachers who were Deaf or children of deaf adults (Codas), were established.

All of a sudden, we were everywhere. Interpreters, Deaf people, and sign language were gaining entry into the cultural landscape of the United States. As the Deaf community moved into new frontiers, our work as interpreters became more visible in public spaces. Interpreters unwittingly became part of the representation of the broader Deaf community. An interpreter is a visible reminder that there are more ways of being and communicating. The presence of the interpreter literally changed the living architecture of public spaces, signifying a new audience in the cultural arena.

COMING OF AGE

During the vibrant '70s and '80s, the world of interpreting and the Deaf community were dramatically shifting. In art, poetry, performance, theatre, music, film, and television, Deaf artists were being seen. For the first time since the golden era of George W. Veditz, the Deaf world was experiencing a renaissance of intellectual and artistic expression. It was during this transformative time that the arts, sciences, and the Deaf community turned their eyes to the language of sign and the Deaf experience. This exploration led to discoveries that would challenge the United States's conceptions of Deafness, language, and culture.

It was only in 1965 that linguistic research by William Stokoe, Dorothy Sueoka Casterline, and Carl G. Croneberg verified ASL as a legitimate language. Padden and Humphries comment, "scientific investigations into signed languages . . . have confirmed what in some sense Deaf people have known all along: that signed languages are human languages with the potential for rich expression."[17] This recognition inspired many Deaf artists to create works about the many years of oppression and discrimination against their language as well as the pathological view of the Deaf body.

Worlds were changing, identities expressed and/or re-expressed, and power claimed from these new insights. People were exploring their intersectional lives in these new spaces and communities. The San Francisco gay and lesbian community made access a priority for their events, everything from rallies and performances to the boisterous Gay Day parade. Olivia Records, a women's record company based in Oakland, California, made a commitment to have all their concerts interpreted,[18] making Holly Near, Meg Christian, and Cris Williamson familiar names in the Deaf women's community. Going a step further, the a cappella ensemble Sweet Honey in the Rock included interpreter Shirley Childress Johnson as a company member[19] as they toured across the country. Equal access in public spaces was understood to be desegregation,[20] a fundamental right to be won. Interpreters became symbolic icons for access, an emblem of rights secured.

Just as Tom Humphries's term "audism" captured the experience of oppression in words, Betty Miller's art captured it in images. Her work focused completely on the Deaf experience, depicting the oppression Deaf people face at the hands of hearing people, as well as on exhibiting the joy of sign that can be found throughout the Deaf community. Artwork that focused entirely on the Deaf experience was an entirely new form in the 1970s and came to be called "Deaf View/Image Art" (De'VIA).[21] Miller, an early pioneer of this form of art, was considered the "mother" of the "De'VIA movement."[22]

Miller's painting *Ameslan Prohibited* (1972) addressed the discriminatory educational practices that denied generations of Deaf people their natural right to signed language. She depicts a row of puppet-like children shackled with hearing aid apparatuses, void of expression, eerily conjuring these Deaf children as ventriloquist's puppets of the colonizer. Miller's works reframe the master's view of "benevolence"[23] and reveal it as a form of colonization of the Deaf body. Her art became a symbol for resistance, a cry to throw off the shackles, and a cry for a culture to speak their truth in their own language, and not (in Adrienne Rich's term) the "oppressor's language."[24]

Miller branched out into performance as well and went on to become one of the cofounders of Spectrum, Focus on Deaf Artists,[25] in Texas in 1975. Surdists United explains, "Spectrum was a Deaf artists' colony in the mid-1970s that predates the coining of the term Deaf View/Image Arts, but it was important in the evolution of the term, concept and assertion of a genre about the Deaf experience."[26]

DEAF THEATRE

The wellspring for Deaf theatre in the United States was, of course, The National Theatre of the Deaf (NTD). This first professional acting company of Deaf performers was founded in 1967. Original company members included Bernard Bragg, Charles Corey, Gil Eastman, Phyllis Freilich. Dorothy Miles, Mary Beth Miller, Audrey Norton, Harold Palmer, June Russi, Tim Scanlon, Andrew Vasnick, Joe Velez, and Ralph White, with hearing company members Lou Fant, Ed Fearon, Joyce Lasko, and Will Rhys, with David Hays as artistic director.[27] Their touring productions gave the American public a glimpse into the mind and eye of the Deaf community.

With its 1971 production of *My Third Eye*,[28] the NTD broke free from the bounds of translated works and created an original work in ASL. Humphries and Padden explain, "the language itself [became] both the medium and the subject of the performance."[29] This was the first time that NTD's translations were developed from ASL into English.

Candace Broecker Penn had the good fortune of seeing a performance during the inaugural season of NTD when it was presented at Gallaudet University. As *Time* magazine's review in 1967 said, "They paint pictures in the air, it is language."[30] Candace recalls,

> The power of the language, movement, and theatricality on the stage was incredibly inspiring. As a child, I had always loved theatre and seeing NTD at that moment was truly life-altering, especially because I come from a Deaf family and Sign Language was my language. From then on, I dreamed of working with the company as a speaking actor. After attending their summer

> school program in 1976, I was honored to be invited to join as a company member in 1977 and toured with them for three and a half years, a truly transformative experience in my life. *Sir Gawain and The Green Knight*, adapted by the Jamaican poet Dennis Scott for the NTD Little Theatre of the Deaf, was the first show I was in. It premiered at The Kennedy Center as part of the first National Children's Art Festival.[31]

Candace's first full company production, *The Three Musketeers*, was an original adaptation directed by Joe Layton. In "Deaf Artists Backstage," Caverly interviews former NTD cast member, Joseph Sarpy. Caverly comments, "I was very surprised and impressed to learn that NTD [as early as 1977] had cast three Black actors as the lead musketeer trio, you—Joseph Sarpy, CJ Jones, and Jimmy Turner."[32] Sarpy recalls, "It was inspiring and it felt 'really good'; I was proud that Black deaf actors were chosen to be the leads, it was really cool. It showed audiences that as Black actors, we can take on these roles. Working with CJ and Jimmy was great, working on our characters, developing our repartee, sparring and fencing with each other, we were a tight ensemble, and audiences loved the show."[33]

NTD hosted the first Deaf Playwrights Conference and continued to produce new works both in ASL and English. The play *Counterfeits*, written by NTD resident playwright, Shanny Mow, was nominated for the American Theatre Critics Association New Play Award.[34] NTD launched its professional drama school in 1967, and "a number of NTD alumni started their own Deaf-theatre companies across the country and abroad."[35]

In 1979, NTD created Theatre in Sign (TIS) specifically for Deaf audiences. The first production was *The Gin Game* by D. L. Coburn with actors Patrick Graybill and Phyllis Freilich, under the direction of Linda Bove. "The play was presented entirely in American Sign Language without any voice actors, much to the delight of deaf playgoers, who appreciated the more natural rhythm of signs."[36] This was a departure from the tradition of NTD, where translations were designed to be spoken and signed for a hearing and Deaf audience. Translations without the additional constraint of matching the spoken modality freed the actors to explore the natural discourse of ASL in their performances. This play was later performed by other Deaf actors around the country.

Starting in the 1970s, innovative productions were seen in Los Angeles, including Dorothy Miles's *Love of Seven Dolls* (written in ASL),[37] *Godspell*,[38] *Peppermint Fantasies*,[39] and *Trojan Women*.[40] Stephanie Feyne recalls, "I was thrilled and honored to be cast in these four shows. I was so fortunate to be in the right place at the right time with amazing people. Couldn't have had a better entry into Deaf arts."[41] Additional LA productions with Deaf artists included *Twelfth Night* (translated by Lou Fant),[42] and *Equus* (with Lewis Merkin).[43] Further exploration of *Twelfth Night* occurred in 1999. Yale University funded the ASL Shakespeare Project, pulling together a team of Deaf and hearing actors as translators. *Twelfth Night*, directed by Peter Novak, was performed at Amaryllis Theatre in Philadelphia, and a digital recording of that production in a DVD format is available through Gallaudet University Press.[44]

Deaf theatre was establishing itself across the country. Cleveland's Fairmount Theatre of the Deaf (founded in 1975, later the Cleveland SignStage Theatre)[45] was "the first residential sign language theatre company in the United States."[46] The broadcast of their 1981 production *Beauty and the Beast* won an Emmy.[47]

In 1979, the New York Deaf Theatre (NYDT) was formed "by a group of Deaf actors and theatre artists who wanted to create opportunities for the production of a dramatic art form that was not found elsewhere in New York City: plays in ASL."[48] Notable early NYDT artists included Charley McKinney and Alan Barwiolek (the performing duo "CHALB"), Mary Beth Miller, Dorothy (Dot) Miles, and Sam Edwards, among others. NYDT produced works by Deaf playwrights, including *A Play of Our Own* by Dorothy Miles, who directed this production, as well as Bernard Bragg's *Tales from a Clubroom.* They also established the Sam Edwards Deaf Playwright competition and produced works by some of the winners.

Wanting to present stories based on the life experiences of Deaf and hard of hearing people of color, Deaf artists Michelle Banks, Opal Gordon, Monique Holt, and Christopher Smith founded the Onyx Theatre in 1989 in New York City, the first Deaf theatre for people of color in the United States. Banks explains she chose its name because "Onyx is a black stone—the black represents people of color, and the stone represents Deafness."[49] Their production of Jaye Austin Williams's play, *A Not So Quiet Nocturne,* was workshopped at the Vineyard Theatre in 1997.[50]

Over the past three decades, Deaf theatre companies have continued to proliferate across the country, including Deaf Austin Theatre (DAT), Deaf Spotlight, Deaf West Theatre, and Visionaries of the Creative Arts (VOCA), among others.

ARTISTRY IN ASL

Artistry has a long history in ASL. Some of the earliest ASL translations on record were created by Deaf individuals in response to attacks on signed languages, both to preserve and protect their beloved signed language and to assert Deaf people's human right to their own language. These translations emerged as a form of resistance, a declaration of their language's worth, an assertion of identity, and a weapon against language oppression.

The Milan Conference of 1880, an international convention of educators for the deaf at which only a few deaf educators were present, banned the use of signed language in the education of the deaf. "As a result, deaf teachers lost their jobs, as there was an overall decline in deaf professionals, like writers, artists, and lawyers,"[51] and the impact of this decision is still felt today.

In the wake of this decision, in 1910, George W. Veditz, the seventh president of the National Association of the Deaf (NAD), embarked on a mission to preserve signed language. At that time, the NAD was concerned that "pure" sign language might disappear under the pressures of oralism and began a film campaign to document signed language presentations "so that future generations might see master signers of the past. *The Preservation of Sign Language* was part of a collection of films produced by the Motion Picture Committee of the NAD specifically to preserve early ASL on film from 1910 through 1920"[52] and raised $5,000 (equivalent to more than $166,000 in 2025) for this project. Veditz documented Deaf leaders presenting translations of poetry, biblical passages, and popular stories. Veditz's memorable quote from the 1913 film, *The Preservation of Sign Language,* "As long as we have deaf people we will have sign language" has long been the inspiration of many a Deaf artist.

By the 1970s, artistry in ASL was being explored in other genres. Ella Mae Lentz and Clayton Valli, two early ASL poets, were paving the way for a new medium, ASL poetry. Lentz explains, "I thought poetry must be written. I never thought it could be created in ASL. . . . When I was in high school, I had a Deaf teacher, Eric Malzkuhn, who encouraged us to explore the creative potential of sign language."[53] Clayton Valli was the "first to develop a kind of taxonomy of ASL poetry, replete with its equivalents of the line, rhyme, and other parameters."[54]

Deaf poets claimed their genre of ASL poetry by discarding the conventional sign for "poetry" (produced with the same movement and placement as the sign for "music," which implied a spoken/written form), replacing it with a sign emanating from the heart. It "reflected the sensibilities of our work; the collective experiences of oppression and love for our language, culture, and community."[55]

In 1984, ASL poetry began a dialogue with Beat poet, Alan Ginsberg, when Jim Cohn organized a Deaf–Beat Summit on the National Technical Institute for the Deaf (NTID) campus.[56]

> Ginsberg asked for an ASL translation of the famous juxtaposition from "Howl"—the words "hydrogen jukebox." Professor [Robert] Panara offered a translation into signed English . . . Professor [Patrick] Graybill volunteered a translation into ASL that was visually precise, vivid, memorable, and spontaneous . . . afterwards ASL poets began to emerge in earnest with a new kind of poetry that had certain formal and thematic compatibilities with Beat Literature, a crossing over effect that had not occurred in past American Deaf poetic history.[57]

Bernard Bragg, performer, actor, and founding member of the NTD, integrated the mimetic and cinematic features of ASL in his approach to "visual vernacular" storytelling, a term he coined in the 1960s.[58] Building from this tradition, ASL storyteller and linguist Sam Supalla took the exploration of ASL storytelling one step further, adding close-ups, pans, quick cuts, and dissolves, introducing new and exciting cinematic grammar to ASL.[59] This exploration of visual language talking to visual language was a new innovation in ASL storytelling conventions.

Inspired by the advent of Music Television (MTV), a medium that made music visual, Rita Corey, Ed Corey, and Bob Hiltermann (with frequent collaborator Marjorie Tanzar) created a signing music performance group, Musign,[60] and took the ultimate icon of hearing culture, MTV music, into the realm of the Deaf experience. They emulated the MTV style as they signed the songs. Pop culture was fast becoming part of the vocabulary. It was hot, fresh, and a new venue and exploration for Deaf artists. Not satisfied with interpreting the music of others, a few years later, Deaf musicians Bob Hiltermann and Ed Corey went the next step with Steve Longo and created their own band, Beethoven's Nightmare,[61] challenging cultural assumptions that only hearing people create music.

Many of these artists appeared on stage for a one-night performance, *Sign On*,[62] showcasing their work as performance art in San Francisco in 1983. This sold-out event was produced by Art Com / La Mamelle, a contemporary art space with support from the theatre department of San Francisco State University, and the San Francisco Public Library. The performers were Ben Bahan, Ella Mae Lentz, Mary Beth Miller, Musign (Rita Corey, Ed Chevy, and Bob Hilterman), Sam Supalla, and Nat Wilson as Emcee, with original music composed by Phil Perkins. This staged performance led to the making of the short film, *Language Landscape*,[63] in 1988, bringing their work to a wider audience. Made a few years later, *The Treasure*[64] features the poetry of Ella Mae Lentz and chronicles her journey to becoming an ASL poet. The live performance and both films were directed by Lynnette Taylor.

In the late '80s, recognizing, in the words of Fanny Yeh, "This is the time to do it, right now," three women—Sue Gill-Doleac, Rita Corey, and Fanny Yeh—founded the National Deaf Dance Theatre, exploring the worlds of sign language, dance, and music.[65] Around the same time, Irvine Stewart was watching music videos on Vh1, Yo!, and MTV and was inspired to form an all-male Black Deaf dance troupe in Washington, DC. Original members include Irvine Stewart, Warren "Wawa" Snipe, and Fred Beam. Wawa explains, "Irvine wanted something different from ballet, jazz, and modern dance and more related to rap, hip hop, and more." Stewart on how the Wild Zappers was born: "I got the idea from the music video of Michael Jackson's 'Beat It.' . . . That's Black culture! . . . I wanted *that* in the dance."[66] This vibrant form of entertainment has continued through to the present. A recent example from the Kennedy Center was the 2021 Livestream: Deaf Enlightenment and Arts Festival, which featured performers DJ SupaLee, Sunshine 2.0, Evon Black, Fred Beam, and Ronnie Bradley.[67]

Another work challenging the colonial pathological narrative of the Deaf body comes from storyteller Ben Bahan, who—in his powerful work, *Bird of a Different Feather*—addresses the ethics and consequences of the rise of the cochlear implant industry and genetic engineering through his story of a bird whose family decides to have surgery done to the fledgling to make him "normal."

DEAF TALENT ON THE BIG AND SMALL SCREENS

Even Big Bird got in on the act. Linda Bove appeared as a regular on *Sesame Street* (1975–2002).[68] Her charismatic smile and personality inspired millions of viewers to learn sign language. Bove, in an interview on WNYC radio talks about the importance of authentic representation. "When a hearing actor plays a Deaf character, audiences are denied a more authentic experience . . . [An] audience . . . may not know . . . the portrayal they are given . . . may or may not be accurate."[69] Bove stressed that authentic representation was critical because without it, "you're perpetuating cultural . . . and linguistic misunderstandings."[70] And millions of viewers must have felt the same way, for they responded to her authenticity by embracing sign language and Deaf people as part of the fabric of American life. Sesame Street has continued the relationship with young Deaf audiences. In a relationship brokered by NTD, Sesame Street brought in Deaf director Jules Dameron, who directed sixteen videos on Sesame Street's YouTube site, featuring Deaf signing performers alongside the Sesame Street family.[71]

In 1978, Deaf Media produced *Eye Music* (with Ella Mae Lentz, Howie Seago, Stephanie Feyne, and several others), winning a Northern California Emmy.[72] Next, emulating a *Sesame Street* format, Deaf Media produced *Rainbow's End*,[73] the first nationally televised program for Deaf children, with three seasons airing on Public Broadcasting Service (PBS) in 1979, 1981, and 1983. A robust creative team with Deaf talent (Freda Norman as SUPERSIGN, writer Howie Seago, director Jane Norman, and a stellar Deaf cast) won an Emmy Award, and their episode "Rules, Laws, and the U.S. Constitution" was cited by the US Commission for the Bicentennial of the Constitution as exemplary programming and is currently used by the Supreme Court in its public programming.[74]

During the 1970s and 1980s, several other award-winning signed television productions were being aired. The San Francisco Bay Area produced several television shows in ASL. Audrey Norton and, later, Joyce Lynch were anchorwomen for a local signing news program in San Francisco, California, *NewSign 4*, which aired during the National Broadcasting Company's (NBC) *The Today Show* on KRON TV, winning an Emmy in 1973.[75] Beginning in 1974, Ed Ingraham produced a sign language talk show, *Silent Perspectives*, with rotating Deaf hosts and discussions on Deaf interests with Deaf and hearing guests, interpreted into English for hearing viewers, and even catering to young audiences with performances by the "Happy Handfuls."[76] *Silent Perspectives* won an Emmy Award in its first season.[77] On the East coast, Gallaudet produced a weekly talk show, *Deaf Mosaic* (1985–1995), hosted by Gil Eastman and Jane Norman, which received eighteen Emmy Awards.[78]

In 1979, "*. . . and Your Name is Jonah*,"[79] a made-for-television movie starring Sally Struthers, James Woods, and a young Jeffrey Bravin, depicted a family's struggle with their son's Deafness until they embrace sign language and the Deaf community, and by doing so, embrace their Deaf son. In an interview with Lynnette Taylor, Nora Tegni shared that this film inspired her Argentinian family to move to the United States where they felt their son would have more opportunities. They enrolled their son in a Deaf school and the family learned sign language.[80] This exemplifies the power of art, narrative, and representation that can shape realities and dream new worlds.

Two more films exploring Deaf and hearing family dynamics soon followed. The first was *Love is Never Silent* in 1985,[81] starring Ed Waterstreet, Phyllis Freilich, Lou Fant, and Mare Winningham. Deaf performer Julianna Fjeld was one of the coproducers. This television film won a Primetime Emmy Award for Outstanding Drama. In 1989, Marlee Matlin and Lee Remick starred in *Bridge to Silence*,[82] which included Phyllis Freilich, Bob Hilterman, Nigel Howard, and Anthony Natale, along with Candace Broecker Penn.

Deaf artists were expressing a language that was not the speech of assimilation, but the language of possibility. As early as 1975, *Deafula*, an indie movie written and directed by Deaf performer Peter Wolf, was "probably the first horror film shot using ASL,"[83] predating *A Quiet Place* by more than forty years.

Lest we forget, Ernest Marshall, the first Deaf filmmaker, produced his first feature in 1937 and continued producing films for decades. His films incorporated sign language and centered on the lives of Deaf characters. They had title cards, just as seen in the silent movies. Later, he added subtitles for nonsigning audiences and even had a bouncing ball move across the subtitles for the lyrics of signed songs. Marshall traveled across the United States, bringing his films to Deaf clubs, schools, and churches, only stopping with the advent of captioned television in the 1980s.[84]

DEAF TALENT ON BROADWAY

In 1978, Deaf actor Bruce Hlibok had a starring role in The Public Theater's production of Elizabeth Swados's *Runaways.*[85] This show soon moved to Broadway, which made Hlibock the first Deaf actor to portray a Deaf character on a Broadway stage.[86] Unbeknownst to many, the first Deaf appearance on Broadway occurred in 1943. The Gallaudet Drama Troop had mounted a signed production of *Arsenic and Old Lace,* and when they visited New York City, Eric Malzkuhn wrangled permission for the Gallaudet cast to perform their signed version for one night on the Fulton Theatre's stage (which was running that very show).[87]

Then, in 1980, Mark Medoff's award-winning *Children of a Lesser God* premiered on Broadway.[88] Starring Phyllis Freilich and John Rubenstein, this play explores whether love can overcome cultural obstacles. Freilich walked away with a Tony for Best Actress,[89] becoming the first Deaf performer to win the coveted award in theatre. Director Kenny Leon's 2018 Broadway revival of *Children of a Lesser God* starred Lauren Ridloff and Joshua Jackson. Following in the footsteps of her predecessor, Ridloff's performance was recognized with a Tony nomination for Best Actress.[90] In 1986, *Children of a Lesser God* was made into a film with Marlee Matlin in the role of Sarah and William Hurt in the role of James. For her performance, Matlin received the Best Actress Award that year.[91]

With the original production of *Children of a Lesser God* came the beginnings of theatres offering interpretation. Deaf audiences were eager to see themselves reflected onstage and in sign language. The show had scenes that were only spoken, and therefore, needed interpretation. While the Broadway production was not interpreted, the national tour was. Soon after, Broadway followed suit, with the Theatre Development Fund (TDF) providing interpreted theatre.

Sign Language Interpreting on Broadway

In New York City, Linda Lowy, project coordinator for TDF's Theatre Access Project (TAP), received funding to conduct a one-year study to investigate the viability of interpreted theatre, providing interpreted shows aligned with TDF's mission, to "enable diverse audiences to attend live theatre and dance in all their venues."[92] As part of her research, Lowy attended signed language interpreted performances in "Boston, Washington, Los Angeles, St. Paul, Minneapolis, and Atlanta."[93]

According to Lowy, "initial efforts to interest producers in this novel kind of audience building began in the fall of 1979. Early response was receptive but somewhat tentative. However, on the morning after *Children of a Lesser God* won the 1980 Tony Awards for Best Play, Best Actor, and Best Actress, Miss Lowy was on the phone making a new pitch for TAP's boldest endeavor,"[94] and the powers that be were now interested in offering Broadway's first interpreted performance.

"In good theatrical tradition," Lowy explains, "the project began with auditions."[95] Carole Lazorisak, a Deaf instructor, and Candace Broecker Penn, a certified interpreter and former NTD actor, were on the TDF panel that auditioned the first interpreters for Broadway, looking for ability in interpretation, translation, and performance. The auditioners were asked to interpret both a short scene with live actors as well as a song. Lowy recalls, "Of the twenty professional sign language interpreters who tried out, five were chosen."[96]

On December 2, 1980, *The Elephant Man*[97] at the Booth Theatre became the first Broadway production to be interpreted in sign language. The interpreters were

ABOUT THE INTERPRETERS

PAM MAYNARD interpreted on Broadway for *Miss Saigon*, as a participant in the TDF/Juilliard "Signing for the Theatre" program last fall. This production of Annie marks her first full-length interpreting debut. She is currently president of NYC Metro RID and has worked with the Deaf community for 11 years as a freelance interpreter.

Pam Maynard

JON WOLFE NELSON interpreted on Broadway for *Victor/Victoria*, *Miss Saigon* (TDF/Juilliard "Signing for the Theatre" program); and recently Off-Broadway for *The Devils* at New York Theatre Workshop. Other credits include New York Deaf Theatre's Language of One at the Vineyard Theatre, touring productions with National Theatre of the Deaf, and interpreting for Ellen Degeheres live at the Guarde Theatre in New London, CT. Jon is an actor as well as a freelance interpreter.

Jon Wolfe Nelson

KATHLEEN D. TAYLOR has interpreted on Broadway for *Bring in 'da Noise, Bring in 'da Funk*; *Seven Guitars; Smokey Joe's Cafe;* and *Jelly's Last Jam* and Off-Broadway for *Born to Sing!* Other interpreting credits include *A Laying of Hands* and *There's Butter But No Bread* at the Onyx Theatre, *Once on This Island* at the GateWay Playhouse; *Telling Tales* and *Body of Work* with Pickney Productions, and the children's television show *Story Barn* of ECLA. She studied theatrical interpreting at Juilliard in the TDF co-sponsored "Signing for the Theatre" program.

Kathleen D. Taylor

CHARACTER NAME SIGNS

Queen
"A" on left shoulder

Miss Hannigan
Sign for scold with "H"

Oliver Warbucks
"W" on side of head

Rooster Hannigan
Sign for rooster on forehead

Grace Farrell
"G" sideways upward over heart

Sandy
Sign for yellow

Figure 1.2. Centerfold of *Playbill* insert for the sign language interpreted performance of *Annie,* June 26, 1997. Drawings by Jean Jenkins. Used by permission, Theatre Development Fund. All rights reserved by the original rights holders.

Alan Champion and Phil Giambaresi.[98] Since then, thousands of shows have been interpreted in New York and across the country.[99]

In the early days of interpreted theatre in New York City, Broadway houses would include the interpreter photos and bios in the TDF inserts in *Playbill,* recognizing the interpreting event as a part of the whole production. For several years, illustrations of the major characters' name signs were included in the program. De'VIA artist Ann Silver was one of the artists creating these illustrations.

At times, these included creative titles of the play illustrated in sign language, showing a commitment to the artistic delivery of sign language programming. These classic ASL line drawings often paired the name sign with the interpreter who was interpreting for that character. The images in figures 1.2 and 1.3 are examples of *Playbill* insert art.

Figure 1.3. Composite of *Playbill* Insert titles for sign language interpreted performances. Drawings by Jean Jenkins. Used by permission, Theatre Development Fund.

The first Broadway show with Deaf interpreters was *Having Our Say*,[100] a show about African American centenarian sisters. The Deaf interpreters were Patrice Joyner-Creamer and Michelle Banks, with hearing interpreter Lisa Weems working as their "feed" interpreter/co-interpreter.[101] In an interview, Joyner-Creamer recalled that when she was asked, she said yes, even though she had no idea what this work would entail. She recalls that, while the process was challenging and time-consuming, it was worth it.[102]

Since then, Deaf interpreters have often been part of the interpreting teams on and Off-Broadway. While not an exhaustive list, New York City interpreting teams have included Kailyn Aaron-Lozano, Michelle Banks, David Bowell, Joshua Castille, James Caverly, April Cheng, Patrice Joyner-Creamer, Frank Dattolo, Patrick Graybill, Lewis Merkin, Jackie Roth, Zavier Sabio, Janna Sweeney, Christopher Tester, Anne Tomasetti, and Alexandria Wailes.

Just as our thinking about interpreted theatre was evolving, so was the role of Deaf advisors. There was no template. Some offered feedback to the team on interpreted utterances that did and did not work. Those who had more theatre experience acted as directors by creating the character division and blocking the positions of the interpreting team during the show. Others worked as translation masters by producing a finished translation for the show that the team would try to "wear." We all learned through these various roles and approaches, which are still evolving in interpreted theatre today. (A more extensive description of the role of the Deaf advisor [now referred to as "director of interpreters"] is found in chapter 2.)

Intersection of Experimental Theatre and Interpreting

Of course, Broadway wasn't the only show in town. There has always been a lively arts scene Off-Broadway and Off-Off Broadway. While TDF was offering interpreted Broadway shows, there was a niche to be filled. Hands On Sign Interpreted Performances realized there was a budding interest from Deaf and signing audiences in the productions that were happening in these more experimental venues. Hands On was founded by four women with backgrounds in the theatre: Beth Prevor, Candace Broecker Penn, Janet Harris, and Janis Cole. Cole, a Deaf actor and translator passionate about the intersection of theatre and signed language, remembers: "I'll never forget. Candy and I went to see a play to prepare for an interpreted performance at the Circle Repertory Theatre in Greenwich Village. That was the start of an incredible journey, blending art, creativity, and inclusivity in the vibrant NYC theatre scene."[103] In an interview for *6SqFt*, executive director Beth Prevor recollected, "We [co-founders] looked at what the Theatre Development Fund was doing on Broadway with interpreting shows, but no one was focusing on the Off-Broadway and the nonprofit theatre community."[104] Hands On began by auditioning and developing a pool of interpreters whose skills were suited to interpreting for the theatre. Their combination of on- and backstage expertise, interpreting skills, and relationship with the Deaf community offered theatres the know-how to connect with this new audience.

When interviewed for this book, Prevor explained why making the arts accessible is so important, "because in this society there are still people who are not as open as they should be. Public visibility is important. Seeing Deaf people on stage and Deaf people in the audience is going to help us in more ways than we know."[105]

When David White, the artistic director of Dance Theatre Workshop (DTW), invited West Coast-based Musign (Rita Corey, Bob Hiltermann, and Ed Chevy) to perform at DTW, the budding Hands On knew that the local Deaf community would want to see this show. Prevor recalls, "We pulled out our address books and put together a list of people we knew, and that's how we created our mailing list. It just started growing from there."[106]

Hands On offered to connect DTW with Deaf audiences, volunteered their time as ushers, and provided interpreting for the pre-/post-show discussions for the audience. DTW's invitation of Deaf artists into their space spawned a longstanding collaboration between Hands On and DTW.

The first interpreted show at DTW by Hands On was the *Traveling Jewish Theatre.* The advantage of being a local organization that was well connected to the Deaf community was that Hands On knew how to reach an untapped audience that had a deep connection with this show. Tanya Towers, a residential center in lower Manhattan, was home to many Deaf Jewish Holocaust survivors. Hands On reached out to a local Deaf services organization, New York Society for the Deaf, to arrange for tickets and transportation to this show, in addition to advertising to the local Deaf community.

Given that DTW was a home for experimental theatre and dance, the artists considered the aesthetic elements of the interpreter as part of their overall piece. At times, this included the interpreter wearing costumes and makeup to be integrated into the show. What were the creative possibilities and boundaries in this interpreter/performer/space/audience relationship? If interpreters appeared in theatrical makeup and costume, would audiences feel they had overstepped their role as interpreters? Or would they feel exhilarated by seeing a new way of presenting and integrating an interpreter into the show? All of us were exploring the role and possibilities of theatre interpreting.

For Dan Hurlin's one-man show, Candace was dressed like him as she shadowed him on the stage. Alan Champion, in a sublime stroke of casting, was selected to interpret for Bloolips, a radical drag performance of satirical political comedy. The director, Betty Bourne, wanted to "find the 'gay clown' in each person" and so invited Alan to dress in drag to match the company. While Alan had no hesitation about dressing in drag, he wondered whether the Kabuki-like theatrical makeup would interfere with grammatical conveyance of ASL. In the spirit of exploration, he interpreted alongside the performers all in the same makeup, and the audience accepted it (figure 1.4).

Interpreters were exploring the line between performing and interpreting. What is the balance between honoring the performative aspects of a production and maintaining an interpreter's presence? The audience's experience was always a primary consideration—with the goal of resonance, rather than unintentional dissonance.

Bloolips with Alan Champion

Candace Broecker Penn shadowing Dan Hurlin

Figure 1.4. Interpreters integrated in DTW performances. Photos courtesy of Hands On.

This was fertile ground for innovative approaches with nontraditional placement of the interpreters, sometimes positioning them in front of, alongside, or behind and above the performers. Other strategies included choreographing the interpreters throughout the piece; at times, this was achieved by not incorporating the body at all and utilizing technology to project the interpretation onto an onstage monitor, as Mabou Mines did with Candace in their show, *Hajj*. Although not every attempt was successful, what was important was the freedom to experiment, to find new ways to express this new world of "interpreted theatre."

This relationship didn't just stop at interpreted performances. It generated more artistic possibilities. Ain Gordon costumed and choreographed interpreters Nancy Frishberg and Candace into his first production of *Women in Black and White* at DTW. He was so inspired by the integration of signed language that he went even further by creating *Epic Family Epic*, in which Deaf characters (originally played by Carole Addabbo and, later, by Lewis Merkin and Anne Tomasetti) were incorporated along with spoken word and sign language interpreters.[107]

DTW continued its relationship with Deaf and signing artists. Hands On and DTW commissioned Deaf artist Mary Beth Miller and director Lynnette Taylor to develop *I Always Wanted to be an Opera Singer*,[108] with Stephanie Feyne as the offstage voice talent. This show received enthusiastic responses from both Deaf and hearing audiences.[109]

These forays into new territory led to surprising new relationships between artists and interpreters, as well as between venues and audiences. DTW remained committed to developing audiences. They invited Deaf seniors to attend avant garde theatre! What seemed an unlikely pairing became a treasured experience of the arts.[110]

These opportunities allowed those of us in this nascent field to experiment with and to expand our understanding of interpretation. We asked questions that continue to shape our work today: How do we create for the signing audience an experience that supports a connection to the show? How do we convey culturally embedded material in an efficient manner that reflects the aesthetics and sensibilities of the performance?

Since there were no rules, we developed our approach based on the values we had learned from community interpreting. We understood that, first and foremost, an interpreter in theatre settings had to have good interpreting skills and a facile command of both ASL and English.

HOW MANY INTERPRETERS DOES IT TAKE . . .

We were also exploring how many interpreters were needed to convey the story on stage. The interpreting field during the late 1970s and early 1980s was quite different from where it is now in terms of how we understood, approached, and practiced our work. At that time, interpreting alone for three hours at a time was common practice, so interpreting solo for a three-hour play wasn't so dissimilar from anything else. However, we soon came to recognize that it was more effective to have two interpreters conveying dialogue between two characters, rather than having one interpreter role-shifting while portraying myriad characters in a play.

As time went on, we realized that, to convey the arc of a story, three interpreters were usually more effective. Most plays are not merely populated by a protagonist and an antagonist; additional characters engage in the dialogue and create alignments and conflict throughout the play. For the sake of clarity in storytelling, we found that it was more coherent and more compelling when there was a team of three interpreters: one to present the point of view of the protagonist, one for the antagonist, and one to portray the other characters or the go-between with these opposing points of view.

We came to see that the essence of all theatre is conversation (as is interpreting), and this became the foundation of our approach. The conversation had to be with the Deaf audience, the theatre, the play, the actors, and the interpreting team. This understanding led us to a more fluid and responsive approach.

The initial pool of interpreters and Deaf directors had the luxury of frequently working together, observing each other's work, and discussing our interpreting choices, leading to deeper understandings about the techniques and nuances of interpreting and the values embraced as a community of theatre interpreters.[111]

We were able to take risks, experiment, and explore because we had the good fortune to work with two important organizations in New York: TDF's TAP and Hands On Sign Interpreted Performances. These two very successful and innovative programs continue to provide quality access for interpreted shows and function as liaisons with the theatre management in order to ensure a successful interpreted event.

Training for Theatre Interpreters

Across the country, interpreters were exploring not only what interpreted theatre was but were also identifying the necessary skills to do it. In 1979, NTD company members and theatre experts collaborated with the Registry of Interpreters for the Deaf (RID) to provide a five-day workshop for interpreters in the performing arts, which was funded by the National Endowment for the Arts (NEA). Participants came from around the country. This was a one-time occurrence that culminated in a singular conferral of the Specialist Certificate in the Performing Arts (SC:PA) to ten interpreters.[112]

It would be close to twenty years before NEA funded another national training. This initiative was spearheaded by Lisa Carling, director of the Theatre Access Project at TDF in New York City, who said the inspiration came when she saw her first interpreted Broadway show: "I loved it. The interpretation was so beautiful, theatrical. . . . Having come from the Yale Drama School, it was apparent to me, even though I was not fluent in ASL, that the performance interpreter needed to have both the language skills and performing skills as well as the knowledge of the conventions of theatre." She recognized a need to expand the pool of interpreters and, therefore, for providing them training. She began a series of roundtable discussions with local Deaf performers and theatre interpreters with whom she had been working for some time.[113]

Lisa conceived of "Interpreting for the Theatre" as a collaborative effort among interpreters, actors, and the Deaf community. She contacted the Juilliard School, a preeminent school for the performing arts. Lisa and Candace Broecker Penn met with the head of the Drama Division, where they received strong support. Lisa was able to secure funding from the NEA, and the course was officially launched in 1991 as a two-semester program taught by Candace, who later brought in Alan, Lynnette, and Stephanie as instructors.

In 1998, the training was redesigned to be a week-long intensive program for interpreters in and beyond New York City, ultimately drawing participants from thrity-seven states and three countries. The curriculum developers and core instructors for the one-week intensive program were Candace Broecker Penn, Alan Champion, Stephanie Feyne, and Lynnette Taylor. In seven rigorous days, students were introduced to the NYC theatre interpreting approach.

Lisa exclaims, "We got twelve Broadway shows to agree to be used for the class projects throughout the life of the program, and an additional twelve shows that demonstrated the Interpreting for the Theatre approach. We pitched it to the theatres by saying, these are interpreters who are going to go out there and interpret your road tours. Isn't this great to have them learn from the Broadway production?"[114]

The program culminated in participants producing teamed interpretations of a segment of a Broadway show in front of an invited Deaf audience.

The Deaf community was integral to this program. They were involved from beginning to end: as screeners, translation coaches, panelists, audience members, and diagnosticians,[115] delivering individualized feedback throughout the program. In fact, there was often a one-to-one ratio of Deaf advisors to interpreter participants. Lisa recalls, "Part of the feedback we got consistently was how wonderful it was to have so much involvement from the Deaf community."[116]

The week was a whirlwind world of theatre. Participants attended an interpreted show that demonstrated our approach to interpreting for the theatre. Deaf audience members who had seen the interpreted performance were invited as panelists to share their perspective on both the play and the interpreting. Attendees discovered what audience members remembered, what caught their attention, what they liked and didn't like about a show, and what they responded to about the interpretations and the teamwork.

In addition to attending theatre daily, participants also practiced the Alexander Technique for body awareness with Juilliard instructor Lauren Schiff, while instructors Champion, Feyne, Broecker Penn, and Taylor guided them through performance techniques for interpreting, taught strategies for partnering while interpreting, and examined translation from a meaning-based approach that emphasized producing dialogic interpretation in natural ASL. Participants were exploring the ways in which their interpretations could be responsive to their team, to the audience, and to the show.

In preparing for the class project, Carling explains, "We used to walk about twenty-eight people into the theatre each night for the students to rehearse. This was no small logistical undertaking!"[117] This would not have been possible without the cooperation of the house managers and ushers, in addition to support from the theatre administrators. These relationships with the theatre personnel were integral to the success of an interpreted program.

In 2002, blogger Dave Boles interviewed Lisa Carling about the annual seminar. She stated, "What is so exceptional about this program is that in a few short years, we have helped raise the national standard for theatre sign language interpretation . . . The program not only benefits interpreters who come to study the art of theatre sign interpretation from masters of the craft but more importantly ensures a more professional quality of interpreting for audience members across the country who are Deaf."[118]

In sum, being based in New York City, a "theatre capital of the world," gave us ample opportunity to interpret both on and off Broadway, finding our way to a cohesive approach to interpreting in these venues. This book is the culmination of many years of conversations, thinking, and practice with different cohorts, communities, and artists.

We offer this book to generate more conversations and thoughts about interpreted theatre, its evolution, and its potential.

Notes

1. Judy Heumann, *Being Heumann: An Unrepentant Memoir of a Disability Rights Activist* (Beacon Press, 2020).
2. "Meet Levi Holloway of Neverbird Project," VoyageChicago.com, April 3, 2018, http://voyagechicago.com/interview/meet-levi-holloway-neverbird-project-na/.
3. Rachel Kolb and Timothy Y. Loh, "How Deaf and Hearing Friends Co-Navigate the World," *Sapiens*, August 17, 2022, https://www.sapiens.org/language/friendterpreting/.
4. Judith Butler and Stephanie Berbec, "We Are Worldless Without One Another: An Interview with Judith Butler," *The Other Journal* 27 (June 26, 2017), accessed July 24, 2024, https://theotherjournal.com/2017/06/worldless-without-one-another-interview-judith-butler/.
5. Kitty Cone, "Short History of the 504 Sit-In," Disability Rights Education and Defense Fund, accessed December 20, 2014, http://dredf.org/504-sit-in-20th-anniversary/short-history-of-the-504-sit-in/.
6. Cone, "Short History."
7. Section 504: "no otherwise qualified handicapped individual in the United States shall solely on the basis of his handicap, be excluded from the participation, be denied the benefits of, or be subjected to discrimination under any program or activity receiving federal financial assistance."
8. Paul Simmons, "Spotlight On: Dr. Frank Bowe—The Father of 504," *Rocky Mountain ADA*, September 29, 2020, https://rockymountainada.org/news/blog/spotlight-dr-frank-bowe-father-504.
9. Andrew Grim, "Sitting-In for Disability Rights: The Section 504 Protests of the 1970s," *National Museum of American History*, accessed January 29, 2023, https://americanhistory.si.edu/blog/sitting-disability-rights-section-504-protests-1970s.
10. *Crip Camp*, directed by James leBrecht and Nicole Newnham (2020; Higher Ground Productions), Netflix. Film. Higher Ground Productions.
11. "Virtual Tour | Patient No More," San Francisco State University, accessed December 8, 2024, https://longmoreinstitute.sfsu.edu/patient-no-more/virtual-tour.
12. Butler and Berbec, "We Are Worldless."
13. Lynnette Taylor, personal recollection.
14. Ken Stein, *20th Anniversary Victorious 504 Sit-In for Disability Civil Rights Celebration and Commemoration Committee*, 1997.
15. Thomas K. Humphries, "Communicating Across Cultures (Deaf-hearing) and Language Learning" (PhD diss., Union Institute and University, 1977), 12.
16. "Audism: discrimination or prejudice against individuals who are Deaf or hard of hearing," *Merriam-Webster*, accessed February 20, 2023, https://www.merriam-webster.com/dictionary/audism.
17. Carol Padden and Tom Humphries, *Deaf in America: Voices from a Culture* (Harvard University Press, 1990), 73.
18. B. J. Morris, "How Should We Archive the Soundtrack to 1970s Feminism?" *Smithsonian Magazine*, March 30, 2018, https://www.smithsonianmag.com/arts-culture/how-should-we-archive-soundtrack-1970s-feminism-180968637/.

19. Samantha M. Shapiro, "They Lives They Lived: Shirley Childress Johnson," *The New York Times*, December 18, 2017, accessed July 15, 2024, https://www.nytimes.com/interactive/2017/12/28/magazine/the-lives-they-lived-shirley-childress.html.
20. "The ADA [Americans with Disabilities Act] bans the unnecessary segregation of people with disabilities in a regulation called 'the integration mandate,'" in "Community Integration," ADA.gov, accessed June 29, 2024, https://www.ada.gov/topics/community-integration/.
21. "DE'VIA: DEAF VIEW/IMAGE ART," Museum of Deaf, accessed January 31, 2023, https://www.museumofDeaf.org/de-via.
22. "Betty G. Miller Art Pioneer," *If My Hands Could Speak*, September 6, 2011, http://ifmyhandscouldspeak.wordpress.com/2011/09/06/betty-g-miller-art-pioneer/.
23. Harlan Lane, *The Mask of Benevolence: Disabling the Deaf Community* (DawnSignPress, 1999).
24. Adrienne Rich, "Oppressor's Language" in Adrienne Rich's poem "The Burning of Paper Instead of Children," *Poetry Society*, accessed March 22, 2022, Poetry Society, https://poetrysociety.org/poems/the-burning-of-paper-instead-of-children.
25. Spectrum founders describe its goals, creation, and variety of work in this video: "Spectrum—Deaf Artists Colony," Youtube video, July 13, 2014, https://m.youtube.com/watch?v=2vkl—cR21A.
26. "DE'VIA: DEAF VIEW/IMAGE ART."
27. Stephen C. Baldwin, *Pictures in the Air: The Story of the National Theatre of the Deaf* (Gallaudet University Press, 1993).
28. *My Third Eye*, 1971, created by the O'Neill Center's The National Theatre of the Deaf, directed by Remy Charlip, Joe Chaikin, Bernard Bragg, J. Ranelli, and Joe Layton.
29. Carol Padden and Tom Humphries, *Deaf in America: Voices from a Culture* (Harvard University Press, 1990), 74.
30. Baldwin, *Pictures in the Air.*
31. Candace Broecker Penn, personal recollection. Actors in the NTD company with Candace included Tim Scanlon, Rita Corey, Patrick Graybill, Ray Fleming, Betti Bonni, Freda Norman, Janis Cole, CJ Jones, Jimmy Turner, Joseph Sarpy, Phyllis Freilich, Linda Bove, Ed Waterstreet, Ray Parks, Nat Wilson, Carol-Lee Aquiline, Carole Addabbo, Sandi Inches, Andy Vasnick, Bernard Bragg, Shanny Mow, Tim Johnson, Sam Edwards, Michael Schwartz, Bob Blumenfeld, Rico Peterson, Ben Stout, and David Fitzsimmons.
32. Gallaudet University Theatre and Dance, "Deaf Artists Backstage: Joseph Sarpy," YouTube, August 7, 2020, https://www.youtube.com/watch?v=EszHZwhB6yI&list=PLZnxsntr8dLzWx6BMfqx6f2orb5HC8glZ&index=7.
33. Gallaudet University Theatre and Dance, "DeafArtists."
34. "Shanny Mow," Deaf-theatre.com, accessed March 10, 2023, https://Deaf-theatre.com/profiles/shanny-mow/.
35. "National Theatre of the Deaf," Britannica.com, accessed February 3, 2023, https://www.britannica.com/topic/National-Theatre-of-the-Deaf/.
36. Baldwin, *Pictures in the Air*, 82.
37. *Love of Seven Dolls*, written and directed by Dorothy Miles, adapted from the novella by Paul Gallico, starred Lou Fant and Bobbie Beth Scoggins.

38. *Godspell*, composed by Stephen Schwartz, book by John-Michael Tebelak. Directed by David Bateman. Translation by the company. Touring production included a cast of twelve Deaf and hearing performers including Howie Seago and Greg Koppell.
39. *Peppermint Fantasies*, created by the LA Sign Company (LASCO) ensemble, directed by Judy Welden, performed at the Cast Theater. The performers included Lewis Merkin, Jann Goldsby, Ellice Sperber, Eileen T. K., Stephanie Feyne, among others.
40. *Trojan Women*, by Euripides. Double cast with Deaf and hearing actors, including Diana Douglas and Julianna Fjeld as Hecuba.
41. Stephanie Feyne, personal recollection.
42. *Twelfth Night*, by William Shakespeare, translated by Lou Fant, and performed by a Deaf and hearing cast.
43. *Equus*, by Peter Schaffer, directed by Sue Wolf, staged at the Pasadena Playhouse and then at the Pan-Andreas Theatre, produced by the West Coast Performing Arts Center for the Deaf. It was performed by a Deaf and hard of hearing cast with Lewis Merkin in the lead role, bringing him to the attention of casting directors as *Children of a Lesser God* was being cast.
44. "William Shakespeare's *Twelfth Night*," DVD, Gallaudet University Press, accessed January 7, 2025, https://gupress.gallaudet.edu/Books/W/William-Shakespeare-s-Twelfth-Night-DVD.
45. Jane Kaufman, "Bridging the Sound Barrier," CANVAS.com, accessed March 2, 2023, http://canvascle.com/signstage/.
46. "Deaf Theatre," San Francisco Public Library, accessed March 27, 2024, https://sfpl.org/locations/main-library/Deaf-services/Deaf-theatre.
47. "Deaf Theatre."
48. "Who We Are," NewYorkDeafTheatre.org, accessed March 1, 2023, https://newyorkDeaftheatre.org/about.
49. "Michelle Banks," Encyclopedia.com, accessed February 26, 2023, https://www.encyclopedia.com/education/news-wires-white-papers-and-books/banks-michelle.
50. "Play Production Spring 2024," *A Not So Quiet Nocturne*, accessed July 10, 2024, https://www.vocarts.org/production2023-2024/anotsoquietnocturne.
51. "Deaf History—Europe—1880: The Milan Conference," Deafhistory.eu, https://deafhistory.eu/index.php/component/zoo/item/1880.
52. "National Association of the Deaf—NAD," National Association of the Deaf, https://www.nad.org/2010/12/28/historic-nad-film-selected-for-preservation-by-library-of-congress/.
53. *The Treasure: Poems by Ella Mae Lentz*, directed by Lynnette Taylor (DawnSignPress, 1997).
54. Thomas K. Holcomb, *Introduction to American Deaf Culture* (Oxford University Press, 2012), 162.
55. *The Treasure.*
56. "The Heart of the Hydrogen Jukebox—ASL." The Allen Ginsberg Project, February 5, 2020. https://allenginsberg.org/2013/10/the-heart-of-the-hydrogen-jukebox-asl/.
57. "Deaf–Beat Summit," Poets {atj}, accessed January 18, 2025, https://www.poetspath.com/deaf_beat_summit.html.
58. "Visual Vernacular: A Global Phenomenon," Connecticut Deaf Theatre, accessed July 24, 2024, https://www.conndeaftheatre.org/posts/visual-vernacular-a-global-phenomenon.

59. Ben Bahan and Sam Supalla, *ASL Literature Series: Bird of a Different Feather and For a Decent Living* (DawnSignPress, 1994).
60. Jennifer Dunning, "Dance Musign Group," *The New York Times*, August 28, 1983, http://www.nytimes.com/1983/08/28/arts/dance-musign-group.html.
61. *Beethoven's Nightmare*, accessed February 17, 2022, http://www.beethovensnightmare.com/.
62. *Sign On,* created and directed by Lynnette Taylor (San Francisco State University, 1983). Voice interpretation by Stephanie Feyne. NEA-funded with support from Roberto Esteves, San Francisco Public Library Deaf Services, and Carolyn Beichle, Catholic Charities Deaf Services.
63. *Language Landscape*, directed by Lynnette Taylor (San Francisco Public Library, 1988).
64. *The Treasure.*
65. "Deaf Women United 'Empowerment Is Contagious—When We Light Each Other's Path, We Create a Brighter Future for All,'" Deaf Women United, Facebook, November 25, 2024, www.facebook.com/story.php?story_fbid=971985191727473&id=100067480027433&_rdr.
66. "Interview with Wild Zappers Founding Members," *Daily Moth*, February 24, 2021, https://youtu.be/0PLn8uUA_yw?si=8vR6MsrrlquEet5I.
67. "Deaf Enlightenment and Arts Festival | Kennedy Center," Kennedy Center, accessed January 25, 2025, https://www.kennedy-center.org/whats-on/millennium-stage/2021/september/deaf-culture-arts-festival/.
68. "Linda Bove," Internet Movie Database, accessed February 13, 2018, https://www.imdb.com/name/nm0100581/?ref_=fn_al_nm_1.
69. Janaya Williams, "Deaf Artists Demand Equal Stage Time," WYNC , November 27, 2009, https://www.wnyc.org/story/1382-deaf-actors-demand-equal-stage-time/
70. Williams, "Deaf Artists."
71. Jules Dameron's videos on Sesame Street YouTube: https://www.youtube.com/playlist?list=PLx1wHz1f-8J8Mk6C-bK76YaRdl26daKvU.
72. Outstanding Achievement Artistic/Historical/Cultural/Religious: Special. Eye Music—Open Studio, KQED. Producers Deaf Media—Elizabeth Mandel. "1978/1979 San Francisco/Northern California Awards," Emmysf.tv, April 21, 1979, https://emmysf.tv/files/2015/11/Emmy79PressRelease.pdf. Performers included Howie Seago, Ella Mae Lentz, Betsy Ford, Lori Seago, Stephanie Feyne, among others.
73. *Rainbow's End* regulars included Freda Norman, Howie Seago, Lou Fant, Rico Peterson, Julie Goebel, and Rico Barlow, and later Ivanetta Ikeda and Jeff Bravin, with additional characters played by CJ Jones, Mary Beth Miller, Ella Mae Lentz, Carol-Lee Aquiline, Adrian Blue, and Chuck Baird, among others. They also featured famous Deaf guests such as stuntwoman Kitty O'Neill, anchorwoman Joyce Lynch, and *Sesame Street*'s Linda Bove. Voice actors included Rico Peterson, Stephanie Feyne, and Betsy Ford, among others. Writers included Rico Peterson and Howie and Lori Seago. Directors included Jane Norman.
74. "Deaf Media Programs," Deaf Media, accessed April 2, 2018, http://www.Deafmedia.org/programs/programs.htm.
75. Mark Chester, "In My Mind's Eye—Deaf Awareness," *Falmouth Wicked*, accessed April 2, 2018, https://www.wickedlocal.com/story/archive/2010/10/18/in-my-mind-s-eye/39517458007/.
76. Shelley Lawrence, personal recollection.

77. Arden Neisser, *The Other Side of Silence: Sign Language and the Deaf Community in America* (Gallaudet University Press, 1983), 259.
78. Jane Norman, interviewed by Kennedy Center, accessed April 2, 2018, http://www.kennedycenter.org/text/accessibility/opening_stages/issue25/peo_norman.cfm.
79. *. . . and Your Name Is Jonah*, directed by Richard Michaels and written by Michael Bortman, (Charles Fries Production, 1979).
80. Nora Tegni, with Lynnette Taylor, *RID/IDP Community Forum*, Summer 2013.
81. *Love Is Never Silent*, directed by Joseph Sargent and written by Darlene Caviotto and Joanne Greenberg (Hallmark Hall of Fame Productions, Marian Rees Associates, and Telepictures Productions, 1985).
82. *Bridge to Silence*, directed by Karen Arthur and written by Louisa Burns-Bisogno and Tom Bisogno (Briggle, Hennessey, Carrothers, and Associates, 1989).
83. *Deafula*, directed and written by Peter Wolf (Sign Scope/Holstrom, 1975).
84. "Moving Pictures, Moving Hands: The Story of Ernest Marshall," Gallaudet University, https://media.gallaudet.edu/media/Moving+Pictures%2C+Moving+HandsA++The+Sotry+of+Ernest+Marshall/1_9enr1u7k.
85. The Public Theater has continued to feature Deaf actors in their productions over the past forty-five years, notably Jeffrey Bravin in *Antigone* (1982), Monique Holt in *The Skin of Our Teeth* (1998), Alexandria Wailes in *Mother Courage and Her Children* (2006), Howie Seago in *Little Flower of East Orange* (2008), Alexandria Wailes in *for colored girls who have considered suicide / when the rainbow is enuf* (2019 and Broadway 2022), Monique Holt and Maleni Chaitoo in *Richard III* (2022), and Dickie Hearts in *Dark Disabled Stories* (2023), in addition to including Deaf talent in their Public Works performances.
86. *Runaways*, book, music, and lyrics by Elizabeth Swados. Additional ASL text by Bruce Hlibok. Directed and choreographed by Elizabeth Swados. Produced on Broadway at the Plymouth Theatre in 1978.
87. Eric Malzkuhn's email to Stephanie Feyne, April 22, 1988—Photos of this event can be found in Baldwin's *Pictures in the Air*.
88. *Children of a Lesser God*, directed by Gordon Davidson, 1980 Broadway production at the Longacre Theatre.
89. "*Children of a Lesser God*, Broadway Awards," Internet Broadway Database, https://www.ibdb.com/broadway-production/children-of-a-lesser-god-3694#Awards.
90. "*Children of a Lesser God*, The Broadway League," Internet Broadway Database, https://www.ibdb.com/broadway-production/children-of-a-lesser-god-515596.
91. "*Children of a Lesser God*, Awards," Internet Movie Database, https://www.imdb.com/title/tt0090830/awards/.
92. "Theatre Development Fund," accessed April 2, 2018, http://www.tdf.org/TDF_Landingpage.aspx?id=109.
93. John Beaufort "Theater in Sign Language—The Drama's Still There," *Christian Science Monitor*, August 12, 1981, https://www.csmonitor.com/1981/0812/081201.html.
94. Beaufort, "Theater in Sign Language."
95. Beaufort, "Theater in Sign Language."
96. Beaufort, "Theater in Sign Language."
97. *The Elephant Man*, directed by Jack Hofsiss, 1980 Broadway production at the Booth Theatre. Interpreting team was Alan Champion and Phil Giambarisi.

98. Playbill, "TDF-TAPS Broadway Shows," *Playbill.com*, accessed April 2, 2018, http://www.playbill.com/news/article/31886-TDF-TAPS-Broadway-Shows.
99. While Broadway had interpretation starting in 1980, it did not have captioning services until 1997, when the first captioned show was *Barrymore*, written by William Luce, directed by Gene Saks, produced at the Music Box Theatre, and starring Christopher Plummer and Simi Horowitz. "Broadway's Open-Captioned Theatre: Welcoming the Hearing Impaired," *Backstage*, Last updated November 5, 2019, https://www.backstage.com/magazine/article/broadways-open-captioned-theatre-welcoming-hearing-impaired-45224/.
100. *Having Our Say*, directed by Emily Mann, written by Emily Mann, adapted from the book by Sarah L. Delany, A. Elizabeth Delany, and Amy Hill Hearth; original music composed by Baikida Carroll. 1995 Broadway production at the Booth Theatre. The interpreting team was Patrice Joyner-Creamer, Michelle Banks, and Lisa Weems.
101. "Feed interpreter" is a term often used for the hearing team member who cues the Deaf team member and supports the rest of the team as needed. Currently, the term "co-interpreter" is also in use.
102. Patrice Joyner-Creamer interviewed by Candace Broceker Penn, September 9, 2022.
103. Janis Cole, personal communication with Candace Broceker Penn, January 19, 2025.
104. Susan Cohen, "Spotlight: Hands On's Beth Prevor Connects the Deaf and Theater Communities in NYC," *6sqft.com*, November 13, 2015, https://www.6sqft.com/spotlight-hands-ons-beth-prevor-connects-the-Deaf-and-theater-communities-in-nyc/.
105. Beth Prevor, interview with Lynnette Taylor, Candace Broecker Penn, and Stephanie Feyne, August 13, 2022.
106. Cohen, Spotlight."
107. A performance of an early incarnation of *Epic Family Epic* was videotaped for the NYC Library of the Performing Arts. Deaf performer Carole Addabbo is in the credits along with interpreters Candace Broecker Penn, Cathy Markland, Bill Moody, and Claude Shirts. Hands On is also listed as a contributor. Jerome Robbins Dance Division, "The Epic Family Epic," *The New York Public Library Digital Collections*. https://qa-digitalcollections.nypl.org/items/8a5c4a40-6f28-0131-e9ae-3c075448cc4b.
108. *I Always Wanted to be an Opera Singer*, directed by Lynnette Taylor, cocreated by Mary Beth Miller and Lynnette Taylor, 1991 Off-Off Broadway production at Dance Theatre Workshop. Onstage performer: Mary Beth Miller, offstage voice: Stephanie Feyne.
109. One of the performances and the postshow conversation of *I Always Wanted to Be an Opera Singer* was recorded and is available at the main branch of the New York Public Library. https://researchworks.oclc.org/archivegrid/collection/data/43488074.
110. David White on Deaf audiences in his interview about Musign for the *New York Times*, "In most cases, I try to see the work first," Mr. White said. "And occasionally I've suggested pieces to bring to New York. But you can't dictate the kind of work they do here. And there have been a few mistakes. But in every case, the companies have reached new audiences. And with Musign, Dance Theater Workshop may itself reach an audience that is new to its theater-gallery complex." Jennifer Dunning, "Out-of-Town Dancers Welcomed Anew," *New York Times*, August 21, 1983, https://www.nytimes.com/1983/08/21/arts/out-of-town-dancers-welcomed-anew.html.
111. In the early-to-mid-1980s, local NYC theatre interpreters met regularly to engage in translation work and get feedback on their presentations. This working group was

written up in *Interpreting: An Introduction* by Nancy Frishberg (Registry of Interpreters for the Deaf, Inc., October 5, 2015).

112. Project coordinator, Julia Hays, described the training as, "a pilot workshop . . . designed to explore skills needed by interpreters to assure successful crossover into the theater world . . . We were fortunate to have a star-studded and talented faculty: Phyliss Freilich, Michael Posnick, Andy Vasnick, John Broome (Movement Director of Royal Shakespeare Company); Bernard Bragg, Ed Waterstreet, and Susie Kirchner (RID representative). Classes included acting, voice, movement, translation, role, and discussions of practical interpreting concerns." SC:PA holders included Darlene Allen (CA), Janet Bailey (MD), Debbie Brenner (GA), Becky Carlson (MN), Andrew L. Diskant (OH), Steve Fritsch-Rudser (CA), Laurel Goodrich (CO), Rob Granberry (TX), Margaret James (WI), and Anna Witter (NY). Information from Janet Bailey, "Special Certificate: Performing Arts, An RID History Lesson," *RID Views*, May 1998.
113. Deaf artists Mary Beth Miller and Alan Barwiolek (AlB) and interpreters Alan Champion, Candace Broecker Penn, and Lynnette Taylor.
114. Lisa Carling interviewed by Lynnette Taylor, February 18, 2020.
115. The diagnostic assessment of interpreters used in the program was based on a training offered by Dennis Cokely, Anna Witter-Merithew, and Sharon Neumann Solow. This training was codified in D. Cokely, A. Witter-Merithew, and S. Neumann Solow. "Principles for Providing Feedback and Discussing the Work" in *Diagnostician Preparation Training Manual*, (Advancement Seminars, 1995).
116. Lisa Carling interviewed by Lynnette Taylor, June 2019.
117. Carling, interview.
118. David Boles, "Juilliard Interpreter Training," *David Boles's Blog*, November 2, 2002, https://bolesblogs.com/2002/11/02/juilliard-interpreter-training/.

2

Foundations for Collaborative Interpreting

Interpreted performances shift the theatre space to become, for one night, a space where mainstream and "infrequent societies" can commingle.[1] These cross-cultural interactions offer "everyone a way to see oneself in the world in a different way, a way to see oneself becoming in a different world."[2]

Interpreting for theatre is a collaborative art, part of an ecosystem that includes the theatres we work with, the interpreting community, the Deaf and signing communities, and greater audiences. Our aim as mindful practitioners is to bring a dynamic and responsive approach to our exploration of meaning and the role of the interpreter in the theatre.

Our approach to interpreting for the theatre is multidisciplinary, in that it draws from translation studies, sociolinguistics, interpreting, performance, and interactive embodied communication. These additional disciplines help shape our understanding and our following questions: What is interpretation in a theatre venue? How does one approach the performance of a translation when it is a dialogic, embodied, performative, transmodal interpretation (signed language, spoken language, performance, and theatrical elements), and how does the difference in modality (signing vs. spoken) affect our understanding and our choices? What are the sociopolitical implications of theatre interpreting? What operative philosophy(ies) guides the work? What are the ethical considerations?

The guiding principles that shape our practice were formed by years of experience, intellectual inquiry, and the many wonderful, engaging, and sometimes challenging conversations with our fellow collaborators and stakeholders.

We believe that to do this work with integrity, interpreters must be fluent in the languages that they work with. Fluency requires "living" these languages. Translator Damion Searls explains: "Learning a language does not mean learning grammar and vocabulary *per se*, it means learning the genres of what is and isn't natural to say and when and where and how . . . [Fluency] channels our appropriate responses, and our possible inappropriate responses too, into a relatively small subset of all the words and gestures that exist in the world."[3]

Just as in community settings, the recipients of our interpretations hold linguistic and personal expectations that interpreters be fluent and able to express meaning clearly. They also expect interpreters to walk in with cultural and content fluency (Suggs),[4] to be trustworthy, and possess an understanding of Deaf norms and values, in short, to be skilled professional interpreters who are guided by a framework that honors the Deaf community.

The following principles guide our work and help us open avenues of thought during the process:

- Without Deaf people, we have no reason to be interpreting.
- Theatre interpreting is an opportunity to build community, not a vehicle for stardom.
- We collaborate with Deaf people in all parts of the process as interpreters, directors of interpreters (DOIs), and audience members.
- We respect and recognize the protocols of the spaces we enter and engage in appropriate professional interactions.
- The interpreting team views the stage as a partner and, therefore, fidelity of interpretation means fidelity to the staged performance.
- The interpreting team considers both linguistic and nonlinguistic information when developing the collective interpretation.
- The team engages and designs the interpretation in a dialogic manner using natural language.
- The interpretations are crafted to express the intentionality of the characters and their interactions.
- The interpreter body is a contextualized body, and the politic of what our bodies signify and represent is considered.
- We take actions to include diverse communities in the interpreting pool.

We also need to be mindful that our actions and choices do not perpetuate harmful systemic practices and behaviors that reinforce issues of power, privilege, and oppression.

What makes interpreting for the theatre different from written/spoken translations is the embodiment (wearing) of the translations and the performativity of the interpretations (breathing, responding, looking to each other, and looking to the stage) in a simultaneous performance. The signed language interpretation needs to be designed for an audience whose gaze traverses between two spaces (stage and interpretation).

In spoken language interpretations, the listener can identify who is speaking through the sound of their voice. The listener's gaze can be directly to the speaker or can track the speaker via auditory cues. For audiences who are listening in a visual language, the interpreter incorporates visual strategies so the audience knows who is speaking and to whom.

While this seems relatively straightforward, in a theatrical space, it becomes quite complex when importing multimodal information into a unimodal visual medium. The interpreters navigate the conversation, not only audience-to-stage but also audience-to-interpreters and interpreters-to-stage, choreographing the lines of communication in the interpreter-mediated space.

The interpreting space is often adjacent to the stage, making it an extension of the mise-en-scène, the stage picture. Theatrical elements are transported and condensed into this coexisting interpreting space (what we call the "co-constructed shared meaning space"). Theatre interpreters spatially map the onstage referents and actions, becoming "cartographers" of speakers, places, and things—re-reifying the world on the stage in the interpreted space in front of the audience.

An individual interpreter will interpret for multiple characters throughout the play and needs to distinguish between them. Because the interpretations are dialogic, the relationship between the speakers needs to be considered when assigning the characters to individual interpreters in the team. This becomes a performative translatory consideration, an additional content strand to be considered in the development of a performed interpretation. Once the character/interpreter alignments have been decided upon, depiction strategies are built into the interpretation so that the interpreters can efficiently signal to the audience which character they are interpreting at the time. Interactions are depicted by the interpreting team in a dialogic and responsive manner.

The interpreter must explore what it means to "inhabit" and then convey the other's message through one's body and then, how does the embodiment of another's voice re-represent the message as well as the bearer of the message? In other words, how will this re-embodiment shape the message? And in what ways can the possible misalignment or misrepresentation be addressed? This is particularly significant for signed language interpretation in the theatre, when transmodal embodied performative translation is enacted.

The embodied re-presentation of characters in a signed language interpretation requires deeper reflection to ensure that performance intent matches performed output. In the process of re-presenting a message in an embodied performative language, our goal is to ensure our interpreting choices aren't "othering" the speaker.

As the field of interpreted theatre evolves and the approach to the practice becomes more sophisticated, so, too, will the conversations. The complexities of theatre interpreting are many, with varying perspectives on best practices. As interpretation in the theatre evolves, it is important that we continue to engage in ongoing conversations about interpreted theatre with all the stakeholders, so that the practice evolves in response to the community.

Origins of Translation in the Deaf Community

Translations are a natural occurrence in any multilingual community. These bilingual bicultural interactions, whether for theatre or for community needs, inform the structure, phrasing, and breath of a translation. There have always been resident Deaf translators. Janis Cole explains:

> Deaf people have been performing *ad hoc* translations within their community for hundreds of years (Adam et al., 2011; Bartley & Stone, 2008) . . . Deaf bilinguals appear to draw on a

> reservoir of extralinguistic knowledge (ELK) developed from their experiences as individuals living within the intersection of two languages, one of which employs a modality that is seldom used by majority populations.[5]

Translations and play between English and ASL have been going on for close to two hundred years, but outsiders to the language and community were not always privy to the creative process of these Deaf translators. MJ Bienvenu talks about watching Ella Mae Lentz "late at night perform[ing] creative signed versions . . . translations from English . . . of songs such as, 'I Left My Heart in San Francisco,' and I would watch wide-eyed over and over again."[6]

The first forays into the realm of artistic translations are from Deaf translators whose works continue to inspire current generations. One of the earliest recognized ASL translators, Eric (Malz) Malzkuhn, is known for his translation of "Jabberwocky." Intrigued by Lewis Carroll's play with nonsensical language, he wondered whether ASL could do the same and still convey the spirit of the poem. Searls reminds us, "a translator is not just a copyist, trying to replicate the original as closely as possible: a translator is necessarily producing new work in and for a new context . . . different from the original's."[7]

DawnSignPress notes that "Malz broke away from the traditional style of signed poetry, which then was more literal translation, with little expression."[8] Malzkuhn's translation surpassed expectations in his creation of a sensical nonsensical ASL version of "Jabberwocky," placing it among the greats in the canon of ASL literature. Malz shared that "Jabberwocky was my trademark, from 1940 to 1967, for almost 30 years."[9]

When the National Theatre of the Deaf (NTD) approached Malzkuhn for permission to use his translation, it raised the question of how a translation designed for one body could live in another. Malz explained, "The reason I picked [NTD actor] Joe Velez was because he had wonderful control of his body . . . so I asked him, 'Why don't we work together?' [In adapting the translation for him,] I developed things that fit his face, his body."[10]

While written translations are frozen and retain the same form, Malzkuhn realized early on that the performed translation in sign language could not be copied and *worn* in exactly the same way by someone else. The linguistic body that *wears* the translation also becomes a consideration. Is the performer able to deliver not just the signs, but also the rhythms and the layers of meaning that need to be expressed?

Since ASL translations live in a signing body, in essence, they are a kind of "bespoke translation." The conveyance and conveyor of the translation are intertwined. So the signing body becomes another consideration. In the words of Walter Benjamin, "It is the task of the translator to release in his own language that pure language that is under the spell of another, to liberate the language imprisoned in a work in his re-creation of that work."[11]

In much the same way that the music director adjusts the orchestration for a particular singer (e.g., those for Bernadette Peters would be different than those for Laura Benanti) or a choreographer adapts the choreography for an individual artist (e.g., those for Christina Applegate would be different than those for Molly Ringwald), the translator also takes into consideration the performer and adjusts the translation for the individual performer's nuances that each performer brings to the work.

When interpreting shows, not only the staged performance but also the composition of the interpreting team, the assigning of characters, the fidelity to meaning, and the artistry of the translation are all elements to be considered. Directors of Interpreters (DOIs) are an integral part of this conversation when working with interpreting teams for theatrical productions. Michelle Banks, artistic director of Visionaries of the Creative Arts (VOCA), points out, "Having deaf people whose first language is ASL working in artistic sign language direction brings a whole other perspective—a deaf one—to a production."[12]

Recently, there has been a surge in the number of productions that include Deaf talent and signed language both on stage and in film and television. This in turn has led to more demand for the services of Directors of Artistic Sign Language (DASLs). In the Alliance of Resident Theatres (A.R.T./New York) panel discussion, *Spotlight on DASLs*, Monique Holt explains,

> It was around 2006 or 2007 that we came together and talked about the scope of our work, which included technical consultations, such as framing, editing, blocking, lighting choices in film and television and cinema, as well as language translations, and language coaching . . . "Director of Artistic Sign Language" best reflected the scope of our work, since it included both linguistic and nonlinguistic elements.[13]

In a theatrical production, DASLs, as members of the creative team, create the signed language that lives in the actors' bodies on the stage, Andrew Morrill, the DASL for the Broadway show *Grey House* with actress Millicent Simmonds,[14] introduced his role by explaining, "We are here to ensure there is an equitable experience for the Deaf talent throughout the production and to ensure the representation of the characters and language is authentic."[15]

Deaf Directors of Interpreters

There have been many terms used for the role of Deaf individuals who work with the team to prepare for an interpreted performance. For this book about theatre interpreting, we are distinguishing the work of the DOIs from that of DASLs.

While DOIs and DASLs both focus on the clarity of translations and signed delivery, working with interpreters is different from working with performers onstage. The conversations of an interpreted play are mediated (interpreted) and exist in two distinct spaces: the interpreted space and the onstage performance space. DOIs consider how to weave these two conversational spaces together. They also work with the team to unpack the play, explore translation choices, character division, and blocking. Michelle Banks adds that DOIs, "can also have a say in hiring, and can choose interpreters who are a better fit for the characters, the culture represented and the chosen signing style."[16] The DOI guides the team throughout the entire process.

We asked several DOIs to share their thoughts and experiences. Veteran DOI Anne Tomasetti draws from her early experiences as a Deaf actor, and shares her insights about the process of translating scripts:

> During my time at Gallaudet Drama and then in NTD, I had learned from a Deaf ASL master who taught "Don't sign every word—that is not what the script means. Play. Find the meaning and sign that." I try to bring those qualities when working with hearing and Deaf interpreting teams. I encourage everyone to play a little bit more. Be less afraid, free up the work, work as a team, be creative.[17]

Tomasetti often talks about adjusting to the linguistic repertoire of the team members:

> Each interpreter is different. I respect what each brings to their work and what they offer. I build from their strengths. This includes giving a range of translation choices that may suit them best and blends well with the team's interpretation. Part of my approach is to make the team feel comfortable and confident in their choices so they can produce the best interpretation.[18]

In addition, Tomasetti often offers dramaturgical support to interpreting teams:

> I do a tremendous amount of preparation before rehearsals begin. This gives me a strong foundation to build from and support the team. Initially, an interpretation may seem fine, but based on my research, I have a different understanding of what a particular line means in context and offer this to the team. even if their translation doesn't change, something shifts in the interpreter's delivery because the interpreter now has a deeper understanding.
>
> I respond differently to the needs of each play. For example, *Travesties* had a lot of references to Russian history and terms such as capitalism and socialism,[19] which have no standard signs in ASL. I did a lot of research into the time period, history, and politics of the play and put together a packet of information that I gave to the interpreting team. With this foundation, we then had time during rehearsals to discuss how the team would express the terms derived from Marxist philosophy.[20]

Andrew Fisher, most recently the DOI for the Broadway production *Enemy of the People*,[21] offered his thoughts:

> Rather than viewing myself as the Director of ASL, I see myself more as a collaborator, since I don't develop the translations—the ASL interpreters do. My role is to collaborate with them throughout the process. As a collaborator, my job is to consider the Deaf audience and how they might perceive the translations in terms of accessibility, visibility, theatricality, and accuracy. I communicate my thoughts and concerns with the interpreters and support them as they develop their translations, acting as a sounding board and providing feedback as needed. I believe that trusting the process is crucial, and it needs to happen organically.

> To facilitate this, I believe it's important to schedule as many rehearsals as possible in advance, allowing the team to develop the translations, bond, and feel comfortable with each other. The DOI should work with the interpreters to schedule meetings and rehearsals and lead in assigning roles. These roles can change during the process based on factors such as comfort, suitability, and visibility, rather than being based on gender or age. Theatrical interpreting is not acting. It's about capturing the essence of the character and providing accessibility. However, interpreters should be comfortable interacting with one another as if they were in conversation with each other, maintaining eye contact and looking at the audience as needed.
>
> Also, I believe the DOI should act as a bit of a dramaturg,[22] introducing signs tailored to the show and providing important information and a character breakdown before the performance. Providing accessibility does not mean giving information that the hearing audience may not have access to. It's okay to use context-specific words that the general audience may not be familiar with if they're central to the story. The goal is to make sure that the Deaf audience feels like they're 'hearing' the dialogue directly, whether they're familiar with every term or not. And making sure there's space for the audience to watch the actors on stage whenever possible.[23]

At times, a DOI may choose to address the signing audience and share the strategies the team will use to signal the visual information, to indicate character shifts, or to introduce uncommon, esoteric, or nonstandard signs (such as signs created specifically for the world of the play, names of people, use of foreign signed languages, etc.), making the interpreting decisions more transparent for the audience. The DOI considers the production, the audience, and the interpreting team and makes decisions about what would lead to a successful event.

Joyce Hom, the DOI for *Here There Were Blueberries*,[24] identified challenges about character switching, language use, and sensitive content that could potentially cause confusion. She decided to prepare the audience by identifying specific theatrical devices and interpreting devices they would see in the play:

> I wanted the audience to have a clear expectation of what would be on the stage. For example, I explained that important visual information would be projected on screens while actors were speaking. In order to give time for the audience to see those important visual moments, I asked the interpreters to pause their interpretation at certain times. I wanted to reassure the audience that this asynchronous interpretation was a deliberate choice, and not to worry because all the information would be interpreted, just not always at the same time as the actors speaking the lines.
>
> I also alerted them to a convention the play was using—changes in lighting to identify character shifts. The actors were playing multiple roles but not changing costumes. When the color changed, the actor switched to a different character. Even though I knew the audience would get used to that convention, I just wanted to give them a heads-up.[25]

For the interpreted performance of *Enemy of the People,* prior to the start of the show, Andrew Fisher addressed the signing audience about the sign choice for the term "servant" used in the play. This sparked a lively conversation, with many offering their local signs for the "servant." This engagement with the audience (a sharing of signed vocabulary, and the way the interpreting team arrived at choices, as well as eliciting buy-in) called upon Deaf cultural norms in the "hybrid"[26] theatre space. Fisher added, "In addition to making the space a welcoming place for the

Deaf audience, it lets them know that having interpreters is more than providing accessibility—they're also invited to be part of the process. It's also a good way to let the audience know that they're in good hands, literally and figuratively."[27]

DOIs collaborate with the interpreting team throughout the process as they discover and apply techniques and strategies designed to connect the audience to the interpretation and to the stage. The DOI plays an integral role in the interpreting team and is nonnegotiable. It is also a paid position with a fee commensurate to the others on the team.

Representation and the Interpreter Body

> "All of our bodies carry meaning on stage, whether or not we want to acknowledge that. And that's going to affect storytelling."
>
> —Ayanna Thompson, Shakespeare scholar for the Public Theater[28]

Interpreters work across and between many cultures, races, and ethnicities, often brokering languages and cultures not of our own background. Signed language interpreters are now beginning to examine the content that our bodies signify and convey while interpreting, challenging the notion that the interpreting body is perceived as a neutral body.

The field of signed language interpretation has long accepted the "Myth of Neutrality," perceiving interpreters as neutral language conduits.[29] That unexamined assumption ignores the fact that our very bodies tell stories. This belief perpetuated a practice that excluded interpreters from diverse backgrounds from being in public-facing venues.

In their 2018 annual report, the Registry of Interpreters for the Deaf (RID) identified 87 percent of sign language interpreters as women. In addition, nearly nine in ten interpreters identified as white.[30] There were no statistics on interpreters who identify as part of the LGBTQIA+ community. While the statistics may be slightly different among the pool of theatre interpreters, most of the teams historically have been white, and the majority have identified as women. Character breakdown was often based on simple assumptions without considering the complexities of gender casting, let alone racial, ethnic, LGBTQIA+, or other identity alignments. Although the interpreter's attributes were considered, there wasn't a deep analysis of the implications of "wearing another's gender or identity" and/or the residue of transitive identity switching of multiple characters during a performed interpretation.

As humans, we are often unaware of our implicit biases, and these may unwittingly appear in our translations. What gestures, mannerisms, use of language, and signed accents are being used when performing utterances? Are these choices also examined with the same scrutiny that should be applied with any other cultural representation? As Hatim and Mason remind us, "The translator acts in a social context and is part of that context. It is in this sense that translating is, in itself, an ideological activity."[31] A seemingly innocent gesture, a character depiction, sign choices, and delivery all become content. And it's possible to cause harm. What we think we are signifying and what the audience sees may not be the same thing.

The transformative practices outlined in the "Principles for Building Anti-Racist Theatre Systems," promulgated by the "We See You White American Theatre" movement,[32] extend to the interpreting team as well. In 2022, National Black Deaf Advocates, the National Association of the Deaf, and RID issued a powerful joint statement on culturally appropriate interpreters. It begins, "Recently, there have been situations where some interpreters have taken jobs that should have been offered to Black, Brown, Indigenous, and persons of color (BIPOC) interpreters, Deaf interpreters, and Deaf persons. Such acts are cultural appropriation, and they disempower BIPOC and Deaf interpreters and consumers. This must stop."[33]

In *Embodied Sociolinguistics*, Bucholtz and Hall explain, "Bodies and embodiment are central to the production, perception, and social interpretation of language. In spoken languages, the body is the locus of the speaking voice and the listening ear, while in the case of sign languages the body supplies the grammar for the entire linguistic system."[34] Because interpreters' bodies are understood in their situated context (place, time, in alignment with or contrast to the others who share the space, etc.), it is important to consider how the content signified by our bodies and the language(s) we use may or may not align with the story being told onstage.

Exploration of identity and race may be expressed in different ways in each production. During an audience talkback for David Henry Hwang's *Yellow Face*, one of the cast members commented, "Every piece of art creates its own rules."[35] This does not mean there has to be a racial, gender, or ethnic alignment of interpreters' bodies to actors' bodies in every show. In most cases, a multicultural team could (and should) be assigned to any genre or production, in contrast to the tendency to hire interpreters of color only when there is a show that is about their particular culture.

However, the play's cultural lens becomes an important consideration for selecting the interpreting team when playwrights design their works with racial, gender, cultural, or ethnic specificity (such as August Wilson, Marisela Treviño Orta, Larissa Fasthorse, David Henry Hwang, Mary Kathryn Nagle, Hilary Bettis, Tony Kushner, Lauren Lee, Paula Vogel, Young Jean Le, James Ijames, and Ntozake Shange). In addition, sometimes, the cultural content is not in the script but expressed in the director's production. If the composition of the interpreting team does not reflect the story, then the interpreting team runs the risk of misrepresenting the meaning presented on stage. The context and intention of the show help guide the team composition.

Alexandria Wailes works as actor, director, choreographer, theatre interpreter, DASL, and DOI. When asked about her thoughts on representation in theatre interpreting, as someone who identifies as a light-skinned biracial artist, she shared,

> If the cast is all POC and the interpreting team is all white, that doesn't sit well. How can they interpret the cultural vocabulary if the vocabulary of the culture is not in them? Can they really understand the cultural nuances? If you are interpreting this show and have none of the lived cultural experiences, how can you interpret the play? I mean you could be transmitting information and it would be a clinical interpreting job, but it wouldn't have the texture and real authenticity.[36]

Erica West Oyedele explored interpreters' cultural competence and social capital in her research. She interviewed a focus group of African American/Black Deaf consumers and found, "They perceived African American/Black interpreters . . . to be more culturally competent . . . [and] felt more confident and more empowered when they had access to an interpreter who shared their same race."[37]

It is important to see the play and understand the director's vision before making the interpreter selection. Sometimes, it's not possible to do this before beginning the process. If, after agreeing to interpret a show, an interpreter recognizes that their body tells a different story, that interpreter can ethically step back so that another interpreter who can better represent the character(s) can step up. Michelle Banks "believes that theatrical interpreters can also be more thoughtful when booking interpreting roles . . . and really do some self-assessment: Am I the right person for this role? Am I the right interpreter for this job?"[38] Jina Porter, "a hearing theatrical interpreter and a person of color . . . [said] 'I feel like you should look at the team and then look at the show and feel like they would all kind of be in the same place together.'"[39]

In 2020, the Roundabout Theatre presented a revival of Charles Fuller's *A Soldier's Play*. In discussing this production, the director, Kenny Leon, explained "I want it to not only be the story of a murder mystery that takes place in the 1940s, I also want it to say something about now, about what it means to actually stand tall as an African American in this country."[40]

The play has a large cast, with twelve men, nine of whom are African American. The Hands On interpreting team consisted of one African American interpreter, one Latino interpreter, one white interpreter, and two male DOIs (one African American and one white).[41]

In the initial character division, the white interpreter was assigned to some of the African American soldiers. During a "hands-up" interpreted rehearsal (a run-through in ASL in real time), the team discovered that they felt uncomfortable with the white interpreter signing for these characters. They felt there was a dissonance between the interpreter's body and the story being told on stage. The intent of the play and the delivery of its message were not in alignment. In order to honor the narrative and character arcs, the team realized it needed an additional interpreter of color to take on the characters that had been originally assigned to the white interpreter.

Roundabout Theatre agreed to Hands On's request to add an additional BIPOC interpreter to the team. The DOIs then reassigned the roles so that the white interpreter was assigned only to the white characters. This aligned better with the story being told onstage.

Zavier Sabio, one of the DOIs for this show, remarked, "I liked the idea of supporting the story in that way. All the soldiers onstage were POC and had a kind of 'swag' that the three POC interpreters could convey. It made watching the whole experience feel powerful and authentic."[42]

Linguist Alastair Pennycook suggests that "performativity opens up several significant ways of thinking about language and identity, languages as entities, and language as part of the transmodal performance."[43]

Social and political narratives—and consequently social practices—are not fixed but rather evolve in response to changes in culture and society. Judith Butler reminds us that we are, all of us, trapped into the narrative we've been brought into, and it is up to us to become aware of the trappings of the narratives and change them. [44] Because these performative transitive (shifts to and from multiple characters) representations are more visible in theatre interpreting, the layers of signification when representing an-other need to be carefully considered.

David Henry Hwang, speaking about race and identity politics in his semi-autobiographical play, *Yellow Face,* stated, "I think the culture has moved toward the play . . . issues of casting, appropriation, identity, and 'woke'-ness seemed more like niche concerns to a general audience in 2007, whereas now they have become central to American popular discourse."[45]

The Lion King, often referred to in this book, is an example of an evolving response to the need for social transformation and more diverse representation in the entertainment industry. This was reflected in Disney's 2019 remake of the animated version of *The Lion King.* Voices.com, a blog for voiceover talent, noted, "If you compare the previous version's voice actors to *The Lion King's* 2019 cast, you see how Disney made major decisions to incorporate heterogeneity and authenticity into the live-action film."[46]

Responding to historic inequity, practices in the field of interpreting are undergoing examination. Theatre interpreters, as well as the organizations that hire them, recognize a need for greater inclusion of a more diverse cultural pool. The first Broadway production of *The Lion King* was interpreted in 1997 and has continued gaining more ethnic and racial diversity in the teams as the years have gone by.

The push for representation in the arts not only applies to interpreters but also to Deaf talent and diversity in the entertainment industry. While there have been strides in the industry, the push for more radical inclusion on every level will always be needed. DJ Kurs, artistic director of Deaf West Theatre, when interviewed by *Variety,* cautioned that he has seen support and attention to Deaf arts wax and wane. "The pendulum swings one way, and we get a lot of good representation. Then the pendulum swings back to the other side, and we have to wait another three to five years before we're on screen again."[47]

Deaf West Theatre has been involved in several initiatives on the need for more representation in the media and entertainment industry. In 2022, the National Research Group (NRG) and Deaf West Theatre published a downloadable report of their research on Deaf representation.[48] As a follow-up, Deaf West "partnered with NRG to host a wide-ranging roundtable about the issues facing the Deaf community."[49] Members of the roundtable included Lauren Ridloff, Daniel Durant, Michael

Epstein, Jessica Flores, Shaylee Mansfield, Erik Nordlof, and Raven Sutton. The recording of this event, "Spotlight on Deaf Representation: A Roundtable Discussion," can be viewed on YouTube.[50]

Interpreters, as members of both the arts and Deaf communities, need to support Deaf representation as well as a broader culturally diverse interpreting pool wherever we can.

Approach to Collaborative Interpreting

The minute we walk into the theatre, we have already begun the search for meaning: What is the experience of being in the venue? What greets us when we enter; what are the visuals, sounds, and smells? Yes, even smells—audiences were greeted with the aroma of baking pies in Diane Paulus's Broadway production of *Waitress*[51] and the smell of frying bacon in David Cromer's production of *Our Town*.[52] At times, the theatre reconfigures its space, as in several Broadway productions of *Cabaret* when the venue was re-designed to become a nightclub.[53]

In the world of the theatre, playwrights design the experience that they want the audience to receive. And the theatre creatives (director, performers, musical directors, etc.) make decisions about how to deliver those messages to the audience, in effect, being the "first interpreter" of the playwright's language.

Audience members bring their own contexts, experiences, understandings of the conventions of the theatre, and distinct relationships to the play. Whatever drew the audience to the play, these individual, social, and artistic aspects are all integral parts of the experience of being an audience member. Interpreters, too, bring their own context, experiences, understandings of the conventions of the theatre, and individual relationships to the play.

While there are distinct and personal experiences of a play, there is also a collective audience response to the play or story. What is the visual experience of the play? The auditory experience? The sensory experience? Where does information reside? Is the story unfolding primarily through action, dialogue, music, or other conventions? What is visually arresting? How do characters interact? Where do audience members laugh, cry, or cringe?

These responses are part of the content that interpreters must explore. They inform the interpretation. This is why in the training that we provided for the Theatre Development Fund's "Interpreting for the Theatre Seminar," housed at the Juilliard School, we always began with seeing the play.

Finding Meaning

The lights are dim. Tom stands alone, talking to the audience. As he speaks, his sister, Laura, ethereally recedes from view, following the request in his line, "Blow out your candle Laura, and so goodbye."

In a revival of *The Glass Menagerie* on Broadway,[54] directed by John Tiffany, we in the audience collectively held our breath when Laura disappeared. It was not just the words that created that magic moment. It was the combination of the emotional, visual, auditory, and linguistic life that was shared with us.

Theatre creates worlds that bring forth a new set of relationships, a new internal language, and new understandings of interactions with every play. The interpreter's task is to transmit these new understandings in a way that the signing audience can appreciate both the art of the actors and the meaning presented in the interpreted utterances.

The root of the word "theatre" is observation, and just as in the ancient Greek theatron (θέατρον), the modern theatre is a place to watch and to observe in order to understand. As our task as interpreters is to transmit meaning, we need to observe and understand meaning before we pick up our hands and sign it. Theatrical interpreters become "both a receiver [of the source message] and [later] a producer [of the translated message]."[55]

The theatrical experience is communicated through far more than just words. Therefore, meaning is found not only in the lines but also in the way the actors say the lines, in their nonverbal behaviors, in the action on the stage, in the music, in the lighting, and in the interaction of all the elements that create the full piece. As linguistic guides into the world of the stage, we must know what the elements convey so that we can be prepared to interpret.

Theatre often responds to what is happening in the culture. Is there contemporary social and political commentary or content that is being brought in from the outside world that needs to be identified? Audience responses are also a source of information that guides our interpretation choices. Marinetti, a theatre translation scholar, calls attention to the fact that, "There is a need for more flexible concepts and broader approaches to the interface between theatre and translation in the context of our increasingly performative world."[56] Interpreters can look to contemporary sources outside of the theatre and outside of the text that audiences may be familiar with to produce meaning. The relationship between the drama on stage and the drama unfolding in the now in other arenas is a living, evolving part of the stage-to-life conversation to consider.

The conversation between the performance and the audience is not static; it is not only contained within the theatre but is also a conversation with the current social and political life. In the 2023 Broadway revival of *Purlie Victorious* by Ossie Davis, director Kenny Leon included social commentary through his staging. After a racially biased event along an Alabama riverfront, white folding chairs became a symbol of resistance and a viral meme. Greg Evans from *Deadline* commented about the play's use of this symbolism: "[Billy Eugene Jones as Gitlow is] the one who holds up a folding chair while none of the other characters are watching, a marvelous little actor-to-audience stage moment that signals Gitlow's true spirit and is just one of the production's details that places *Purlie Victorious* squarely within contemporary discourse."[57]

The work of unpacking meaning (translating the world of the stage) may require the team to go beyond the familiar and to journey into the shared understandings of the production and the audience, even when the interpreters may not immediately recognize the references. They also need to look at the play in its current social context and the conversation between the play of then and the world of now.

There are many avenues to finding meaning in the theatre: through lights, sound, set pieces, staging, and acting. This may even begin before the curtain rises. When audience members walk into the theatre, what kind of mood is being set? Are the lights dim or bright? What kind of music is playing—Upbeat? Period? Is the curtain already up, revealing the world of the play? If the curtain is down, is there information displayed on it?

When the curtain opens, what kind of a stage is it? Cluttered? Empty? Contemporary? Fantastical? Are there people walking through it or does it stand on its own, as an imposing presence? Is it indoors or outdoors? Or some undefined landscape? Does it instill a feeling in the audience?

What does the lighting tell us? Is it brightly lit, feeling festive, like a summer day? What time of day? Is it brooding and dim? Does it presage a ghost telling Hamlet tales of murder? Or does it suggest a lilting comedy?

What does the soundscape tell us? Is the wind howling behind the cackles of the three witches in *MacBeth*? Are there bagpipes playing offstage in *Brigadoon?* There is no need to make a decision about the interpretation yet, but at this moment, merely seek to understand the message of these elements.

How are the actors moving? In *Copenhagen*, the actors circled each other, like electrons, never touching. Certainly, that visual information is helpful as we construct our ideas of how to interpret. If the characters don't really connect physically, what is the impact on their communication?

Do the actors touch each other? When they touch, how is it? Lovingly? In a threatening manner? If an actor says, "Do that again and I'll break your neck" but is hugging his brother, how serious is the threat? How can we know unless we watch the actors and the company bring it to life?

DOI Anne Tomasetti expounds on the value of seeing the show:

> I know the first thing that I need to do is just go see the play. I often read the script or an online summary before seeing the show, so I have a general idea of what the play is about. I often go alone for the first viewing. Most of the time, I just want to see what I can understand from what's happening on the stage. Where are the actors entering and exiting? What is the configuration on the stage? What's the story happening on stage? Where are the contrasts, opposing forces, tensions, and how are they manifesting?
>
> Where are my eyes drawn? At what times or what moments? I might see something and know it's important, even if I don't know what it means yet, and I know I will sort that out later. So the first viewing is a visual experience for me. I see how much, and which parts of the play come through solely through the visual information.[58]

The director of the play has created specific staging to create meaning. The script only takes life when the actors perform it—so it is important to attend to how the actors communicate their lines. What is the actor intending with their delivery? Is it stated as a simple fact? With derision? As a warning? A cry for help? The meaning is different in each possibility. The actors have worked to create living characters who have relationships with each other and the environment. How they say the words, what they are doing as they say the words, and the impact of those words on the other characters all have meaning. Interpreters need to understand the interconnectedness of the production elements if the interpretation is to come alive. The process of discovery is ongoing, even during the interpreted performance.

Dialogic Interpretation for Theatre

Theatre is a collaborative experience throughout its development, its performance, and its interaction with the audience. So, too, is the collaborative dialogic approach that we offer. Interpreters use many of the strategies listed in this book in daily interpreting work, but what sets this work apart is the interactive component in both the source (the play) and the product (the interpreted performance). This is the DNA of team-constructed discourse in interpreted theatre. It begins with team engagement and culminates in a teamed delivery of a live interpretation of a show.

The performed play is the primary source that the team members draw from while developing their translation and interpretation agreements. Because the nature of the primary source is performed and the interpretation is also performed, the examination of meaning for translation includes the information found in the performance: the delivery of expression, staging, lighting, character relationships, interactions between the stage elements and the audience, and so on. In this setting, interpreters have extended time to view the show, analyze it, and work with the team to make choices prior to the interpreted event.

To make a robust interpretation that expresses the dynamic interactions of the play, the interpreting team needs to consider each of these elements as strands of meaning to be assessed, unpacked, and incorporated via linguistic and/or performative means. The team examines these strands of meaning not only as they stand alone, but how they cohere, both in individual expression and in the overall team expression in relation to the performance. In Searls' understanding, the translator "*re-creates the arc,* fashioning a new text that incarnates 'the same' movement, but starting off from the baseline of a different language."[59]

Producing a dialogic interpretation is what makes our approach to interpreted theatre different from most others. Most theatrical experiences consist of planned and rehearsed interactions that reflect the norms of spontaneous communicative interactions. As renowned acting teacher Sanford Meisner points out, "Acting is the ability to behave absolutely truthfully under the imaginary circumstances."[60] This is what the interpreting team should strive for as well. They do this through deep listening to the actors' delivery and observing their interactions both physical and verbal. The team explores the characters' interactions and how those relationships are expressed on the stage and then looks to capture and re-produce their interactive essence. Siobhán Rocks points out, "Just as the actor, when speaking his or her dialogue . . . as if it is being uttered for the first time in a moment of spontaneity, the interpreter must also reflect that apparent spontaneity in their signed rendition."[61]

In our dialogic approach to theatre, interpreters are expressing "a chain of utterances" in the context of the play. Cecilia Wadensjö speaks about dialogic interpretation in her book, *Interpreting as Interaction*:

> A dialogical point of view . . . implies that an utterance is seen as a link in a chain of utterances, as a thread in a net of intertwined communicative behaviour. Meanings conveyed are seen as resulting from joint efforts between the people involved. Hence, the meanings of an original utterance will depend on how it is reacted to by people present at it . . .[62]

In our dialogic approach to theatre, interpreters are expressing "a chain of utterances" in the context of the play. To understand these chains of utterances, interpreters must explore them in their full theatrical context. When crafting a translation, interpreters keep in mind, as Searls says, "the kinds of things speakers of that language naturally do and listeners or readers naturally expect."[63]

We call attention to the core of our task, as defined by Danika Seleskovitch in *Interpreting in International Conferences*:

> Interpreters should not be focusing on word-level equivalents but rather on the sense of what a text conveys . . . The sensing of what is meant as opposed to knowing a language as such is the very foundation of interpretation.[64]

This reminder is true for both spoken and signed language interpretation.

Next, because the team is interpreting the discourse of the characters onstage, we offer Erlich and Romaniuk's definition of discourse as "language embedded in social interaction."[65] Most dialogue onstage is interactive, and the meaning within the dialogue is derived from the context and from the manner in which the characters interact socially.

In *Interpreting as a Discourse Process*, Cynthia Roy discusses how people communicate and co-construct meaning in conversation. "As people talk, meaning is created in and by the relationships established, by previous knowledge and experience interaction, by words, and sentences, and by the way utterances occur sequentially."[66] Roy goes on to quote Deborah Schiffrin, who elucidated a framework for understanding interpersonal communication:

> One of Schiffrin's central principles of discourse is that "how something is said, meant, and done . . ." is guided by relationships among the following:
>
> 1. Speaker intentions
> 2. Conventionalized strategies for making intentions recognizable
> 3. The meanings and functions of linguistic forms within their emerging contexts
> 4. The sequential context of other utterances
> 5. Properties of the discourse mode—narrative, description, and exposition

6. The social context—participant identities and relationships, structure of the situation, and the setting
7. A cultural framework of beliefs and actions.[67]

Interpretation includes the meaning intended and transmitted by the original speaker. Cynthia Roy sums up the factors to consider:

> [An] interpreter's primary concern while interpreting is to make sense of what any one person means when saying something and to convey that same sense to another person. How something is said and meant is guided by a number of relationships, the same sort of relationships that a discourse analyst uses when determining what speakers mean, such as speaker intentions, conventionalized strategies for making conventions recognizable, the meaning and function of linguistic forms, the sequential context of utterances, discourse genre, the social context, and a cultural framework of beliefs and actions.[68]

The interpreting team's task is to analyze these social cues, find ways to express them, and weave them into the interpretation. This collective construction leads us to better cohesion in the interpreted discourse of the play.

The translatory strategies applied in this dialogic approach help the team thread discrete character utterances into natural signed discourse, reflecting ASL communicative norms. Interpretations should be responsive to team partners' utterances. There are dangers of freezing individual translations in isolation in that it can impede the interactive dialogic expression of the team. When interpretations are not developed in concert, the responsive interactions can get lost. They live in a parallel discourse rather than an interactive and responsive discourse, a discourse that breathes and responds to changes in the actors' presentations and in teammates' translations. Of course, there may be moments that are frozen (such as agreed-upon cues, moments in songs, Shakespearean soliloquies, etc.), but the goal is to intimately know the play so that the well-rehearsed interpretation is still responsive to the moment.

These translatory practices help the team develop a collective understanding of the characters' interactions. The rehearsal process helps the team arrive at an interpretation that demonstrates cohesion of thoughts, themes, affect, character relationships, and narrative. Assigning of characters is also explored in the early stages as it is also a translatory consideration. The team monitors the cohesion of its output with the goal of individual translation, team translation agreements, and the performance of the interpretation all aligning with the performance on the stage, with the requirement that everything is produced in a linguistically and culturally appropriate manner in ASL.

To convey these cultural interactions within the parameters of interpreted theatre, our team must bring linguistic and cultural competencies to help us become, in Kate Briggs's words, the "producer of the relations."[69] Collaboration with Deaf team members as interpreters, as advisors, as DOIs, as translation coaches, as language and culture resources, and so on is more than standard practice—it is a requisite to produce authentic expressions of the play in signed language.

TOOLS FOR TRANSLATION

> "In any case, there is a thing that exists in one place, and the translator brings it, keeping it as intact as possible, to another place. After this process, the same thing exists in another place."[70]
>
> —Damion Searls, *The Philosophy of Translation*

While teaching at the Theatre Development Fund (TDF) Interpreting for the Theatre Seminar, we drew from the tools offered in Mildred Larson's *Meaning-Based Translation: A Guide to Cross-Language Equivalence*,[71] to develop cohesive and interactive signed interpretations, in which she addresses translation between written and oral face-to-face languages. Here, we discuss how her theory is applicable to teams preparing an interpreted show. Larson uses the terms "source" and "target." These terms can seem linear and aggressive. We authors see the process as more of a journey and offer the terms "starting point" and "destination," because these terms suggest traveling through and among languages and cultures. However, "target" is the term most commonly used in the field, and we will continue to use it for the remainder of the book.

Larson addresses the "Four Ts" that the translator (or, in our case, the interpreting team) considers while preparing a translation:

- Text—The source text
- Team—Who are involved with the translation
- Tools—What tools are used in the course of the translation
- Target—The language of the audience that you are interpreting for

Interpreting in the theatre entails working from a performed language into a performed language, rather than from a frozen text into a frozen text. This means that our source is not the script, but rather a live performance. Her work inspired us to contextualize Larson's Four Ts for the theatre:

- THEATRICAL PRODUCTION—staging elements, visual and auditory information, dialogue, character interactions
- TEAM—interpreters + directors of interpreters
- TOOLS—dramaturgical community sources and online information
- TARGET—audience language and familiarity with theatre conventions

Larson also offers a translation continuum that ranges from literal–unduly free, with idiomatic as the goal. "Idiomatic translation is meaning-based translation which makes every effort to communicate the meaning of the source language text in the natural forms of the receptor language."[72] Figure 2.1 shows the designations for Larson's continuum.

This continuum can be both an evaluative tool and a reflective tool to explore the translation. For example, if you identify portions of the translation that are "very literal," then it is an opportunity to engage in a practice of inquiry—why was that choice made? The reasons could vary from still forming an understanding of

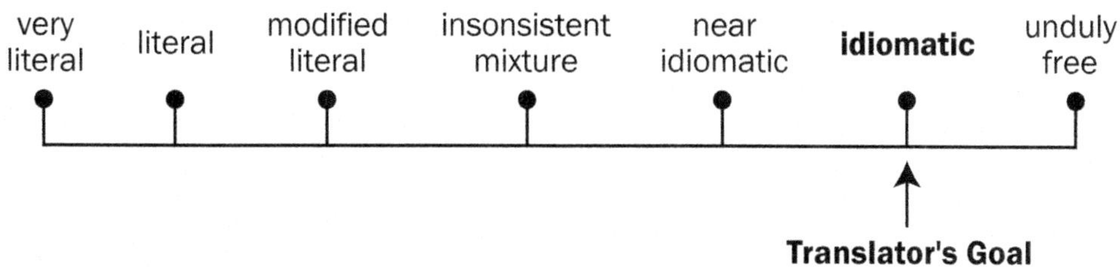

Figure 2.1. Larson's continuum.

the source material, to searching for a way to express that concept in the target language, to mulling over the idea that a direct literal importation would be most effective.

Note that the translator's goal of "idiomatic" language is found relatively close to "unduly free" translations that, as Larson explains, may add extraneous language, change the meaning, or "distort the facts of the historical and cultural setting of the source language text."[73] The goal is to stay in the idiomatic and not jump over into "unduly free."

While "idiomatic" expression is the target on Larson's continuum, all translations are relative to each utterance and its context in the play. At times, there may be moments when interpreters intentionally choose to produce unidiomatic translations. There is no fixed point that signifies the "right translation" for a particular moment or scene. It isn't a rigid marker or destination. Rather, it is a journey along the continuum and measured in relation to all the strands of meaning throughout the play. The goal is to find what works for the scene, the play, and the team.

According to Marinetti, "The greatest advantage of seeing translation as *performative* is that it allows us to place originals and translations, source and target texts, dramatic texts and performances on the same cline, where what counts is the effect that the reconfigured text (as performance) has on the receiving culture and its networks of transmission and reception."[74]

Larson's continuum helps identify where the individual translation lies, but in addition, we propose that the team's interpretation needs to be examined in its interactive sense along several continuums, each of which is a strand of the "performed dialogic" interpretation (fig. 2.2).

Understanding where the work is on each continuum helps interpreters assess which strand needs to be dialed up or dialed down, so to speak. Exploring these interactive strands for meaning coherence on individual, team, and performance levels helps align the teamed interpretation with the production (fig. 2.3).

Marinetti sees translation as

> a linguistic, cultural, literary, sociological, hermeneutic, historical, ideological and aesthetic practice. The aim then would not be one of constructing revolutionary new paradigms or frameworks that do away with everything that came before, but rather to offer new concepts (such as the notion of *performativity)*, which can be used alongside existing analytical tools (linguistic, semiotic, cultural analysis) to approach translation in the theatre.[75]

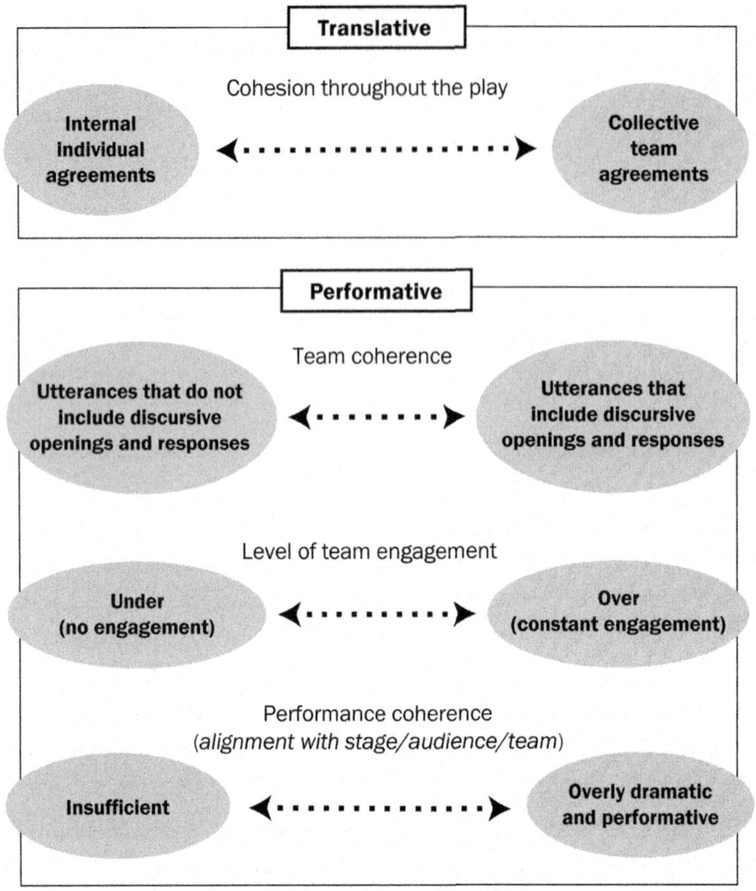

Figure 2.2. Translative and performative continuums. Copyright © 2024 Taylor, Feyne, and Broecker Penn.

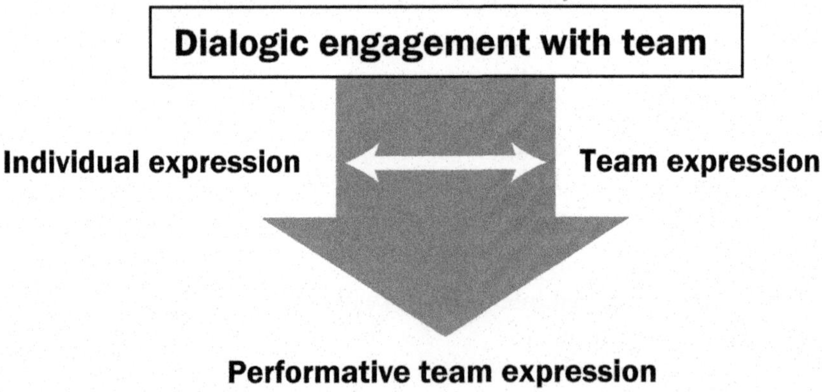

Figure 2.3. Dialogic engagement with team. Copyright © 2024 Taylor, Feyne, and Broecker Penn.

COHESION IN INTERACTIVE INTERPRETATION

A cohesive teamed idiomatic interpretation requires consideration of both individual construction and teamed construction of meaning. The team recognizes and finds moments to include the stage as a partner in the construction of the interpretation.

Onstage discourse is constructed to elicit responses in a dialogic manner; likewise, the teamed interpretation must ensure that meaning is intact and cohesive throughout the characters' conversations. As a single utterance, a translation may be replete, but when it is seen in context, it may not work as a discursive agreement. The team assesses whether the meaning is clear not only in an interpreter's individual translations but also in the teamed dialogic interpretation.

We suggest that interpreters look for interpretation coherence in three areas: within individual discourse, within team discourse, and within the performance. All three areas require expression of meaning that is responsive to the production. Without cohesion among all three, interactive contextualized meaning will not be intact.

Individual Coherence

- Individual translation that has semantic, affective, and spatial coherence with expressions that are contextualized and responsive to the production
- Natural dialogic features of ASL incorporated into utterances

Team Coherence

- Teamed translation that has semantic, affective, and spatial agreements that are cohesive and responsive to teamed signed utterances
- Natural dialogic features of ASL incorporated into utterances and responses

Performance Coherence

- Interpreted constructed discourse that aligns with the characters' affect, intent, interactions, and stage information
- Spatial mapping and referencing that aligns with the stage information
- Natural dialogic features of ASL incorporated into utterances and responses

When the expressions of meaning at the individual, team, and performance levels are cohesive, the team produces idiomatic discourse that is aligned with the production.

Engaging in the work with these understandings leads us to engage in collaborative inquiry. This becomes the foundation for a different kind of interactive individual and teamed interpretation, in which both the translation and the performative nature of the interpretation are examined and expressed in response to the live performance.

The foundational understandings and inquiry we have addressed in this chapter will come to play in our next chapters on translation and performance.

Notes

1. "Infrequent society" is a term promulgated by artist Catherine Opie. Catherine Opie, "The Community of Difference," *Surprise.org*, November 30, 2021, https://sunpride.hk/catherine-opie-community-difference/.
2. Opie, "The Community of Difference."
3. Damion Searls, *The Philosophy of Translation* (Yale University Press, 2024), 89–90.
4. Trudy Suggs, "Deaf Disempowerment and Today's Interpreter," StreetLeverage, 2012, https://streetleverage.com/live_presentations/deaf-disempowerment-and-todays-interpreter/.
5. Janis Cole, "Deaf Translators: What Are They Thinking?" *Journal of Interpretation* 28, no. 1 (2020): 3.
6. "The Power of Deaf Artistic Expression: An Interview with MJ Bienvenu," *The HeART of Deaf Culture*, January 17, 2018, https://heartdeaf.com/overview.
7. Searls, *The Philosophy of Translation*, 3.
8. DawnSignPress, "This Never-Before-Seen Video, the Father of Deaf Theatre Eric 'Malz' Malzkuhn (1922–2008) Reflects on Choosing His Successor, the Talented Joe Velez," Facebook, July 8, 2017, https://www.facebook.com/watch/?v=1737130106316087.
9. DawnSignPress, "This Never-Before-Seen Video."
10. DawnSignPress, "This Never-Before-Seen Video."
11. Walter Benjamin, "The Task of the Translator," in Walter Benjamin: Selected Writings Volume 1, 1913–1926, ed. Marcus Bullock and Michael W. Jennings (The Belknap Press, 1996), 261.
12. Ilaria Parogni, "How These Sign Language Experts Are Bringing More Diversity to Theater," *The New York Times*, January 7, 2023, https://www.nytimes.com/2023/01/07/arts/sign-language-experts-diversity-theater.html.
13. In 2021, The Alliance of Resident Theaters in New York (A.R.T./NY) and Hands On hosted an informative panel discussion "Spotlight on DASLs: The Role of Directors of Artistic Sign Language." Panelists included Alexandria Wailes, Anne Tomasetti, John McGinty, Monique Holt, and Zavier Sabo, and it was moderated by Janis Cole. "Spotlight on DASLs: The Role of Directors of Artistic Sign Language." A.R.T./New York, June 2, 2021, https://www.youtube.com/watch?v=pGDPLpEvcY4&t=1241s.
14. Andrew Morrill, personal communication to the *Grey House Company,* March 18, 2023, included with permission.
15. Morrill, personal communication.
16. Parogni, "How These Sign Language Experts Are Bringing More Diversity to Theater."
17. Interview, Anne Tomasetti with Lynnette Taylor and Candace Broecker Penn, August 14, 2021.
18. Interview, Anne Tomasetti.
19. *Travesties*, by Tom Stoppard, dir. by Patrick Marber, interp. Bill Moody, Molly Wilson, and Stephanie Feyne, DOI. Anne Tomasetti, Roundabout Theatre, New York, NY, April 24, 2016.
20. Interview, Anne Tomasetti.
21. *Enemy of the People,* by Henrik Ibsen, dir. Sam Gold, adapt. Amy Herzog, interp. Candace Broecker Penn, Dylan Geil, and Rick Rubin, DOI. Andrew Fisher, Circle in the Square, New York, NY, April 26, 2024.

22. "Dramaturgs are experts in the study of plays, musicals, or operas. It is their job to provide the cast and crew with vital knowledge, research, and interpretation about the theatrical work in question . . . [and] to know as much as possible about the play at hand, including its themes, language, period, history, music, and even past stagings, and to hold the current production to a high standard of historical and textual accuracy." *Berklee,* https://www.berklee.edu/careers/roles/dramaturg.
23. Andrew Fisher, email to Candace Broecker Penn, June 15, 2024.
24. *Here There Were Blueberries*, by Moisés Kaufman and Amanda Gronich, dir. Moisés Kaufman, interp. Jess Ames, Craig Fogel, and Amy Meckler, DOI. Joyce Hom, New York Theatre Workshop, New York, NY, April 17, 2024–June 30, 2024.
25. Joyce Hom, interview with Stephanie Feyne, July 6, 2024.
26. Eileen Forestal and Janis Cole, "translation: socio-cultural space," (workshop, RID Biennial Conference, Providence, RI, July 7–11, 2019).
27. Fisher, email.
28. Marc Tracy, "Who Can Play the King? Questions of Representation Fuel Casting Debates," *The New York Times*, July 28, 2022, https://www.nytimes.com/2022/07/28/theater/richard-iii-casting-debates.html.
29. Melanie Metzger, *Sign Language Interpreting: Deconstructing the Myth of Neutrality* (Gallaudet University Press, 1999).
30. Mariah Stewart, "Deaf and Hard of Hearing Community Suffers from Dearth of Diverse Interpreters," *Insight into Diversity,* October 16, 2020, https://www.insightintodiversity.com.
31. Basil Hatim and Ian Mason, *The Translator as Communicator* (Routledge, 1996), 146.
32. "Principles for Building Anti-Racist Theatre Systems," *We See You White American Theatre*, accessed February 2, 2023, https://www.weseeyouwat.com/.
33. "NBDA, NAD, RID Statement on Culturally Appropriate Interpreters," *National Association of the Deaf,* November 11, 2022, https://www.nad.org/2022/11/22/nbda-nad-rid-statement-on-culturally-appropriate-interpreters/.
34. Mary Bucholtz and Kira Hall, "Embodied Sociolinguistics," in *Sociolinguistics: Theoretical Debates*, ed. Nikolas Coupland (Cambridge University Press, 2016), 173–97.
35. *Yellow Face* talk back at the Roundabout Theatre, November 9, 2024. *Yellow Face,* by David Henry Hwang, dir. Leigh Silverman, Roundabout Theatre, New York, NY, October 1–November 24, 2024.
36. Alexandria Wailes, interview with Lynnette Taylor and Candace Broecker Penn, June 20, 2020.
37. Erica West Oyedele, "Persistence of African American/Black Signed Language Interpreters in the United States: The Importance of Culture and Capital" (thesis, Western Oregon University, 2015), 77.
38. Parogni, "How These Sign Language."
39. Parogni, "How These Sign Language."
40. "*A Soldier's Play*: An Interview with Director Kenny Leon," *Roundabout Theatre,* January 15, 2020, https://www.roundabouttheatre.org/about/our-blog/an-interview-with-director-kenny-leon/.
41. *A Soldier's Play,* by Charles Fuller, dir. Kenny Leon, interps. Dana Fuller, Jose Gomez, Rick Rubin, and Jacinda Damas, DOI. Darren (Dax) Fudenske and Zavier Sabio, Roundabout Theatre, New York, NY, January–March 2020.

42. Zavier Sabio, interview with Lynnette Taylor and Candace Broecker Penn, April 1, 2020.
43. Alastair Pennycook, "Performativity and Language Studies," *Critical Inquiry in Language Studies* 1, no. 1 (2004): 1–19, https://doi.org/10.1207/s15427595cils0101_1.
44. Judith Butler, *Who's Afraid of Gender* (Farrar, Straus, and Giroux, 2024).
45. "David Henry Hwang Discusses His Play 'Yellow Face,' Now on Broadway," *Columbia News*, December 6, 2024, https://news.columbia.edu/news/david-henry-hwang-discusses-his-play-yellow-face-now-broadway.
46. "The Lion King Live Action Cast—Diversity in Voice-Over," *Voices*, August 27, 2019, https://www.voices.com/blog/the-lion-king-diversity-in-voice-over/.
47. Brent Lang, "Despite Success of 'CODA,' Study Finds Deaf Community 'Rarely' or 'Never' Sees Itself Reflected on Screen," *Variety*, November 22, 2022, https://variety.com/2022/film/news/coda-study-nrg-deaf-representation-movies-tv-1235439108/.
48. "Deaf Representation," National Research Group and Deaf West Theatre, November 2022, https://downloads.ctfassets.net/4ivt4uy3jinr/6TDIhMpZdL9iILN2CcNnbn/3e601d88e31a0c00c7c3487d2e72497c/Deaf_Representation_Report.pdf.
49. Jazz Tangcay, "Deaf Representation Is Improving in Film and TV, but Falls Short in Video Games, Animation and Kids TV," *Variety*, April 14, 2023, https://variety.com/2023/film/news/deaf-representation-hollywood-animation-video-games-kids-tv-1235582543/.
50. *Spotlight on Deaf Representation: A Roundtable Discussion*, National Research Group and Deaf West Theatre, April 14, 2023, https://www.youtube.com/watch?v=bjN4salwtUM.
51. *Waitress,* by Jessie Nelson, music and lyrics by Sara Bareilles, dir. Diane Paulus, Brooks Atkinson Theatre, New York, NY, March 25, 2016–January 5, 2020.
52. *Our Town*, by Thorton Wilder, dir. David Cromer, Barrow Street Theatre, February 26, 2009.
53. *Cabaret*, by Joseph Masteroff, music by John Kander, lyrics by Fred Ebb, Studio 54, New York, NY, 1998 and 2014.
54. *The Glass Menagerie*, by Tennessee Williams, dir. John Tiffany, Booth Theatre, New York, NY, 2013.
55. Basil Hatim and Ian Mason, *The Translator As Communicator* (Routledge, 1996), 2.
56. Cristina Marinetti, ed., *Translation and Theatre: From Performance to Performativity* (Benjamins, 2013), 319.
57. Greg Evans, "'Purlie Victorious' Broadway Review: Leslie Odom Jr. Keeps Ossie Davis' Groundbreaking Comedy True to its Title," *Deadline*, September 27, 2023, https://deadline.com/2023/09/purlie-victorious-broadway-review-1235555904/.
58. Interview, Anne Tomasetti.
59. Searls, *The Philosophy of Translation*, 94.
60. "The Meisner Technique Studio," *The Meisner Technique*, January 9, 2019, https://themeisnertechniquestudio.com/meisner-technique/.
61. Siobhán Rocks, "The Theatre Sign Language Interpreter and the Competing Visual Narrative: The Translation and Interpretation of Theatrical Texts to British Sign Language," in *Staging and Performing Translation: Text and Theatre Practice*, ed. R. Baines, C. Marinetti, and M. Perteghella (Palgrave Macmillan, 2011), 72–86.
62. Cecilia Wadensjö, *Interpreting as Interaction* (Routledge, 1998), 43.
63. Searls, *The Philosophy of Translation*, 89.
64. Danika Seleskovitch, *L'interprète dans les conférences internationales, problèmes de langage et de communication* (Paris: Minard Lettres Modernes, 1968). Translated into

English as *Interpreting for International Conferences*, 2nd rev. ed. (Pen and Booth, 1994).

65. Susan Ehrlich and Tanya Romaniuk, "Discourse Analysis," in *Research Methods in Linguistics*, ed. Rovert J. Podesva and Sharma Devyani (Cambridge University Press, 2013), 466–99.
66. Cynthia Roy, *Interpreting as a Discourse Process* (Oxford University Press, 1999), 110.
67. Roy, *Interpreting*, 110–111.
68. Roy, *Interpreting*, 22.
69. Kate Briggs, *This Little Art* (Fitzcarraldo Editions, 2017).
70. Searls, *The Philosophy of Translation*, 17.
71. Mildred Larson, *Meaning-Based Translation: A Guide to Cross-Language Equivalence* (University Press of America, Inc., 1998).
72. Larson, *Meaning-Based Translation,* 17.
73. Larson, *Meaning-Based Translation,* 17.
74. Marinetti, *Translation and Theatre*, 2013.
75. Marinetti, *Translation and Theatre*, 10.

3

Translation: Developing Agreements

Sign Language Interpreting for Theatre: A Collaborative Approach is the title of our book because we believe the team as a whole is responsible for co-constructing the expression of the meaning presented in a play. The challenge that the interpreting team faces is how to manage the multiple forms of content strands: language to language, culture to culture, aural to visual, visual to visual, performative to performative, and, at times, textual to textual.

Theatre interpreting, unlike many other venues, affords an opportunity to work collaboratively and synergistically with a team. It is a much-needed salve to what many interpreters often complain of—isolation in their work. By working with a team, interpreters are invited in to see each other's working process, discoveries, sketches of translations, language use, and multiple ways of expressing a thought—a rich world of surprises, where we can see the possible variants of an interpretation and borrow from each other's palettes.

We offer a three-pronged process of meaning exploration, translation refinement, and translation presentation during the interpreted performance. This iterative process of discovery continues throughout our work. The strategies and techniques crucial to crafting a performed interpretation apply to both the individual interpreter's construction and the team's collective construction. The translation exists in relation to the play as a whole and to each scene, as well as to each interpreter's individual translation, and the team's translation.

We are, all of us, translating the world around us at every moment. Every interaction awakens the innate translator in all of us and, according to I. A. Richards, "Translation probably is the most complex type of event yet produced in the evolution of the cosmos."[1]

This section begins with a discussion of how to identify meaning, where it resides, and its myriad possibilities of expression in our interpretations. Translation (chapters 3 and 4) and performance (chapter 5) are in separate sections, but that is an artifact of the writing process. In actuality, this is a fluid and responsive process.

Fidelity is the main concern for any interpreter or translator. The question for the sign language interpreter in the theatre is, "Where does my fidelity lie: to the script, to the performed word, or to the production as a whole?" In our Interpreting for the Theatre Seminar, many participants arrived with a belief that fidelity should be to the playwright's words and that conveying those words through transliteration honors the source. However, when their transliterated version was presented, fellow participants responded that they only understood bits of information in isolated moments, not the overall meaning of the passage. When the participants included the contextual information that is implicit in the lines as well as nonverbal information from the stage, the interpretation became more vibrant and aligned with the source. When that happened, everyone responded more favorably; they felt that they now understood the story.

Our belief is that fidelity must align with the story presented onstage as it is unfolding in real time. This means that our fidelity lies to the whole production in its full context, and not to a word or a line—or even a scene—in isolation. We think of our work as a conversation with the audience, with our interpreting team, and with the stage, the text, and the performance. In fact, we conceptualize the stage as a member of our interpreting team; hence, the interpretation is designed in response to and in concert with the events unfolding on the stage.

The stage functions as both our primary source and partner because our goal is to connect the audience to the stage. The more we "listen" and respond to the stage, the more cohesive the interpreted conversation. We treat the stage as an active collaborator in our interpreting process by drawing from its rhythms and cues, shifting focus between it and the interpreters, and engaging with it as part of the unfolding drama. Integrating all of these elements requires a different mindset. Translators recognize that translations rest on a fulcrum and strive to find a balance that will honor the meaning and, when possible, the form as well. As Jhumpa Lahiri explains, "Translation requires creativity, it requires ingenuity, it requires imagination. So often, you have to radically rework the text, and if that isn't the work of imagination, I don't know what is."[2]

> "to translate is to transthink."
>
> —José Martí[3]

"Transthinking" means considering the respective relational worlds in the target and source languages, the differences in their modalities and cultures, as well as the nature of the live source material, which is, in this case, the performative world of the play. Transthinking also requires interpreters to consider the sociopolitical context in which the play originated and is being performed.

Of course, a translator's eye is always looking "true north" to fidelity. Much like video calling on a mobile phone, we keep adjusting to get a clear picture or a clear signal. Think of fidelity in the same way—a dance in space, in the moment, looking and aiming for the place where we can both receive and transmit the clearest signal. Transthinking posits that there isn't a fixed point for "fidelity." Fidelity is considered to be both relative and responsive to the stage, the interpreting team, and the audience.

As "transthinking" suggests, there is movement—a crossing between thought worlds. This propels the translator to keep tuning into the conversations between the social/cultural/linguistic/theatrical aspects of each show. This is why we encourage a more collective interactional development of a translation. Engaging with team members from diverse communities can bring the multiple expressions of these ideas to life.

Simply said, the team strives for a living interpretation, not a fixed translation. This requires the interpreter to be committed to a living translatory process, one which allows, as David Hare says, "your sample dialogue to develop, change, strengthen in the course of time, as a result of the translator's deepening experience of the text and of comments from the outside."[4]

To engage in this process requires a different kind of attention and awareness than interpreters normally use to approach their daily interpreting. The complexities are not only cultural, ideological, and linguistic, but also logistical. Drawing from the performance on stage (our source), our practical considerations include the lexical, semantic, visual, interactional, and performative layers of meaning. The presentation of our translation is an additional factor because our source and our live interpretation are both performative.

These layers operate simultaneously, but at each moment, interpreters must make decisions about which one takes precedence. In one moment, the visual information may be primary, while in the next, the lexical content in the lines may take precedence. Theatre interpreters do not ignore all the other strands; they monitor to see which one brings the clearest meaning into focus in each moment.

Interpreters' underlying beliefs guide their decisions, whether these beliefs are conscious or unconscious. Exploring these and developing a set of shared beliefs about the approach to the practice with the interpreting team provides a foundation for collectively co-constructing a cohesive interpretation inspired by shared principles.

Here are some important beliefs that inform the practice:

- The translation is produced in signed language in a natural dialogic manner.
- We are there as interpreters, not as performers.
- The team is collectively responsible for the transmission of meaning.
- The team co-constructs the interpretation.
- The script is a tool; however, our primary source is the performance.
- The team is composed of the director of interpreters (DOI), interpreters, and the stage.
- The team interpretation is designed to let the stage speak for itself as much as possible.

In addition, this work is built on respect for both languages, both cultures, the language of the theatre, the cultures represented onstage plus the diversity reflected within Deaf culture, our audience, our colleagues, and the team interpreting process.

Meaning Is Not Only in the Words

What is unique in the theatre is that interpreters derive meaning from multiple sources simultaneously. The time, setting, and stage visuals (e.g., Harlem in the 1970s or Iowa in 1912) are "unspoken" elements that a translation draws from in order to create as authentic a world as possible. In addition, the interpreting team's translations are informed by the text, the actors' choices of expression and manner of interaction, stage action, and other elements of the performance.

Interpreters know that meaning goes beyond words and is contextual. The goal is to ensure the information exchanged within the social interactions of the characters on stage is expressed in the interpretations. Sometimes, what is implicit in one language—which may also include culturally specific gestures—must be made explicit in another because each languaculture has its own reservoir of implicit understandings built on shared life experiences and social contexts. For example, in Sainvil's article discussing theatre translations, Prof. Lamartine-Lens of Pace University mentions that even some gestural information is culturally specific, "One roll of the eyes in American culture says a thousand words. That doesn't exist in Spain—that gesture. So you're translating not only words."[5]

Meaning can also be expressed implicitly in one language when the individuals in the conversation have a shared life experience and social context. The question of how information is delivered (implicitly or explicitly, linguistically, or gesturally) when working between American Sign Language (ASL) and English is explored throughout the process of developing the interpretation.

WHAT IS UNDERSTOOD FROM SILENCE?

> "Silence has a myriad of meanings. In the theatre, silence is an absence of words, but it is never an absence of meaning."[6]
>
> —Sanford Meisner

Theatre is replete with meaningful silences. Silence is form. It is deliberate. In Samuel Beckett's *Waiting for Godot*, Gogo and Didi run out of things to say. In Harold Pinter's *The Caretaker*, the characters quietly brood in corners. In many contemporary plays, such as Christopher Demos-Brown's *American Son*, silence is charged with underlying tension and imbued with implicit social/political/cultural meaning. Silence—that lack of spoken lines—can be incredibly powerful and meaningful. The aim is to allow the silences to "speak."[7]

When examining moments of silence, we consider:

- What events or interactions lead up to the silence?
- What is being communicated in the silence?
- What is the tone, subtext, and/or mood of this moment?

SOME MEANINGS ARE IMPLIED BUT NOT STATED EXPLICITLY

There are different reasons for information being unstated on stage. When audiences have a shared contextual understanding, information does not need to be said overtly. Information to interpret is sometimes in the text, sometimes in the manner it is spoken, sometimes implicit, and sometimes in the visual information on the stage.

Consider an onstage moment with implicit information from the musical *Cabaret.*

The scene is set in Berlin during the 1930s. Cliff Bradshaw has been beaten up by Nazis. He is concerned that he doesn't know where his pregnant girlfriend, Sally Bowles, has been all night. Early in the morning, Sally arrives home shivering. She wants a drink, even though Cliff reminds her that expectant mothers shouldn't drink. He asks where her coat (that has been featured prominently in previous scenes) is. She responds that she left it at the doctor's office. Cliff worries that she might not have been feeling well. She tells him how she makes promises and never lives up to them, but Cliff still doesn't understand. She tries to make it more explicit by saying:

Cabaret[8]

Act II–Scene 6

SALLY: *My one regret is I honestly believe you'd have been a wonderful father.*

Later, in the same speech, she implies that her coat was the fee for medical services with her remark,

SALLY: *I've another regret: That greedy doctor. I'm going to miss my fur coat.*

She never overtly states that she had an abortion, but the meaning is finally understood by Cliff in that last exchange.

When theatre interpreters encounter meaning that is not directly stated, questions arise, such as:

- What are the choices when something is not said overtly in English, but the plot revolves around the implicit meaning being understood?
- What does this "implied" idea look like in the target language?

- How can the interpretation be strategically designed, building in references along the way of the importance of the coat to Sally? Thus, when she says, "I'm going to miss my fur coat," the implications of her fur coat being the payment for the abortion will be clear.

The understandings between the characters as well as those between the stage and the audience are important considerations. Sometimes, what is not stated in one language will need to be expressed in another, and vice versa. The translation considers what is understood in the world of the play. What does the character understand and what does the audience understand at a given moment?

Sometimes, information is not stated explicitly because it appears visually on the stage. For example, when the characters are talking about the donuts that they are dunking in their coffee, they may not say "donut," but rather, "It's so much better when you dunk it." The referent is visible on the stage.

When interpreters move into performing the interpretation, the visual information (ASL and the stage picture) are separated. When making interpreting choices, think about the visual elements that need to be incorporated into the interpretation, whether the reason is grammatical, efficiency (the time it takes the audience to see both the stage and the interpretation) or aesthetic, or whether the visual information can live on the stage.

Recognizing Themes and Motifs

Themes are the central ideas of the play, and motifs are recurring narrative elements that carry symbolic significance. Exploration of themes helps the team gain a deeper understanding of a play, which in turn can lead to an interpretation that resonates with the underlying message of the narrative. Thematic information can appear in multiple forms, as motifs or conceptual frameworks or ideas, and is dramatized in language, settings, and/or actions. In order to weave these references into the interpretation, one must first recognize them as elements in the narrative.

In *Cabaret*, there are recurring references to Sally's fur coat. This motif of the coat changes signification throughout the play. These nuanced shifts in meaning also need to be recognized in the translation. To see Sally without the coat is an important visual moment. To ensure that the loss of the fur coat will resonate, references to the coat in earlier scenes will have to be noted and highlighted. The process of building in the references requires us to analyze and then construct an interpretation by moving both forward and backward through the narrative to note its changes in signification.

In Alexandra Alter's article about Jennifer Croft (translator for Pulitzer Prize–winning novelist Olga Tokarczuk), Croft "described her process as 'completely dismantling a book and then completely rebuilding it from the ground up.'"[9] When translating a play from a holistic—rather than a linear—view, the symbolic references that reside in the narrative need to be identified. When building the translation from the ground up, the interpreting team should recognize the function of important motifs so that they can import the motifs into the translation.

Cultural Information

One strand of content that is infused in a narrative, but not always explicitly revealed through words, is culture. Culture is, of course, embedded in everything (dialogue, unstated understandings, physical action, visual setting, etc.). Culture may be represented in social norms, behaviors, mores, and underlying beliefs, which are expressed in the play through dialogue and actions.

Sometimes, the cultural information is more overtly available, such as when cultural specificity is written into a play. Layers of cultural meaning may be found in works such as Lin-Manuel Miranda's *In the Heights* (contemporary New York City [NYC] Latiné), August Wilson's ten-play "Pittsburgh Cycle" (African American mid-twentieth century), Brian Friel's *Dancing At Lughnasa* (1930s Irish), Paula Vogel's *Indecent* (a love story between two Jewish women during the first half of the twentieth century), Beth Henley's *Crimes of the Heart* (1980s Southern USA), Mart Crowley's *Boys in the Band* (Gay community NYC 1968), and Oscar Wilde's *The Importance of Being Earnest* (fin de siècle upper class British), to name a few.

Directors may layer a culturally specific world onto the piece. For example, two versions of *The Taming of the Shrew* produced by the Public Theater's Shakespeare in the Park presented two completely different cultures. One production was built on the premise that the ensemble was a traveling carnival touring the American West. This was performed by a female company, challenging gender norms. This layer of cultural meaning would, of course, have an impact on the translation and performed interpretation, as well as the composition of the interpreting team. This same play was produced in the park by another director who based it in the era of the Wild West and populated it with a mixed race and mixed gender ensemble. The same dialogue with a different directorial intention led to a vastly different production, which required a different interpretation.

Contextual Information

All plays are performed in conversation with the audience and the time in which they live. Within a play, there are contexts within contexts: the era in which it was created, the era and culture in which it is placed by the director's vision, and the contemporary social time in which the audience lives while seeing the production. These conversations between the contexts bring different shades of meaning that interpreters will want to address.

In 2017, the Public Theater produced *Julius Caesar* in NYC's Central Park. It was conceived as a response to the presidential election. Its casting and performance were deliberately evocative of the Trump administration. The public response was strong. Some audience members loved it, and some vociferously did not. Political operatives denounced the production, and some of the funding for the show was pulled. Audiences could not help but see the play through the lens of contemporary politics. This was simultaneously a historical and real-time conversation with audiences who were engaging both with the staged story and the social events of the time.

Director Kenny Leon's 2019 production of *Much Ado About Nothing* for the Public Theater was framed with a contemporary African American cultural lens. It was performed during a time of social examination and reckoning, just as the Black Lives Matter movement was gaining national attention. Leon's company of Black actors challenged the traditional casting of Shakespearean productions by situating the show in a conversation about cultural representation, power, and privilege.

An outsider to a particular culture may not understand or even recognize a play's layered nuances of expression. In the case of *Much Ado,* the 2019 production signaled contextual as well as cultural information in the production elements (including a "Stacey Abrams 2020" banner as well as Jimi Hendrix's version of "The Star Spangled Banner"). Cultural information was also found in the actors' spoken cadence as well as backchanneling and gestures. This created a space where the spoken language contained, in Sharon Masingale Bell words, "the very symbolic function of expressing our intergroup unity and our separateness from other groups in American society."[10] This production was one of many around the country that demonstrated the universality of the human tales of Shakespeare by offering a specific cultural lens.

In sum, meaning is conveyed through silences, implied meanings, motifs, themes, cultures, and contexts, in addition to the text and production elements. Exploring these content strands leads to a deeper understanding of the inherent meaning found within these conversations. Questions to ask include: What is the conversation of context talking to context? Of culture talking to culture? Of performance talking to the audience? Interpreters for the theatre continue to search for where elements of meaning reside.

Questions to Unpack Meaning

We offer an inquiry-based approach that helps develop a robust interpretation, one that considers all the interconnected elements in a production in order to create an interpretation that is true to the production and true to its expression in ASL.

In the theatre, meaning is transmitted not only from the text, but also by the direction, the visual information on the stage, the manner in which the actors present their lines, the social and historical context in which the play is set, and, in short, the entirety of the play. The contemporary time, place, and conditions surrounding a production also have an impact on our understanding of its meaning.

The moment the lights go down, the audience wonders:

- What is the world of the play?
- Who are the characters?
- What are their relationships?

Interpreters (as receivers and producers of meaning) begin the process by asking questions that help uncover the story arc, character arc, character relationships, and thematic through lines.

- What is the genre?
- What are the themes?
- What is the feel/tone/mood?
- What are the characters' journeys?
- What is the narrative arc?
- How does each scene fit into the narrative arc?
- What does each scene reveal about the characters and their relationships?
- What are the key scenes of the play, the cornerstones?
- Is there a recurring concept or image or action?
- Are there specific historical or sociocultural contexts that are being represented?

Opening up this inquiry leads to a cascade of questions specific to the interpretation of each production.

This next set of questions arise from the dialogue:

- What do the characters' lines mean in context?
- What does this exchange reveal about the characters and their relationships and their interactions?
- Do the characters share the same understandings or do their viewpoints differ?

Stage information that should be considered in our interpretation includes:

- What visual information of character behavior is seen by the audience?
- What visual information (props, costumes, sets etc.) is present onstage that the characters refer to?
- What spatial locations do the characters refer to?
- What auditory information needs to be considered?
- What offstage information needs to be considered?

Theatrical devices to be considered when developing a performative interpretation:

- How much information can be understood by the words alone? How much of this is visually connected to what is on the stage? How much of this staged information does the interpretation need to incorporate? How much can be understood by the stage visuals alone?

EXPLORING MEANING IN THE TARGET LANGUAGE

When exploring questions of meaning, the language used in rehearsals is as important as the information uncovered in the discovery process. Talking about the play in the target language (ASL) is a means for discovering and developing language for expressing the play's ideas, feelings, and relationships. In our Interpreting for the Theatre Seminar, the Deaf advisors were actively involved in discussions and explorations of the play, necessitating the participants' use of ASL.

This conversational approach to unpacking meaning in ASL helps guide the interpreters to build semantic domains for the world of the play and discover what the dialogue would look like in natural ASL discourse.[11] This approach provides a basis for shared team agreements. This process also creates a bridge between meaning discovery and the co-construction of the interpretation. The DOI helps choreograph the turn-taking between the signed interpretation and the action on the stage.

Team inquiry helps to identify the sources of the information (e.g., dialogue, visual information, sound effects). The team considers these elements prior to building translations. The goal is to create a shared team understanding of the play in order to create a more cohesive interpretation, moving from "How do I sign that line?" to instead "How do we express this play?"

EXPLORING MEANING IN *BAREFOOT IN THE PARK*

The opening scene from *Barefoot in the Park* by Neil Simon is deceptively simple. It may appear easy to interpret, but once it's unpacked, we will see how much embedded information needs to be considered in our interpretation.

This comedic play revolves around a young newlywed couple (Corie and Paul Bratter) living in Bohemian Greenwich Village in NYC during the early 1960s. They have just moved into a tiny studio apartment, a fifth floor walk-up (no elevator) with a skylight, which is still not completely unpacked or even furnished. The stairs are not seen on stage (if you are viewing the film, stairs are established via cuts to outside the apartment but are not visible from within the apartment).

Back in the 1960s, telephones were owned by the phone company and delivered in person to each home. Telephone lines had to be installed, and phones were connected to their outlet in the wall by the company's service person. Interpreters who are interested in knowing what the Telephone Man is doing can look up the process online. YouTube has several examples. Doing this kind of research helps our translations be more specific.

As the scene begins, the Telephone Delivery Man (MAN) arrives to connect the new phone to the wall. He is completely out of breath. Corie greets him.

Barefoot in the Park

Act I–Scene I[12]

MAN: *Tel - Telephone company.*
CORIE: *Oh, the phone. Good. Come on in.*

MAN: *That's quite a - quite a climb.*
CORIE: *Yes, it's five flights. If you don't count the front stoop.*
MAN: *I counted the front stoop.*

(*Barefoot in the Park* by Neil Simon. Lines reprinted © 1963 Paramount Pictures Corp. All rights reserved.)

The first questions in this opening scene have been answered in the description above—who are the characters, what are their relationships, and when and where is the scene taking place. The next set of questions arises from the dialogue in context and the characters' behavior seen onstage:

1. What does the Telephone Delivery Man gasping for breath signify?
2. What does "That's quite a climb" mean?
3. What does "It's five flights if you don't count the front stoop" mean?
4. What does "I counted the front stoop" mean?
5. Are these details important, and if so, why?
6. What is the tone of this scene?
7. What does this exchange reveal about the characters?
8. What visual information is present in the scene that needs to be considered and included?

In unpacking the scene, we make these discoveries:

1. The Telephone Delivery Man is gasping for breath after climbing stairs.
2. "Quite a climb" refers to what he just did offstage—climb many flights of stairs. It is implied that there is no elevator.
3. "Five flights if you don't count the front stoop" refers to the indoor stairway and the additional set of stairs outside the building, also offstage. From the Telephone Man's perspective, this was particularly exhausting.
4. The Telephone Man's perception of the stoop is that it's an additional flight of stairs to climb. His breathless response indicates that it is a hardship. Corie's perception of the stairs is that she hadn't considered it to be a hardship at all.
5. The tone of this scene is light comedy, as evinced by the dialogue and the characters' behaviors in the scene. For example, in this short exchange, the lines are delivered in a specific manner in order to elicit a laugh at the third line:

   MAN: *That's quite a–quite a climb.*
   CORIE: *Yes, it's five flights. If you don't count the front stoop.*
   MAN: *I counted the front stoop.*

6. This five-line exchange reveals that Corie has just moved in and she is excited about the possibility of living in a new space. Unlike Corie, an additional flight makes a difference to him. It makes for a comedic contrast.

7. Given that the visual information onstage is part of the source, and that interpreters are producing meaning in a visual language, the team will develop visual (interpretation)-to-visual (stage) agreements when appropriate. As the team co-constructs its interpretation, the questions to consider include: How much of this information can be understood by the words alone? How much of this is visually connected to what is on the stage? How much of this visual information does our interpretation need to refer to? How much can be understood by visuals alone? Can the stairs be seen on the stage or are they merely alluded to? What actions and dialogue help in storytelling?

Onstage, the audience sees an empty apartment, but cannot see the stairs or the stoop, which are referenced solely in the dialogue. Visible character actions include the Telephone Man gasping for breath at the door. Later, when the team is developing their interpretation, this visual information will shape their output. The team considers when to reference the stage for information and when to linguistically embed it in the interpretation.

Let's see what we need to understand in these next few lines from *Barefoot in the Park*.

As the scene unfolds, the Telephone Delivery Man (MAN) is installing the new phone. He's incredulous that she plans on making that climb up those six flights every day. She reveals that she is a newlywed, and that the furniture is due to be delivered that day.

Barefoot in the Park

Act I–Scene 1

The doorbell rings.

CORIE: *OH! I hope that's the furniture.*
MAN: *I don't want to see this.*
CORIE: *Helloooo! Bloomingdale's?*
VOICE: *Lord & Taylor.*
CORIE: *Lord & Taylor? Up here. Top floor.*
CORIE: *Lord & Taylor? Probably another wedding gift . . . From my mother. She sends me wedding gifts twice a day. . .*

(*Barefoot in the Park* by Neil Simon. Lines reprinted © 1063 Paramount Pictures Corp. All rights reserved.)

Questions:

1. What's the function of the line "I hope that's the furniture"?
2. Why doesn't the Telephone Delivery Man want to see "this"?
3. What does "Helloooo! Bloomingdale's?" mean?
4. What does "Lord & Taylor" mean?

5. What visual information is present in the scene that might need to be considered?
6. What is the tone of this scene?
7. What does this exchange reveal about the characters?

1. At the top of the scene, the apartment is empty. When Corie hears the doorbell and says, “I hope that’s the furniture,” she is referring to furniture that would be hand-carried up the stairs to her fifth-floor apartment. This line is the setup for the comedic response that immediately follows.
2. When the Telephone Man says, “I don’t want to see this,” he is commiserating with the delivery person’s plight—carrying furniture up all those flights.
3. When Corie calls out, “Helloooo! Bloomingdale’s,” she’s checking if the delivery is from Bloomingdale’s, a store that sells furniture. From the previous lines and from the excitement with which Corie asks if the man is from Bloomingdale’s, we can infer that she is hoping that the furniture has arrived. On the surface level, Bloomingdale’s signifies a store, but in context, it also signifies her anticipation of furniture being delivered.
4. Lord & Taylor refers to an upscale store that Corie’s mother frequents, spurring her explanation of wedding gifts. In this context, it signifies “not furniture delivery.”
5. If the stage version were the same as the film, visual information that might need to be considered includes Corie’s body language as she leans over the stairs looking down toward the delivery man, the Telephone Delivery Man’s understated comic take on not wanting to see the furniture brought up, and the Telephone Delivery Man’s reaction at the foot of the stairs when he is told to walk up to the top floor.
6. The tone is still light comedy, with joke setup and delivery. Stairs, again, are a topic of discussion, which flags them as a possible recurring joke that the team may want to watch for as the play goes along.
7. This exchange reveals Corie’s disappointment that the furniture is not being delivered. She mentions that the packages are probably wedding gifts from her mother, who sends them twice a day. From the names of the two upscale stores, Lord & Taylor and Bloomingdale’s, the team now has information about the affluence of her mother who can afford to send so many gifts. From Corie’s body language and how she tosses away the line about her mother’s gifts, she communicates her cavalier acceptance of these gifts as a natural occurrence. All of these cues help to illuminate the social status that Corie comes from.

Look how much information is found in two minutes of dialogue! From these simple opening lines and the way they are delivered, the function that each line serves, as well as the costumes, the set, and the characters’ actions and behaviors, the world of the characters at the top of the play has been introduced. We will later consider how our understanding of this information guides our translation choices.

Dialogic Character Assignment

> "Imagine you're watching (not interpreting) a play with lots of characters, how do you keep track of everyone's names?"
>
> —Carol Padden[13]

Character assignment is one of the techniques used to support clear storytelling. We consider this to be another aspect of the translation task. Each character is imbued with meaning that has to be unpacked and represented in our interpretation. As much as possible, assignment is determined by the storylines of the characters. This is strategic, rather than automatic.

Characters are assigned by considering their relationships. Who are the characters telling the protagonist's story? The antagonist's story? Which characters support each side? Which characters are neutral? Our ultimate goal is for the signing audience to easily follow who is talking to whom and the progression of ideas throughout the story.

At first glance, one might think assigning characters is simply a matter of one-to-one correspondence, irrespective of what happens onstage. However, that approach does not take into consideration the action of the play and scenes, nor of relationships and dynamics between and among the characters. Strategic character division is not solely about the characters of the play. DOI Andrew Fisher explained that when assigning characters, "I think it's important to consider how the three interpreters will interact. Are your characters more like rivals or friends? Ideally, the relationships between the characters (and interpreters) should feel authentic. It's similar to casting actors based on how they connect with others, not just their individual performances."[14]

When assigning characters, the DOI and the team also take into account the individual attributes that each interpreter brings to the team. If, for example, an interpreter resembles Kristen Chenoweth, then it will be easy for the audience to track that interpreter as her character. Other factors may be the interpreter's comfort level and fluency with the content, their own "personality," and how that aligns with the story—are they comedic, poetic, intellectual, etc. Do these qualities align with specific characters in the play?

An interpreting team of three (and, occasionally, more) interpreters allows more options to address the complexities of stories with multiple main characters. Often, the third interpreter operates as the "go between" in the narrative, taking on roles of the supporting characters. The fact that the "go between" interpreter is not strongly aligned with either the protagonist or the antagonist frees them to be in dialogue with any of the main characters. This supports storytelling and is one of the strategies designed to help the audience more readily identify the relationships of the characters.

CONSIDERATIONS

Character assignment begins with a panoramic overview of the play, looking for patterns, plot points, and relationships. Considerations include the characters' relationships, thought worlds, and story arc, which guide the decision-making process. Character assignments should support the distinct motivations, alliances, and/or relationships that propel the story. Identifying the interpreters for the lead characters early on allows the team to then engage in a strategic assignment of the supporting characters.

Factors that guide our choices:

- Lead characters
- Relationships
- Who talks to whom
- Ideological positions
- Action on stage
- Plot development
- Stage picture

In *West Side Story*,[15] for example, an interpreter who has been assigned to Jets characters may also need to interpret for a member of the Sharks. However, the interpreter assigned to Riff, the leader of the Jets, would not also interpret for Bernardo, the leader of the Sharks, at any time because those two characters have scenes where they will be in dialogic opposition. When multiple characters have different motivations and agendas in a scene and/or the play, character division becomes more complex. During rehearsals, the team may discover that initial character assignments may need to be changed to better suit the needs of the scene and the team.

Considerations for assigning secondary characters include:

- Frequency and recency of character appearance, meaning how often the character is seen and/or when the character was last seen on stage
- How integral the character is to the plot
- Intensity and duration of the character's interaction

Dramaturgical exploration of relationships can be helpful in determining character assignment. Mapping these relationships is another strategy. The following CourseHero.com study guide (fig. 3.1) for Shakespeare's gruesome *Titus Andronicus* is a great example of a character map.[16] It identifies relationships between the characters, their alliances, actions taken, and final outcomes. This visual shorthand clarifies complex social structures and relationships and can be beneficial both for character division as well as translation.

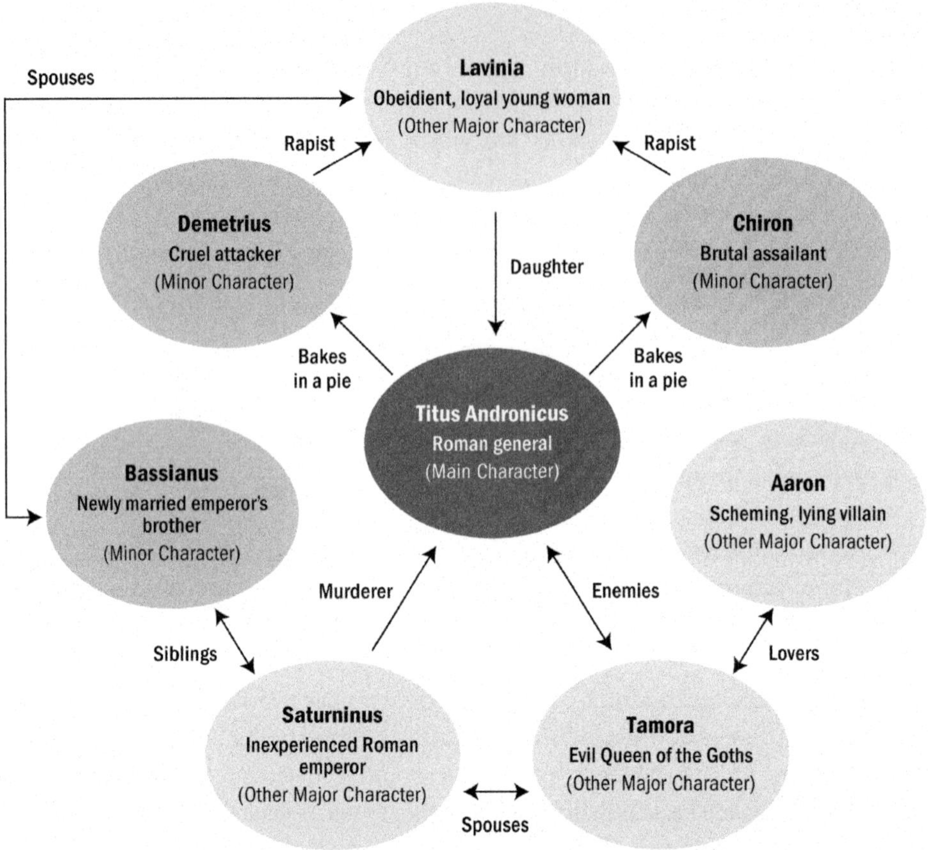

Figure 3.1. Titus Andronicus character map. Image included with permission from Course Hero.

We will now examine several scenes from Shakespeare's *Romeo and Juliet*, looking at factors that inform choices in character division. The relationships among the characters throughout the play can be clarified through interpreter assignments. It is a given that one interpreter will be assigned to Romeo and another to Juliet. The goal is to maintain character consistency as much as possible for these two roles. The third interpreter would handle some of the supporting characters who propel the play and speak to both *Romeo and Juliet.*

Think about the play as a whole and assign characters in such a way that will help the arc of the play move forward. Rather than approaching the work with a scene-by-scene, line-by-line, or character-by-character sensibility, it helps to look at the show holistically to make sure the assignments make sense throughout the play. An effective division for one scene may not be effective for all scenes. The assignment of supporting characters in each scene is determined in relation to the main character(s), the action, the through line of the play, and the thought world being represented.

With three interpreters for *Romeo and Juliet*, the character assignment would begin with this framework:

Interpreter A: Romeo—consistently (plus other characters as needed)
Interpreter B: Juliet—consistently (plus other characters as needed)
Interpreter C: Nurse and Friar—as consistently as possible (plus other characters as needed)

Consideration—Stage Picture Versus Character Consistency

In the balcony scene, Romeo, hidden in the garden, admires Juliet up on the balcony. She, unaware that he is below, expresses her love for him. Once Romeo reveals himself, they speak of their love for each other. The Nurse (offstage) doesn't know Romeo is there and repeatedly interrupts them by calling out to Juliet to come indoors. Juliet leaves Romeo alone onstage when she goes in to talk with the Nurse. When Juliet returns, they make plans to wed.

Romeo and Juliet

Act II–Scene 2

NURSE: *[Within] Madam!*
JULIET: *I come, anon. – But if thou mean'st not well,*
I do beseech thee –
NURSE: *[Within] Madam!*
JULIET: *By and by, I come –*

The conversation between Romeo and Juliet is intimate, hidden from the view of the others in Juliet's family. Only two people are seen onstage. While the interpreter for the Nurse has been established in previous scenes, at this moment, the Nurse is not visible onstage. The audience only hears and recognizes the voice of the Nurse as she calls Juliet from offstage.

Consider how the stage picture influences character assignment decisions. What are options for interpreting for the Nurse in this scene?

One option would be for the team to continue the same breakdown with Interpreters A and B and have Interpreter C stand up and sign the offstage voice of the Nurse.

Interpreter A: Romeo
Interpreter B: Juliet
Interpreter C: Nurse (offstage voice)

Would it be distracting if Interpreter C pops up for the Nurse when the nurse is not visible onstage? Would that disrupt the intimate moment being seen onstage? What is the impact of that visual incongruity? Is there enough time for the audience's gaze to travel from Interpreter C to the stage and back to clarify the interpreter/character alignment (especially when it's only for a few lines)?

Another option would be for only Interpreters A and B to interpret this scene. The Nurse's lines could be assigned to Interpreter B, the interpreter for Juliet. This option would be:

Interpreter A: Romeo
Interpreter B: Juliet (incorporate the Nurse's offstage lines)

The decision to have only two interpreters (with Interpreter B "incorporating" the Nurse's lines) honors the stage picture and the intimacy of the moment. We believe that for most productions in which the Nurse is not visible during this exchange, this option would best serve the scene.

There are choices in how to interpret this interaction. As mentioned above, the Nurse's call could be incorporated into Juliet's lines. The interpreter for Juliet could role-shift between Juliet and the Nurse or, alternatively, narrate that the Nurse is calling Juliet from offstage. Whichever choice is made, the conversational partner (the Nurse) would be identified, and the interpreter for Juliet would keep the two conversational spaces (Juliet-and-Romeo and Juliet-and-the-offstage-Nurse) distinct.

Choosing to have the information from the Nurse expressed by the interpreter for Juliet is an example of "distribution of meaning." This concept is predicated on the belief that the team shares responsibility for the information that will be interpreted, even if, in this scene, the message comes from a different interpreter than the one usually assigned to the character.

Interpreters incorporating the lines of other characters can be used to support the scene on stage, to clarify thought worlds in larger scenes, to help with turn-taking and timing (simultaneity and performability), and so forth. The content and context of each scene guide the team.

Consideration—Thought Worlds

Teams identify who inhabits which thought worlds, meaning which characters express similar ideas, points of view, sensibilities, understandings, systems of reality, and goals. It will then be easier to assign characters who share similar thought worlds to the same interpreter.

Consider what it takes to make the thoughts expressed in the dialogue coherent. What will bring ease of viewing and understanding events and characters to the signing audience? How can character division support the scene and the storytelling?

Romeo and Juliet

Act III–Scene 1

The scene begins with Romeo Montague's friends Mercutio and Benvolio in conversation. Tybalt and the Lady and Lord Capulet (enemies of the Montagues) enter. Mercutio and Tybalt goad each other. Benvolio tries to keep the peace. Romeo enters and Tybalt tries to bait him by hurling insults to lure Romeo into a duel. Romeo tries to assuage Tybalt by pledging friendship. However, Mercutio draws his sword on Tybalt. Romeo tries to separate them, but Tybalt mortally wounds Mercutio and flees. Benvolio asks Mercutio if he's hurt and takes the dying Mercutio off stage as Mercutio curses both families: *"A plague o' both your houses."* Benvolio returns to report his friend's death to Romeo. Enraged, Romeo kills Tybalt in revenge. The Prince enters and, after Benvolio explains what occurred, banishes Romeo from Verona, and Romeo must flee for his life.

It certainly looks messy! Even with four interpreters usually hired for the Public Theater's Shakespeare in the Park, the scene's character division would still be challenging. The team considers the characters' respective thought worlds and then identifies which interpreters can cross between these thought worlds and when.

Thought worlds:

- **Alliances and opposing camps:** The Capulets and Montagues are enemies. Benvolio and Mercutio reside in Romeo's camp, the Montagues; Tybalt and the others are in the opposing Capulet camp. The Prince, being the ruler, is in neither camp.
- **Storylines and character arcs:** Tybalt is goading Romeo. Romeo's friends want him to fight against the Capulets, but Romeo wants to make peace with Tybalt, Juliet's cousin.
- **Character intentions:** The Prince wants lawlessness to stop. Mercutio and Tybalt want to keep loyalty to their respective houses and enmity as a priority. Mercutio wants Romeo on his side. Tybalt wants to shame Romeo.
- **Stage picture:** Tybalt fights Mercutio, with Romeo intervening. Tybalt's blade goes under Romeo's arm, fatally wounding Mercutio. Enraged, Romeo fights Tybalt.

Visual information on the stage also helps identify thought worlds. Costume designers often use similar colors for members of the same camp. The director's blocking often separates the camps into different spaces on stage, leaving the center free for the dramatic fights. The character relationships are often understood from the actors' demeanors whether they are talking to a comrade or shouting over to the enemy on the other side of the stage.

When assigning characters, consider who talks to whom about what. Are they arguing with each other or are their thoughts in alignment? If the characters represent differing views, it would be confusing for one interpreter to hold and express two opposing thought worlds at the same time.

An additional issue is the performability of the character breakdown. The pace and the complexity of a heated argument would be difficult for one interpreter to convey all the ideas and reactions through role shifting. It is more effective if there are two interpreters, with each representing a distinct thought world.

Next, we consider how to assign the important supporting characters of Tybalt and Mercutio. Interpreter A is assigned to Romeo for the entire play and both of these supporting characters interact with Romeo, moving the plot forward. In Act III, *Scene 1*, Juliet is not onstage, which frees up Interpreter B, who has been Juliet. The pivotal fight between Tybalt, Mercutio, and Romeo will occur in this scene. For narrative and dramatic impact, we want three separate interpreters for these characters.

A possible configuration based on thought worlds is:

Interpreter A: Romeo
Interpreter B: Mercutio, Benvolio (Montague camp)
Interpreter C: Tybalt, Lady Capulet (Capulet camp)

Consideration—Multicharacter Scenes

What about the rest of the secondary characters in Act III, Scene 1? When the cast is larger than the interpreter team, it is inevitable that character switching will occur. Contextual analysis of character assignment guides the decision-making. Determining if and when a character will be thrown and which interpreter will be assigned is always guided by the narrative.

Again, the goal is to maintain consistency with the main characters' assigned interpreter, making the character-to-interpreter connection efficient for the audience. For secondary characters, the aim is to keep the thought world alignments intact. When switching interpreters for secondary characters, it is almost inevitable that some ruptures in the clarity of the interpreter/character alignment will occur, but the aspiration is to keep this at a minimum.

In making these assignments, consider which characters each interpreter has been representing thus far, the narrative before and after these characters' moments, and the major plot points these characters represent. In addition, consider how often the character is seen, when the character was last seen on stage, and how important the character is in a particular scene. These are issues of frequency, recency, narrative relevancy, and clarity.

Let's look at two additional characters, the Prince and Benvolio.

THE PRINCE

The Prince is an important secondary character who only appears in three scenes over the course of the play (frequency and recency), but each time, he exerts a powerful influence on the events of the play (narrative relevancy). Factors that determine who is assigned to the Prince include what occurs before and after the Prince enters, who the Prince talks with, who else is onstage, and the import of the Prince's dialogue. In Act I, Scene 1, the Prince arrives after the Montagues and Capulets have been fighting in the street and announces that if anyone disturbs the civil peace again, they will be put to death. In Act III, Scene 1, the Prince banishes Romeo, affecting both houses and his proclamation leads to Romeo and Juliet's tragic deaths. In Act V, Scene 3, the Prince calls for the families to stop their feud and ends the play with "For never was a story of more woe Than this of Juliet and her Romeo".

In our proposed breakdown for Act III, Scene 1, after Tybalt dies, Interpreter C is available to take on the role of the Prince, representing the power and authority residing outside of the two families.

While this seems straightforward, this character assignment also supports the narrative arc—the Prince (C) banishes Romeo (A) in front of his friends (B), allowing Interpreters A and B to maintain the thought worlds and emotional truths of their main characters and families. In this way, the team character assignment supports the events occurring on the stage.

The aim is to ensure that the interpreter assigned in these moments can take on the character of the Prince without a lot of residue from other characters. This means considering if there has been enough time since the character they just interpreted to be able to slip into the new character without it being too jarring for the audience. When there is no other choice, and the character must be assigned to a particular interpreter, then additional character identification strategies will be used.

BENVOLIO

Benvolio (Romeo's cousin) does not appear often and will need to be assigned to all three interpreters at different moments to support the storytelling.

In Act I, Benvolio has long dialogues with Romeo (A) and would likely be assigned to Interpreter B.

In Act II, Scene 4, Romeo (A) and Mercutio (B) are the most important characters, leaving Interpreter C to take Benvolio. Since there are no Capulets onstage, there is no confusion about which thought world the characters/interpreters are aligned with.

Then, in Act III, Scene 1, Interpreters A and B will need to share Benvolio. At the top of the scene, Romeo is offstage while Mercutio (B) and Tybalt (C) begin their fight. The only available Interpreter is A and will be assigned to Benvolio. Once Romeo returns, Interpreter A resumes Romeo, Mercutio (B) is stabbed by Tybalt (C). Benvolio carries the mortally wounded Mercutio offstage, leaving Interpreter B available. When Benvolio reenters, Interpreter B takes Benvolio for the rest of the scene.

Figure 3.2 illustrates our proposed character assignment for scenes Act II, Scene 2 through Act III, Scene 1. This is a helpful way for the team to track the interpreter/character alignments throughout the play. Of course, these decisions would have been made after viewing the play and taking stage blocking into consideration. During rehearsals, the team would take time to revisit these decisions and, if needed, revise and refine them to best meet the needs of the interpreting team, as well as to support the clearest storytelling on the stage.

Character Assignment Chart Example

Scene	Page	Interpreter A ROMEO	Interpreter B JULIET/ MERCUTIO	Interpreter C NURSE/ FRIAR
Act II Sc 2		Romeo	Juliet	
Act II Sc 3		Romeo		Friar
Act II Sc 4		Romeo	Mercutio	Benvolio Nurse
Act II Sc 5			Juliet	Nurse
Act II Sc 6		Romeo	Juliet	Friar
Act III Sc 1		Benvolio Romeo	Mercutio *After Mercutio dies:* Benvolio Montague	Tybalt LadyCapulet Prince

Figure 3.2. Character assignment chart example.

Approaching these multicharacter scenes is like working a 5,000 piece jigsaw puzzle. The team looks for the most elegant solutions available that make it easier for the audience to track the story unfolding on stage.

We strategically weigh the impact of the character assignment in each scene and consider character relationships, thought worlds, the stage picture, consistency versus storytelling, and the visual-to-visual nature of our work. Throughout the play, the team will determine which factors take precedence. The ultimate question is, "What will lead to the most cohesive transmission of meaning?"

CONSIDERATION–BUNDLING CHARACTERS

In considering the stage as a primary partner, the interpretation is designed to allow the stage to speak for itself. One strategy used to accomplish this is bundling. Because the interpretation is engaging in a visual-to-visual conversation between ASL and the stage picture, interpreters consider how and when to give space for both to be seen.

Bundling is when one interpreter takes the lines of multiple characters. Bundling is both a translation/interpretation strategy and character division strategy. The decision to assign the lines of multiple characters to one interpreter is based on the principles of clarity, economy, and ease of storytelling.

Bundling occurs for several reasons: When having one interpreter incorporate the lines of multiple characters clarifies the narrative (storytelling); when the same idea is stated by several characters in a scene or in a chorus (thought worlds); or when stage blocking identifies the characters as belonging to distinct groups (stage picture) or when multiple characters are a challenge (e.g., crowds and cacophony). At certain moments, individual characters may be less important than the content of the lines, when the "who" is less important than the "what." Some of the bundling strategies might be applied for an entire scene, and others might be utilized only intermittently or briefly. The visual impact of our choices is an important consideration.

Bundling for Storytelling

The interpreters for the 2018 Broadway production of *On Your Feet* used the bundling strategy in a pivotal flashback scene.[17] (Please note that in this book, the interpreting teams are listed in the endnotes along with the information about each show.)

In Act II, Emilio remembers saying goodbye to his mother and grandfather as a child at the airport just before he leaves Cuba forever. While the grandfather understood that this would be their last encounter, the young Emilio did not. Now, as an adult, he revisits these last moments and words of guidance from his grandfather, the import of that last goodbye.

The older Emilio's memory comes alive during the flashback as the conversation is reenacted by three characters (the young Emilio, his mother, and his grandfather). The stage picture is somber with soft lighting. Since there were three interpreters, it would have been simple to assign each character to a separate interpreter for this scene. However, in order to represent the manifestation of Emilio's memory, a moment he creates and observes, the entire flashback was bundled to one interpreter. The literalness of recreating the stage picture was secondary to honoring the emotional impact of the scene.

Interpreter A: Previously Emilio, Now All. Using one interpreter in this scene was a deliberate choice, arrived at by understanding the meaning, affective textures, and aesthetic of the stage. The ambience created by the stage elements of blocking, soft lighting, and sound all inform the audience that the memory is not in the present time. Understanding the language of the theatre helped guide the team to this decision on character division. Too many interpreters might have cluttered the interpreting space and competed with the stage picture. Having just one interpreter accommodated both the quiet as well as the memory aspect of the scene.

The decision to bundle the three characters into the interpreter for Emilio then informed the translatory decisions of that interpreter. The interpretation explicitly framed the scene as an activated memory and produced the conversation replete with constructed discourse. Had three interpreters worked the scene, the ASL might have appeared to be a conversation in the present rather than a memory.

Bundling to Collaborate with the Stage

Another way to use bundling can be seen in this dynamic scene from *Wicked*.[18]

Wicked

Act II–Scene 9

Glinda, who was engaged to Fiyero, is unwittingly used by the Wizard to lure Elphaba to the site where his guards can capture her. Elphaba taunts Glinda with the fact that Fiyero only loves Elphaba, which sparks a witches' duel. The Guards rush in to arrest Elphaba. Fiyero enters, engineering Elphaba's escape by threatening Glinda. Therein ensues a struggle between the Guards, Fiyero, and Glinda. The Guards capture Fiyero in order to torture him while Glinda begs for his release.

Here is the original character assignment breakdown:

Interpreter A: Glinda
Interpreter B: Elphaba
Interpreter C: Fiyero, Guards

At the top of the scene, all three members of the team are interpreting. When Ephelba runs offstage, even though multiple characters are still present onstage, the team decided to have Interpreters B and C sit. Interpreter A remained standing and continued interpreting for Glinda, and incorporated the Guards' and Fiyero's lines. The audience having time to view and an unimpeded line of sight to the physical action on stage was a guiding factor in the team's decision.

Interpreter A: Previously Glinda, Now All. Having only one interpreter for this moment allows the stage picture to become the focal point of the narrative. The choice to bundle characters occurs after the team determines that the visual action onstage is providing important information. The team intentionally creates the opportunity for the audience's gaze to attend to the stage picture.

The DOI, who has both the audience and the story in mind, is the best person to orchestrate the visual score of interpreters' entrances and exits, when discursive spaces are at rest or are in action, effectively weaving in the action on stage with the interpretation. The ultimate goal is for these elements to no longer be discrete, but rather cohesive strands unfolding and revealing the story.

Bundling for Crowds and Cacophony

The next examples demonstrate the bundling of characters as well as the bundling of lines (which we also refer to as "truncating" or "paraphrasing"). This strategy can be effective for complex scenes with multiple characters. Decisions are guided by character through lines, story arcs, and intent of the scene. The goal is to convey the meaning of the scene in an accessible manner for the audience.

The bundling strategy is often effective in crowd scenes, especially those where individual characters are not easily identifiable. Let's explore a crowd scene in Shakespeare's *Julius Caesar*.[19]

Julius Caesar

Act III–Scene 2

A cabal has just murdered Roman Emperor Julius Caesar on the floor of the Senate. In this scene, Brutus (*et tu Brute*) explains to the citizens of Rome that his honor required him to kill Julius Caesar for the sake of Rome because Caesar was too ambitious. The crowd applauds his murder until Caesar's friend, Mark Anthony, speaks to them, ostensibly to support the conspirators. Anthony's speech, in which he ironically calls Brutus *"an honourable man"* while extolling the virtues of the slain Caesar, turns the populace against the conspirators and incites them to demand vengeance.

Bundling could be an effective strategy in this scene. For three interpreters, the breakdown for this scene would be:

Interpreter A: Brutus
Interpreter B: Mark Anthony
Interpreter C: All Roman Plebeians

The First, Second, Third, and Fourth Plebeians are collapsed (bundled) into Interpreter C, as they all follow the same thought line. These lines are not dialogic in that they are not responding to each other. They are reactions to the speeches given by the leads or are encouragement to others to take action. This supports the decision to have no distinct character portrayed, but rather collective responses.

At the end of this scene, after the crowd exits to avenge Caesar, Octavius's Servant arrives to deliver a message to Mark Anthony. Their dialogue serves to further the plot. Depending upon previous scenes and what occurs next, the team will decide if it makes more sense to have Interpreter A or Interpreter C take on the character of the Servant. If there are more than three interpreters, then there are more options.

Next is an example of bundling in which eight characters perform the song "Notes/Prima Donna" in *The Phantom of the Opera.*[20]

The Phantom of the Opera

Act I–Scene 8

The Phantom, in an effort to secure his protege Christine's place as the lead singer in the upcoming production, sends letters with individual directives to members of the Opera company. The scene opens with the company responding to these letters.

The producers of the Opera are incensed by the gall of the Phantom ordering them about. Raoul (Christine's boyfriend) is furious at the producers, not realizing that his letter is from the Phantom. Piangi (the bass) and Carlotta (the diva) rush in, furious that her letter demands she step down. Mme. Giry (the ballet mistress), accompanied by Meg (a dancer), delivers another note from the Phantom issuing further instructions. The Phantom's voice is later heard from offstage threatening disaster if they do not comply. In a state of panic, the characters on stage begin simultaneously singing their individual responses, culminating in a polyphonic auditory experience.

Character assignments at the top of the scene:

Interpreter A: Mssrs. André and Firmin, Raoul, and Phantom
Interpreter B: Carlotta and Piangi
Interpreter C: Mme. Giry and Meg

Decisions are informed by performability factors. As there are many more characters than interpreters, information needs to be distilled from eight characters into a form that three interpreters can present. The beginning of the song is dialogic and manageable. When deciding how to assign interpreters for the moment when all eight start singing different lines simultaneously, the team considers the function of the song, visuals on stage, intention of the characters, scene, and moment, as well as the performability factors.

The main through lines in this moment are Carlotta's demands, the two producers trying to appease her, Mme. Giry's warnings of potential harm if they don't heed the Phantom's warnings, and Meg and Raoul's concern for Christine's safety. Since Carlotta and the producers's through lines propel the conflict in this moment, they are kept at the forefront by assigning different interpreters to them. Mme. Giry then becomes the container for all the other concerns.

There is also the issue of practicality. The interpreter assigned to Giry has time, when Giry is not singing, to include the lines of Raoul and Meg in her interpretation. Performability and content are both considerations in determining distribution of meaning through character assignment for this moment.

The only change in assignment for this moment was moving Raoul to Interpreter C:

Interpreter A: Mssrs. André and Firmin
Interpreter B: Carlotta and Piangi
Interpreter C: Mme. Giry, Meg, and Raoul

These character distinctions merge into one unified voice at the end of the song when the ensemble sings in defiance of the Phantom. The individual interests now become a collective interest representing the company. Following suit, the interpreting team signed the ending lines in unison, to reinforce the shift from the individual through lines to the company's through line. This choice not only supported the narrative but also the performance, conveying their collective defiance of the Phantom's impending threat. The bundling choices for *Phantom* stand in contrast to those in *Wicked*, where the action took precedence, and in *On Your Feet*, where the quiet storytelling took precedence. Here, the intensity of the visual, aural, and performative elements led to the decision to have the full team interpret that moment.

The above examples of bundling for character assignment are detailed examinations of small moments to show how decisions are made in response to the performance on stage. While the resolutions offered are not definitive or applicable for every crowd scene, we did want to provide a peek into our "think aloud" of how we arrive at our choices.

CONSIDERATION–TEAM ATTRIBUTES

The translatory considerations of character assignment are funneled through our bodies, the literal body space through which we have to express the ideas, conditions, and narrative of the play. If our bodies function as the paper on which we are writing, our page—the space on which we write—becomes a factor in our translation and performance decisions.

Consider which character imprint has left the strongest traces on the interpreter body and which character imprint can more easily be written over so that a new character can come to the foreground. Our bodies carry residual signification from scene to scene. In a way, interpreters for the theatre are living palimpsests, as characters are written on our bodies and then written over.

Within a team, certain interpreters might be more suited to inhabit particular characters based on signing style, linguistic competencies, background knowledge, sensibilities, or other qualities. The assignment of a character might even be for an arbitrary reason. There may be something about a particular interpreter that seems to fit or is reminiscent of the character onstage. Sometimes, visual likeness helps the audience make quick interpreter/character connections. The Broadway revival of *The Mystery of Edwin Drood* had a team of three interpreters.[21] Onstage, Chairman Cartwright was played by a man. At first, it was assumed that the male interpreter would be assigned to him. On closer inspection, the team realized that one of the female interpreters, Molly Wilson, more closely resembled that performer and was assigned to interpret that character regardless of gender.

Character assignment is also an opportunity to rethink and challenge assumptions and "isms" about what bodies convey. The complexities of re-presentation in the casting of interpreters are worth exploring.

It's important to recognize that the audience can and does look beyond the interpreter body. One year, the class project for the Interpreting for the Theatre Seminar was *Rent*.[22] One of the participants chosen to interpret a segment of the staged performance, Dave McCloskey (affectionately known as the "Santa Interpreter"), had a long white beard and was much older than the actors onstage. At first, the audience was surprised to see an elderly man interpreting for a cast of actors in their twenties in a story about the turmoil of youth. Dave's performative abilities along with the beauty of his language and the strength of the performed interpretation carried the audience along with him. Interpreting teams have the power to disrupt or challenge some of the preconceived notions (in this case, ageism, but equally other "isms") simply through the choice of assignment of characters, liberating our traditional thinking and allowing for more expansive views of the body in space and time.

The character assignment process in *A Soldier's Play* on Broadway was one of ongoing discovery, factoring in individual attributes of the interpreters.[23] During the rehearsal process, the DOIs felt that Dana Fuller's authoritative presence projected a strong sense of command that matched the two lead characters, Sgt. Waters and Capt. Davenport. One week before the interpreted show, the DOIs changed the breakdown and assigned both Sgt. Waters and Capt. Davenport to Dana. One of the reasons this was possible was because these two characters were never in the same scene. The team was able to incorporate these last-minute changes, a credit to their responsiveness and professionalism. Zavier Sabio, one of the DOIs for the show, told us, "We experimented with the new version of character assignment. It was beautiful to watch. We found something that really worked."

Intimate knowledge of the cultural layers in the play is an asset for any interpreting team. In putting the team together for the Broadway production of *Oh Mary*,[24] DOI Andrew Morrill felt it was important to bring in interpreters who were LGBTQ+ identified and would be comfortable with and have the cultural content fluency to interpret drag performances on the stage. With that in mind, Morrill selected Joshua Castille, Craig Fogel, Tolly Tolman, and feed interpreter/co-interpreter Cathy Markland. Fogel explained, "The storyline includes drag performances as well as repressed internalized homophobia that is playfully parodied. The choices were designed to communicate that everyone is in on it (the actors, the writer, even the interpreters are part of the community), so it would feel safe and comfortable for the audience to laugh."[25]

Grammy award-winning Alicia Keys's Broadway musical *Hell's Kitchen*[26] is about the artist's life growing up in NYC. In the words of Frenchetta Perez Kilpatrick, the show contained "elements of young love, self-discovery, race, and the search for that mother–daughter relationship while also finding one's place within a community and discovering a true sense of home."[27] The interpreting team was composed of Jose Gomez, Frenchetta Perez Kilpatrick, Justine Rivera, Gloria Vargas, and DOI Alexandria Wailes. Perez Kilpatrick continued, "As a New Yorker and a Coda [child of Deaf adults], I felt a profound responsibility to honor the essence of the language and culture of New York City, which meant paying attention to the New York slang, colloquialisms, and the mannerisms used in the play. These themes resonated deeply with our intersectionality as Codas, New Yorkers, and minorities."[28] Justine Rivera added, "Based on the audience feedback, I left feeling gratified knowing the audience felt and saw all of the things in the show that I loved. They laughed and cried during all the right moments, and we all shared in an experience with the Deaf community that was unlike any other."[29]

The interpreter's linguistic repertoire, their cultural and experiential knowledge, and their ability to deliver certain concepts are critical components in character assignments. There may be a member of the team who has a knack with humor in signed language, or who has poetic sensibilities, or an authoritative signing style, or another quality that makes them a good fit.

DOI Andrew Fisher explained his thinking for assigning characters for *Enemy of the People*[30] on Broadway:

> I thought about matching each of the interpreters with a role that fits their signing style and speed, rather than just going by gender. I pictured Rick Rubin as the Doctor because of the Doctor's tone and intense rants. Of the play, Ibsen said, 'It may include traits of comedy, but it's also based on a serious idea.' Rick has a real talent for being both indignant and articulate. I keep thinking back to his interpretation during *A Bright Room Called Day* when he delivered the speech accusing the government of being literally full of shit. His ability to convey genuine indignation adds a layer of humor that I felt would be perfect for the Doctor's character.[31]

Some of these decisions, much like casting, are based on the characteristics of the interpreter. Does someone look like a character onstage? Can one interpreter more readily handle the content (poetry, Shakespeare, humor, etc.)? Some of these considerations depend upon the artfulness of interpreters in differentiating each character as well as the sociopolitical aspects, what an interpreter's body can/cannot or should/should not signify.

CONSIDERATION–THEATRE SPACE

An additional consideration that can affect character division is the actual space that the show, the audience, and the interpreters occupy. Factors such as how intimate, how large, whether it is a proscenium stage or juts into the audience (thrust), whether interpreters are seated on high stools or stand during some scenes and are seated during others, audience sightlines, and lighting for the interpreted space and its distance from the performers and the audience all play into the team choices. Different choices are made for expansive spaces than for intimate spaces, as well as for outdoor as opposed to indoor theatres.

For example, the Oregon Cabaret Theatre is a dinner theatre housed in a small old church. For its 2022 production of *A Christmas Carol*,[32] DOI Darren Frazier made character assignment choices based not only on the issues discussed previously but also on the experience of the audience and its relationship to the performers in that space. In the original breakdown, one interpreter was designated as Scrooge throughout, and the other two took on the rest of the characters. After seeing the show onsite and understanding where the Deaf audience would be seated and their vantage point, Frazier made some changes to the character division based on the constraints of this small space. He streamlined the source of the interpreted information by reducing the number of interpreters per scene, so that the storytelling on stage could also be seen. During certain scenes that had shorter dialogues between two characters, Frazier wanted the interpreters for Scrooge and the Ghost of Christmas Present to stand quietly off to the side, while the third interpreter engaged in role-shifting for the dialogue. This character-bundling strategy was used several times for shorter two-person exchanges even in the middle of longer scenes with multiple characters, such as the party scene at Scrooge's nephew's home.

In truth, character division is not always simple. Complex shows with large casts, such as farces, musicals, and Shakespeare are a challenge. As much as consistency is the goal, the original character assignments can't always be maintained, and sometimes, it is more effective for characters to be thrown or bundled.

Ultimately, character assignment should not be driven by consistency alone. Additional considerations include stage action, stage picture, performability, character arc, stage as team member, mood/tone, thought worlds, and the theatre space. Assigning characters in a manner that supports the flow of ideas and conversations can help to avert cognitive overload for the interpreters as well as clarify character relationships for the audience.

DIALOGIC APPROACH IN COMMUNITY PRACTICE

The benefit of having a community of theatre interpreters who share an ideology and approach is that interpreters can quickly identify strategies that support a play and its expression in a visual modality. In 2017, Lynnette and Stephanie were sent to interpret a children's show, which was a collection of Cinderella-like stories from cultures around the world. They had only one day's notice and were given an older version of the script. They had no time to rehearse or to even see a run-through before the school audience arrived. They spontaneously introduced name signs for characters who were being talked about but not seen on stage.

The play began with a young Cinderella-esque character wishing to meet a prince. Lynnette signed Cinderella's first line, and then, logically, working from a dialogic approach, Stephanie knew that she would take the role of the Prince and all the characters talking to Cinderella. This was accomplished with a nonverbal check-in (quick eye gaze and nod).

This tacit agreement for character division became the template for the rest of the show. It followed that Lynnette would then take all the Cinderella-type characters and Stephanie would take all those talking to them. Likewise, when the young Prince characters were the focal point of scenes, Stephanie took up the princes and Lynnette took all the characters who had exchanges with them. This kind of "on-the-fly" dialogic character division could only be accomplished because both Lynnette and Stephanie have a shared practice and approach to interpreting theatre.

This kind of interactive team approach can also apply to our community practice. We interpreters often find ourselves interpreting for interviews, conversations, panel discussions, and the like. Recognizing the dialogic nature of these events, it becomes second nature to use the same kind of conversational strategies in deciding to interpret dialogically, for example, with one interpreter as the interviewer and the other interpreter as the respondent. This approach gives the conversations life and breath and reflects the discursive nature of ASL, as opposed to the arbitrary solo interpreter producing constructed discourse for fifteen or twenty minutes. These strategies are also applicable in virtual settings.

If all conversation is seen as a story, a miniplay unfolding, then the analysis and strategies used in interpreting for the theatre can be applied in dialogic community work.

Conventions for Naming and Referring

Every opening scene has an important function: to introduce the audience to the world inhabited by the characters. The interpreting team has additional functions—not only are we simultaneously introducing the signing audience to the world of the play and the characters, but we are also introducing them to the language that will be used in the interpretation and identifying which interpreter is representing each character.

Actors often, but not always, maintain the same character throughout a play. Because interpreters represent multiple characters, strategies are needed to identify which character is being "worn" in each moment. The aim is to make it easier for the audience to follow who is talking to whom and about whom.

The script and the program list the names for all the characters (the dramatis personae). The impulse may be to invent a name sign for every character listed in the program; however, there are other options that may be more efficient given the constraints of simultaneity and performability and ease of tracking for the audience. When determining how to refer to characters in a play, interpreters explore the characters' roles and relationships to each other. A character can be referred to in multiple ways (by a name sign, by their relationship status, or both), depending on what the scene calls for.

ASL conversational norms are honored as much as possible. Each languaculture has distinct conventions for naming and referring. What a name signifies in English may not carry the same meaning if translated literally. It's good to remember not to impose the conventions of English on the signed translations. For example, if Peter speaks about himself in the third person, "Poor Peter," the meaning is understood to be "Poor me." Consider the function of the name in its context before deciding if or how to express it in the target culture and language.

CONSIDERATIONS

Commonly used options when referring to characters are to fingerspell the name, to indicate the social relationship (e.g., boss, mom, husband), use a descriptor, point to the character on stage, or to invent a name sign. Another option is to strategically omit the reference.[33] When the team analyzes names for meaning and explores what the name signifies in context, then options that make sense for that moment present themselves more readily.

When a character is referred to by others, the team then asks questions such as: What are their social relationships with other characters? What is their position? Is this character present in the scene while being discussed? More often than not, the character's relationship to others or their social position would be the most meaningful and efficient way to refer to them. Translation considerations include the function of the name in its context. Is the name a term of endearment? Is it an attempt to call someone's attention? Is it to show intimacy? To exert power over? When assigning a name sign to a character, other factors to consider are the frequency and relevancy of the character (how often they appear or are talked about, and how central is the recognition of the character's name to the narrative).

If an interpretation is overpopulated with name signs, it can be confusing, especially when the name signs may be used only intermittently. Memorizing an entire new world of name signs is additional work for an audience. Carol Padden reminds us, "I can't remember name signs in interpreted shows, so I'm often lost until I figure out who's interpreting for who, and by the middle or the end of the production, I've managed somehow to learn them."[34]

Referring to Social Relationships

Social relationships and status in the context of the play help guide decisions on how to refer to characters. With some ancillary characters, referring to them by their social status or role rather than a name may be more efficient and convey the same relational understanding. For example, in *Romeo and Juliet*, while the title characters would be assigned name signs, the role of Lady Capulet in each scene may be reflected in her social relationships with other characters. She is the mother of Juliet and the wife of Capulet. When interpreting for the Nurse speaking to Juliet, the decision might be to refer to Lady Capulet as "your mother." When interpreting between Juliet's father and Juliet, the interpreter for Juliet's father (Capulet) might refer to Lady Capulet as his wife or as Juliet's mother. The team may choose to give her a name sign but may also use multiple ways to refer to her.

In developing the repertoire of references for a particular character, the team identifies the primary relationship in each interaction. Based on that assessment, the team decides how to best represent that character in specific moments. Different choices might be made for another scene or for a different character referring to this person.

ASSIGNING NAME SIGNS

There is no one right way to invent name signs for characters. Sam Supalla writes that name signs can be classified as being arbitrary, descriptive, or nontraditional.[35] The team may consider representing character attributes, costume elements, using neutral name signs, or creating something else. It should be recognizable as a name sign and not confused with a lexical item. The DOI works with the team to make these decisions.

When a name sign is invented for a character, the team anchors it by spelling the proper name to introduce it to the audience and then present the sign that will be used. Be mindful that merely inventing a name sign does not necessarily guarantee that the audience will recall that name sign throughout the play. There is always the option to reintroduce the name and its sign.

Fingerspelling the name is also an option. For example, in *Mary Poppins*, the titular character of Mary Poppins is unique in that she seems to magically appear, is considered "practically perfect," and is always referred to by her full name by other characters when speaking to her or about her. None of the other characters are referred to in this manner. Candace and Lynnette explained for the Broadway-interpreted performance that the team made the decision not to create a name sign but rather find opportune times to fingerspell her entire name in order to convey the way in which her name is used in the play.

In sum, name signs are not necessarily fixed throughout the entire play. Identifiers are chosen in response to the needs of each interaction. Especially when plays have a multitude of characters, referring to characters by their function or social position is often much clearer and more natural than referring to them by name. When talking to Carol Padden about the strategy of referring to characters via their social relationships, she responded, "I love the idea of adding the relationship information, brother, etc. That helps until I figure out how to recognize the name sign."[36]

Notes

1. I. A. Richards, Towards a Theory of Translation, in *Studies in Chinese Thought*, ed. Arthur F, Wright (University of Chicago Press, 1953), 13.
2. Alexandra Alter, "Shining a Spotlight on the Art of Translation," *The New York Times*, February 11, 2022, https://www.nytimes.com/2022/02/11/books/literary-translation-translators-jennifer-croft.html.
3. Hugo, V. (1875). Mis hijos (J. Martí, Trans.). Revista Universal.
4. David Hare, *Stages of Translation: Essays and Interviews*, ed. David Johnston (Oberon Books, 1994), 42.
5. Marie Sainvil, "Finding Meaning—The Art of Translation," *Women in Theatre Journal Online*, accessed August 11, 2022, https://witonline.org/2022/08/08/finding-meaning-in-translating-words-and-culture/.
6. Sanford Meisner and Dennis Longwell, *Sanford Meisner on Acting* (Vintage Books, 1987), 29.
7. For a discussion of the impact of silent moments, we refer you to this 2001 article from *Backstage*, "The Rest Is Silence," https://www.backstage.com/magazine/article/rest-silence-mute-moments-move-audiences-20453/.
8. *Cabaret*, by Joseph Masteroff, music by John Kander, lyrics by Fred Ebb.
9. Alexandra Alter, "Shining a Spotlight on the Art of Translation," *The New York Times*, February 11, 2022.

10. Sharon Masingale Bell, “In the Shadow of the Father Tongue: On Translating the Masks in J.-S. Alexis,” in *Between Languages and Cultures: Translation and Cross-Cultural Texts*, ed. Anuradha Dingwaney and Carol Maier (University of Pittsburgh Press, 1995).
11. A semantic domain is “an area of meaning and the language used to talk about it.” *Semdom*, accessed May 2, 2022, https://semdom.org/description.
12. *Barefoot in the Park*, by Neil Simon. Lines reprinted with permission © Paramount Pictures Corp. All rights reserved.
13. Carol Padden, email with Lynnette Taylor, July 30, 2024.
14. Andrew Fisher, email with Candace Broecker Penn, August 1, 2024.
15. *West Side Story*, by Arthur Laurents, adapted by Jerome Robbins, music by Leonard Bernstein, lyrics by Stephen Sondheim.
16. Course Hero, “Titus Andronicus | Character Map,” March 22, 2018, https://www.coursehero.com/lit/Titus-Andronicus/character-map/. Included with permission granted, January 18, 2021.
17. *On Your Feet*, by Alexander Dinelaris Jr., music by Emilio Estefan, Gloria Estefan, and Miami Sound Machine, dir. Jerry Mitchell, chor. Sergio Trujillo, interp. Dana Fuller, Lynnette Taylor, and Emilia Lorenti-Wann, DOI. Alexandria Waile, Marquis Theatre, New York, NY, November 5, 2015–August 20, 2017.
18. *Wicked*, by Winnie Holzman, music and lyrics by Stephen Schwartz, dir. Joe Mantello, chor. Wayne Cilento, interp. Alan Champion, Candace Broecker Penn, and Christina Trunzo Mosleh, DOI. Jason Norman, Gershwin Theatre, New York, NY, September 14, 2024.
19. *Julius Caesar*, by William Shakespeare.
20. *The Phantom of the Opera*, by Andrew Lloyd Webber and Richard Stilgoe, music by Andrew Lloyd Webber, lyrics by Charles Hart, dir. Hal Prince, chor. Gillian Lynne, interp. Alan Champion, Candace Broecker Penn, and Priscilla Cooper Jones, Deaf advisors, George Garcia and George Pehlgrim, The Majestic Theatre, New York, NY, January 26, 1988.
21. *The Mystery of Edwin Drood*, lyrics, music, and book by Rupert Holmes, suggested by the unfinished novel by Charles Dickens, dir. Scott Ellis, chor. Warren Carlyle, interp. Candace Broecker Penn, Rick Rubin, and Molly Wilson, DOI. Anne Tomasetti, Studio 54, New York, NY, November 13, 2012–March 10, 2013.
22. *Rent*, music, lyrics, and book by Jonathan Larson, dir. Michael Greif, Nederlander Theatre, New York, NY, April 29, 1996–September 7, 2008.
23. *A Soldier's Play*, by Charles Fuller, dir. Kenny Leon, interp. Jacinda Damas, Dana Fuller, Jose Gomez, and Rick Rubin, DOIs. Dax Fudenske and Zavier Sabio, Todd Haimes Theatre, New York, NY, January 21, 2020–March 11, 2020.
24. *Oh, Mary*, by Cole Escola, dir. Sam Pinkleton, interp. Joshua Castille, Tolly Tolman, Craig Fogel, and Cathy Markland, DOI Andrew Morrill, Lyceum Theatre, New York, NY, July 11, 2024.
25. Craig Fogel, email communication with Candace Broecker Penn, September 5, 2024.
26. *Hell's Kitchen*, by Kristoffer Diaz, music and lyrics by Alicia Keys, dir. Michael Grieff, chor. Camille A. Brown, interp. Jose Gomez, Frenchetta Perez, Justine Rivera, and Gloria Vargas, DOI. Alexandria Wailes. Shubert Theatre, New York, NY, April 20, 2024.
27. Frenchetta Perez Kilpatrick, email with Lynnette Taylor, September 6, 2024.

28. Kilpatrick, email.
29. Justine Rivera, email with Lynnette Taylor, September 6, 2024.
30. *Enemy of the People*, by Henrik Ibsen, adapted by Amy Herzog, dir. Sam Gold, interp. Candace Broecker Penn, Dylan Geil, and Rick Rubin, DOI. Andrew Fisher, Circle in the Square, New York, NY, March 18, 2024–June 23, 2024.
31. Fisher, email.
32. *A Christmas Carol,* by Charles Dickens, adapt. Rick Robinson, interp. Todd Agan, Stephanie Feyne, and Suzanne Lightbourn. DO. Darren Frazier Oregon Cabaret Theatre, Ashland, OR, November 17–December 31, 2022.
33. Jemina Napier, *Linguistic Coping Strategies in Sign Language Interpreting* (Gallaudet University Press, 2016).
34. Padden, email.
35. Ilaria Parogni, "What Matters in a Name Sign?" *The New York Times*, July 16, 2021, https://www.nytimes.com/interactive/2021/07/16/arts/kamala-harris-name-sign-language.html.
36. Parogni, "What Matters."

4

Translation: Interactive Team-Constructed Discourse

> "It is useful . . . to ask different questions that relate not to the extent to which a performance represents a translated text, or a dramatic text is performable but to the force the text has in performance, what 'it does' and how it functions 'as performance' (Schechner 2002: 32)."
>
> —quoted in Cristina Marinetti, *Translation and Theatre: From Performance to Performativity*

The team creates both individual and collective translations to respond to the lexical, semantic, relational, spatial, discursive, and performative elements of the production, both spoken and unspoken. This becomes the landscape upon which the team interpretation is mapped. As the team crafts the interpretation, they look for ways to refine individual translations while incorporating these understandings into a collective interpretation. Damion Searls quotes Polly Barton in reminding us that "Conversation is not, as we might imagine, 'trading perfectly formed, pearl-like ideas between one mind and another,' but because of 'the enmeshed relationship that exists between behavior and language.'"[1]

When making translatory choices, the team draws from the actors' expressions, the contexts in which these expressions arise, and cultural matter, as well as auditory and visual elements of the staged expression. Additional influences on translatory decisions include the genre, setting (location and era) of the play, social relationships, world of the characters, and their interactions with others in the world of the play. Depending on the play, social factors important in any interpreted event (e.g., race, gender, socioeconomic status, and power relations) will be relevant to our translation choices. These considerations drive the choices, from broad strokes of the world to the details of specific sign choices.

The discovery process is iterative. The team returns always to their foundational experience of attending the play as an audience member. Listening as an audience member and listening as an interpreter are very different experiences. Audience members may understand an utterance enough to enjoy the play, but when interpreters have to transform that idea into another language, they are now pushed to a deeper level of inquiry and a deeper level of understanding. The interpreter's experience as an audience member becomes a resource to draw from as the team forms its interpretation. This also occurs when translating printed text.

Kate Briggs, in "This Little Art," addresses the difference between understanding a sentence and the complexity of translating it. "This sentence, on the other hand: I am able to read it, I feel fairly sure that I understand it. But until I start translating it, I'm not yet in a position to tell you exactly where, of what order or of what combination of orders (lexical, syntactical, atmospheric, psychological, ethical . . .) its difficulties will turn out to be" (Briggs 2017, 69).[2]

When interpreting for the theatre, the team also considers how the script and lines live in the interactions onstage. Character interactions are understood in the context of the moment, scene, and entirety of the play, a more directorial perspective. This lens is beneficial when the interpreting team is in the process of developing their understanding of the world of the play, from which the team constructs a shared meaning space where the signed conversations live. The conceptual and spatial agreements that we introduce below are the building blocks of this shared meaning space.

The strategies introduced in this book are applicable to almost any genre (from farce to drama, from Henrik Ibsen to Eugène Ionesco to Harold Pinter to Suzan-Lori Parks and musicals from Stephen Sondheim to Lin-Manuel Miranda and Jeanine Tesori) and era (Greek, Shakespeare, Grand Guignol, contemporary, etc.). Each makes its own demands on the interpreting team. Additional dramaturgy and time may be needed for language or content that is outside standard contexts, but the approach remains the same.

Teaming in the Rehearsal Process: Building the Architecture of Our Team-Constructed Discourse

Agreements, both performative and lexical, are the architectural elements that help the team collectively construct the world of the play. In order to create a unified expression of the entire play, the team approaches the work with both a macro and a micro lens, zooming in to the discrete and specific moments and zooming out to make sure the whole of the narrative is conveyed. The stage is recognized as a partner and is looked to as the primary source to draw from (rather than the script). For this collective approach to work, everyone needs to come prepared: having seen the play, having questions ready, bringing ideas to share, being open for discussions of meanings and themes, and identifying where meaning resides (e.g., in the stage picture, in the story, or in the characters' delivery of the lines).

There is always individual analysis and development of translations, but without the shared discoveries, an interpretation runs the risk of being disconnected from the whole. Building translations collaboratively allows for a more cohesive and dialogic presentation. If all of the individual translations are frozen or set ahead of time, there is no room for the breath of the team's language, new responses, or the play's specific expression on any given night.

A dramaturgical perspective can help answer some of the questions discovered during rehearsal. Dramaturgy provides play-specific information and/or background knowledge relevant to a specific community or context. Some organizations and theatres offer support to their interpreting teams via their dramaturgs, education department, or online information resources. In addition, some Directors of Interpreters (DOIs) also provide dramaturgical support to their teams.

The shared understanding of the play is also developed by using American Sign Language (ASL) as the language of our rehearsals. Understandings develop through responsive, back-and-forth exchanges. When working in this discursive rehearsal process, the team identifies where agreements need to be made at the lexical, semantic, relational, and performative levels.

The default is not to rely on frozen translations for most of the play; however, there are certainly moments when frozen agreements are helpful, such as for particular lines of dialogue when a certain response is needed, or when building toward a joke's punch line, for shared lyrics, and so on. Teams need to identify those moments when frozen translations are needed for cuing, for discursive agreements, for humor, for signing musical lyrics, and so forth. When there is a mixed Deaf and hearing team, allow time to explore cueing strategies that the team will utilize.

During the rehearsal process, the team reexamines the narrative arc, the character arc, and their progression in the collective translation. During the "hands-up" signed rehearsal process, the team identifies whether character assignments need to be reassessed. Speed-through plot discussions reinforce many of the significant points of storytelling.

DOI Anne Tomasetti helps teams "identify the narrative structure of the work and the narrative devices used to propel the story. . . ."[3] By outlining the key ideas that recur, the interpreter can understand the build of each segment in relation to the others. Tomasetti reminds us, "It helps interpreters identify the big ideas they want to communicate to the audience. Working within that larger framework is helpful when developing their individual translations or monologue."[4]

Teams continuously monitor the collective output, ensuring that multiple strands of content are incorporated into the translations: visual to visual, language to language, thought to thought, and performative to performative. This leads to a deeper connection between the interpreted space and the stage space. The goal is to design cohesive team-interpreted discourse that leads to ease of viewing of both the interpretation and the stage performance.

It takes time to build the architecture of the team interpretation. It requires a robust rehearsal schedule, which is often one of the most difficult things to coordinate! Some shows and teams require more time than others, so we recommend being mindful of that when developing a rehearsal schedule.

When time constraints are a factor, such as when touring shows are only in town for a week, teams can begin their rehearsal process early by getting the script in advance, along with working as a team with the cast album and viewing a video of the show (when possible). Some Broadway shows may be available through streaming platforms. There are also theatres that include permission for digital recordings in the performers' contract. If the team has access to these recordings, they become a valuable rehearsal tool.

The interpreting team for *Jordans* did not all live in New York City (NYC).[5] This created a logistical challenge for rehearsals. The Public Theater provided the team with a digital recording of the production for rehearsal purposes. *Zoom* was the platform for much of the rehearsal process until the entire team could be together on site for the run-through. Of course, it's preferable to have the entire team work in the same space, but this is a viable option when that is not possible. Technology and digital platforms give us a vehicle to expand the community of practice while maintaining a collaborative interpreting process.

Another way to use technology is in crafting and/or refining translations. Interpreters can record drafts of their translation and share them with the DOI and team members. This is a useful way to collectively assess interpretations and ask for feedback and clarity of meaning. Given that ASL has no shared written form, these recorded intralingual dialogues are helpful because they offer language choices that can be incorporated into the final interpretation.

It is important to note that such recordings are production specific and not to be used as a template for future interpretations of the play. Each team develops its translation in accordance with the director's and actors' vision that is represented in a particular production. A different production would merit a new translation, even if it is the same interpreting team, such as for Shakespeare's plays, which are rich material for directors to reinterpret and explore. Earlier translations might be helpful as a reference but may not be relevant to the current production. For example, in the interpretations of the Broadway production of *Hadestown*,[6] the sign used for the underworld was developed from a gesture used onstage. It may be that future productions would not include that gesture, so that sign may not be effective in other interpreted productions.

SERVANT OF TWO SOURCES (APOLOGIES TO GOLDONI)[7]

The interpreting team processes multiple sources of information simultaneously, which then must be rendered in a unified strand. It is important to wean ourselves away from the idea that the auditory is the singular source. Theatre interpreters are "servants of two masters" (the stage and the signed language created by the team), both of which have visual modes of information delivery.

Stage sources include:

- Auditory source (lines, sound)
- Visuals (lighting, character actions, events)
- Story (plot points, character arcs)
- Character interactions (relationships, intentions, actions, and reactions)
- Tone, genre, and mood
- Timing (of lines, actions, blackouts, etc.)

The team's signed expressions are a second visual source, forming the basis for discursive agreements on:

- Translation choices
- Cues
- Spatial referents
- Eye gaze

Recognizing these multiple sources helps develop a "shared meaning space" as the team begins drafting their interpretation.

ASL AS THE LANGUAGE OF REHEARSALS

ASL is produced physically, an "embodied" language. By listening with the eyes instead of the ears, the team begins to forge the shared language of the play, finding natural ways to respond to each other's utterances. Exploring these ideas in the target language allows us to formulate a collective working team interpretation that is responsive to what can arise in the moment.

When starting the interpreting process as a signed conversation, the natural turn-taking, listening, and dialogic features of ASL are already embedded in the interactions. This helps to guide the interpretation to an expression that is more natural in the target language.

This process has the potential of lessening "interpreter-ese" in the final output. "Interpreter-ese" is our descriptor for interpreted utterances that have been influenced by the spoken source to such an extent that the prosodic delivery and/or the grammar is less natural and thus requires more effort to comprehend. As George Garcia, one of our regular Theatre Development Fund (TDF) Deaf advisors, would often say, "I can see you listening to the play as a hearing interpreter, which pulls me out of the life of the play."

When the team is co-constructing this world, each response is built upon the other interpreter's imagery and language. Individual interpretations may be incorporated by other team members, developing a shared semantic domain for the world of the play. In this way, choices for conveying ideas can be repeated and instilled throughout the play by each member because the team is working to build a unified expression.

Initial agreements will morph throughout the rehearsal process because the team is continuously discovering layers of meaning from the source and from watching each other. These agreements are not made in linear stages, even though they are presented here as discrete strategies. The team agreements are strands of the whole and evolve throughout the rehearsal process.

Shared Meaning Space: Spatial Component

Signed language is kinetic and three-dimensional, and the space in which it operates is a potential meaning space, waiting to be activated by the interpreting team.

The live interpretation always coexists with and in relation to the stage space (which includes narrative information, character interactions, and behaviors seen onstage). In the interpretation, these become active, performative, and reified in a three-Dimensional language, which means they become part of the shared meaning space in an ASL interpretation.

Shared meaning space is both the interpreted space and its interplay with the staged performance. The team travels between these two spaces to develop the interpretation and draws from stage elements that will either be imported into the interpretation or referred to on stage. Meaning space can include stage references, character blocking, conceptual placeholders, and mapping of the dialogic interactions of the actors. It becomes a spatial landscape for the interpreting team.

The interpreting team creates and interacts with mutually agreed-upon spatial referents informed by both the stage and the grammatical requirements of ASL. The practice of sharing meaning space is a discursive requirement particular to theatre interpreting. Agreements on referents can be made on an individual and/or a team basis and correspond to what is seen onstage or to team-constructed imaginary spaces. These multiple agreements (maps) converge into a shared meaning space. In a sense, team members become linguistic cartographers, mapping and referencing their spatial agreements. The shared meaning space extends from the stage to the interpreting team, into the audience.

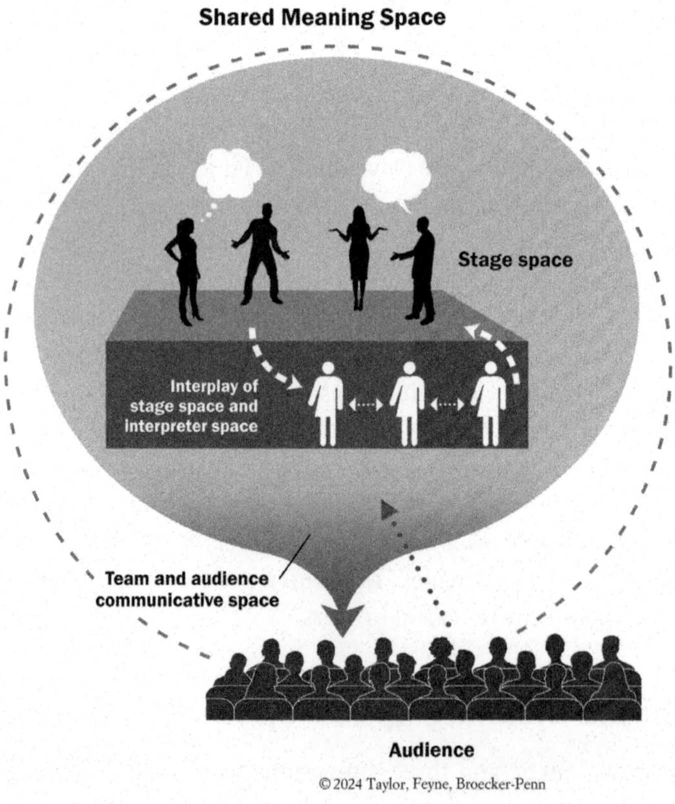

Figure 4.1. Shared meaning space.

We offer a chart to help visualize the spaces that can be activated and interacted with during our interpretations (fig. 4.1).

Mapping can operate singly by one interpreter as well as collectively among the team. The team makes agreements on where the referents will appear in the shared space, by referring to the stage, and when.

This communicative space is activated when the interpreting team interprets directly to the audience in order to engage them (such as moments of audience involvement). In addition, interpreters are always monitoring and adjusting when needed. By observing audience interactions, team members may spontaneously revise or clarify their interpretations.

Questions that help to determine which space will be activated at particular moments in the play include:

- To what extent does the visual stage information speak for itself?
- What visual information from the stage needs to be imported into our meaning space?
- Who do the characters onstage have conversations with?
- How does the team construct shared interactive linguistic space?
- How does the co-constructed activated space express cohesion on an individual, team, and performance basis?

SPATIAL AGREEMENTS FOR SHARED MEANING SPACE

During a play, and even during individual scenes, the team uses many types of meaning space (spatial) agreements: individual agreements, shared partner agreements, and shared agreements with the stage.

Individual Agreements for Imaginary Space

An individual interpreter's spatial translation agreements must also align with the stage. Shakespeare's play *Romeo and Juliet* offers an example. When Romeo expresses his heartbreak that Rosaline doesn't love him, if the actor establishes a spatial location for Rosaline, the interpreter would use that referent during the signed monologue. If the actor does not look to any specific location for her, then the interpreter would choose a spatial location for Rosaline and use it consistently throughout the monologue. By placing Rosaline in a fixed location, the interpretation establishes individual cohesion.

Team Agreement for Imaginary Space

Teams also make agreements to designate a space for something that is discussed but not established by the characters onstage (imaginary space). In Chekov's *Three Sisters,* the family dreams of leaving their current home and returning to Moscow, the city that represents their hopes and best memories of happiness. They often discuss their aspirations for moving there. Moscow signifies the shared longing to return. If the team did not agree, it could be possible for one interpreter to establish Moscow up high and to the left, another interpreter to have it down low to the right, and a third to have it somewhere else. By the interpreters agreeing to place Moscow in the same location, the shared experience of joint longing is reinforced through team eye gaze and shared spatial referent. This decision is not only for efficiency, but it is also a discursive cohesion agreement. In this manner, the shared referent takes on consistent meaning throughout the play.

A similar kind of imaginary space agreement was made in Tom Stoppard's *Arcadia*,[8] in which pivotal information resides in conversations about calculations from a mathematical algorithm. The characters constantly referred to the implications of a graph of that algorithm although there were no visual representations of it onstage. The interpreting team used shared meaning space to represent the graph being developed.

This interactive mapping now required each member of the team to be precise in their individual plotting of the findings from the algorithm, so that each member's map could be built upon by the next interpreter. The team had to attend to both the shared and the individual spaces as the graph was actively being built. As the conversations on stage unfolded, team members could see each other's map and thus respond to and build upon it. Unlike stationary references, the space and representation of this concept continuously evolved throughout the play.

Team Agreement with the Stage

An illustration of an agreement with stage visuals occurs in *The Lion King*,[9] when Mufasa, the king, shows the young prince Simba the lands he will someday rule:

The Lion King

Act I–Scene 4

MUFASA:	Look, Simba, everything the light touches is our kingdom.
YOUNG SIMBA:	. . . But what about that shadowy place?
MUFASA:	That's beyond our borders. You must never go there Simba.

(*The Lion King*, script courtesy of Disney Theatrical Group. © 1994 Disney)

As Mufasa directs his gaze across the Pride Lands, he explains to his son that his realm will encompass the entire area where the sun shines. Simba looks to the far corners of the land and asks his father about the shadowy place. As Young Simba stares off in the direction of the shadowy place, he points to that area. The team would incorporate Simba's spatial references into their interpretation, thus aligning the interpreting picture with the stage picture.[10]

Another example from *The Lion King* highlights the interpreters incorporating multiple agreements between the stage and the conversational partners. Below are photos from a teaching module developed from a twenty-six-second exchange among Timon, Pumba, and Simba, which illustrates interactive discourse techniques.

Five discrete spatial agreements are expressed through body position and eye gaze: interpreters looking to the stage, Timon and Pumba addressing Simba, Pumba talking to Simba (with Timon engaged and receptive), and the team to the audience (fig. 4.2).

In brief, the stage picture informs the interpreting team's decisions about where to place referents in our shared meaning space.

Once the interpreting team establishes spatial agreements, they continue to navigate the virtual and actual maps as part of meaning exploration. They constantly monitor the work for clarity and team consistency, during both rehearsals and the performance of the interpretation. The DOI, as part of the team, guides this work of identifying referents, sharing grammatical conventions for referring, as well as respecting the stage picture.

Depending on your fluency and the material you are working with, your space can reflect what is being seen or discussed onstage—anything from a dilapidated shantytown to a sleek Mies van der Rohe building. The greater the linguistic fluency, the more sophisticated the use of space will appear in the interpretation.

The use of space in the construction of an interpretation can make an interpreted performance go from "2-D to 3-D," as George Garcia used to say. When he was evaluating a piece of work and declared it a "3-D" interpretation, it meant that the meaning was complete and living in the interpretation.

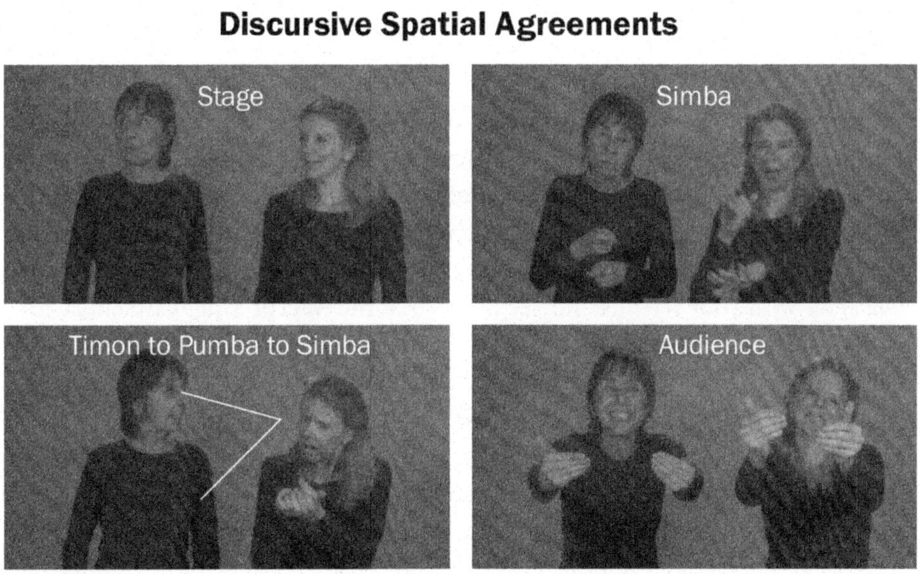

Figure 4.2. Discursive spatial agreements. Copyright © 2024 Taylor, Feyne, and Broecker Penn.

Shared Meaning Space: Conceptual Component

This section focuses on the lexical agreements that need to be made, while the next chapter addresses performative agreements. Both of these types of agreements operate concurrently in the performed interpretation, creating conceptual cohesion throughout the play.

IMPORTING CULTURAL MATTER

In a play, the characters are often members of the same speech community where concepts and ideas are understood implicitly in shared linguistic forms. In the theatre, interpreters are introducing not only the narrative and emotional worlds, but also the intellectual and linguistic worlds of the characters, what we call "cultural matter."[11] Creating shared understandings of implicit meanings normally requires shared social and cultural experiences. This shared knowledge often resides implicitly in language.

When cultural matter familiar to one community (such as a concept or specific terminology) is introduced into another, translators recognize that what was implicitly understood in its original ecosystem may not be understood in its new domain. Some cultural matter reside implicitly in both languages and can be readily imported as implicit into ASL translations. Other cultural matter require a temporarily constructed and agreed-upon form when transporting it. Interpreters need to consider what should be explicit or reframed when transporting cultural matter.

In community interpreting, interpreters and Deaf participants agree on ways to present new concepts and vocabulary, as in college classes, when we quickly check in for an ASL sign for a term, concept, or name. In the theatre, rather than negotiating agreements directly with the audience, the team embeds the process of negotiating agreements into the interpreted dialogue.

Once the agreements are established, the team continues to use these agreed-upon forms throughout the play. These temporary linguistic agreements are conventionalized and become part of the vocabulary for the interpretation of the show. These signs live only in the world of the play and are not necessarily used outside of that context. In other words, it is very unlikely that you're going to be sitting in a coffee shop with your friends and see a sign that the interpreting team chose for a play pop up in conversation.

However, if the signs were created during a staged production with Deaf talent, their use may continue outside of the theater, such as the sign for the title of *Spring Awakening* presented by Deaf West on Broadway in 2015. For the Public Theater's production of Ntozake Shange's *for colored girls who have considered suicide/when the rainbow is enuf*,[12] Director of Artistic Sign Language (DASL) Onudeah Nicolarakis suggested an older Southern sign for "colored" for Alexandria Wailes to use in the play. When the show was interpreted, the team incorporated the sign. That sign has now become a part of the vocabulary of the local NYC signing community.

When considering what cultural matter can be easily transported, we need to identify the shared lexical and cultural understandings. A question that guides the process is who shares the cultural matter:

- the characters?
- the society contemporaneous to the play?
- the general audience viewing the show?

If the cultural matter is shared by the Deaf community, then transporting it is relatively straightforward. This is also true in spoken language translation. A *New York Times* article on the process of translating *Hamilton* into German stated, "A few English phrases—well-known to fans, repeated often, and easy to understand" were included in the German translation, such as a reference to New York as "the greatest city in the world."[13]

However, if there are gaps in shared understandings, then there may not be a ready conveyance, and additional strategies will need to be applied. As translators know, "Figures of speech and wordplay rarely survive translation."[14] In the case of *Hamilton*, Lin Manuel Miranda "encouraged the translators to come up with their own metaphors. One example that Finale [one of the translators] is proud of concerns Hamilton's fixation on mortality. In English, he [Hamilton] says 'I imagine death so much it feels more like a memory.' In German, he will say words meaning, 'Every day death is writing between the lines of my diary.'"[15] It takes time to both find these expressions and to play with ideas that are crossing between cultures and language.

Cultural matter can spring from the style of the play. The following questions can be asked: What genre is the play (e.g., comedy, drama, musical, farce, Greek tragedy)? What meaning does the genre carry? Is the play historical? If so, how does historical language manifest in the ASL community? Are there recognizable signs that can lend the flavor of the era to the team's interpretation? If the play is representative of a particular community, are there signs used within that community in ASL that can be used by the interpreting team? It is important to ensure that team members and advisors have access to the repertoire of signs that support the play.

The manner in which dialogue is presented also carries meaning. Humor, for example, serves several functions. It can demonstrate a character's wit (e.g., famously in Shakespeare with Mercutio, Beatrice, and Benedict; characters in more contemporary plays), as well as reflect relationships. Margaret Edson's *Wit* is a rumination on life and death through reflections on language, with emphasis on wit found in famous English sonnets. Certainly, the manner, content, and form of the English would be important considerations for this work. In Lin-Manuel Miranda's *Hamilton*, those who take center stage in this telling of the founding of America are challenging the very nature of whose voices are heard in the telling of history and in the way these stories are expressed. The lyrics and rhythms of the songs are infused with cultural meanings, so both form and content must be considered.

How characters use language can reveal their social relationships. Do they speak as equals? Do they speak down to others? Do they speak with deference? Are they fluent in the language used by others? Are they fluent in the language used by the other characters or learning a new language during the play, as in Shakespeare's *Henry V*? Are they multilingual, and if so, how is this expressed? For example, in the opening number "Willkommen" in *Cabaret*, the Emcee speaks/sings in English, French, and German. How can the team convey the international flavor of the club's milieu that is expressed in his ease with multiple languages? The DOI can assist the team to find resources to open up the language repertoire of the translation.

Well-known phrases such as "To be or not to be" from *Hamlet* and "Out, out damn spot" from *Macbeth,* lead us to ask what cultural matter is shared? Does it manifest in the Deaf community, and if so, how? Questions that arise include: How important is that cultural matter? Can the form stand on its own and be transliterated? Can the transliteration and the corresponding interpretation both be offered given the time allotted? Or is there only time for expressing the meaning and dropping the form? And, as was mentioned in "Meaning Is Not Just in the Words," as part of the work of unpacking meaning, the interpreting team also considers the meaning in both its historic and contemporary contexts, times, and places.

Decisions about what cultural matter entails, what is easily transportable, and what will be included in the translations/interpretations are influenced by the knowledge bases, personal beliefs, and ideologies of the team. The choices that interpreters make about how much of the original source to include are affected by the interpreters' beliefs about the relative value of each language (linguicism) and beliefs (implicit and explicit) about translation and interpreting. Recognizing our beliefs allows for more conscious and deliberate choices as the team brokers cultural matter.

Importing cultural matter requires a relationship with the community that embodies that cultural and linguistic knowledge. Since ASL is not a written language, knowing who to ask for insights into language that reflects historic and/or culture- or community-specific content necessitates a relationship with members of the community who embody that knowledge. An example of this is found in *A Soldier's Play*, a show situated in the 1940s with language use from that era. Dana Fuller, one of the interpreters, explained, "Dax and Zavier really helped me find the language. I also asked my [Deaf] parents for signs they used from that time. One of their suggestions was an older sign for 'newspaper.' After the performance, a Deaf audience member came up to me. He was very moved and shared, 'I haven't seen that sign in a long time. It brought back a lot of memories.' It was nice to bring back the old signs and see the audience's response."

Zavier Sabio, one of the DOIs for the show explained, "As an advisor, I wanted to ensure that the tone, emotional impact, and authenticity of the language had an equally powerful impact on the Deaf audience. We wanted to include the offensive language and the signed expressions used in the '40s, so the audience would experience that era as well as the emotional impact of hate language used during that time. My co-DOI, Darren (Dax) Fudenske, and I reached out to elders in the Deaf Black community who had lived through the '40s for specific signs used in that era, such as the 'N-word.' Seeing that was quite emotional."[16]

This kind of careful investigation and deliberate choice of signs in the importation of cultural matter is important. As Sabio pointed out, "By adding these signs, even though some are offensive, we will elicit a reaction, an experience, and a connection to what is happening onstage so that the Deaf audience can truly experience it."[17]

Anchoring Strategies

What we call "building the architecture" is actually a series of linguistic strategies that continuously connect the interpretation/translation back to the staged conversations. This ensures that the cultural matter of the stage resonates throughout the interpreted representation. "Anchoring" is the term we use for a cache of linguistic and performative interpreting strategies that can be used to link the interpretation to the play. Anchoring strategies include introduction, expansion and compression, linguistic partnering with the stage, use of schematics, and so on. All are means of ensuring that the connections between the stage and the interpretation are clearly expressed. Many of the techniques used are traditional interpreting strategies; however, some of these techniques were developed in response to the specific needs of the venue.

As mentioned above, because interpreted theatre does not often allow for the negotiated interactions that often occur in community interpreting, the team needs to consider how to efficiently share team sign choices with the audience. Anchoring strategies are used to make signed choices for the cultural matter explicit. In this way, the team introduces the audience to the semantic domains created for the play.

TEAM AGREEMENTS

There are a variety of reasons that lead interpreting teams to make multiple agreements that build toward a shared linguistic outcome. These agreements are the building blocks of the architecture of our translations and are developed during the rehearsal process.

Lexical Team Agreements

The interpreting team would agree on signs that would be appropriate for specific time frames and characters. For example, the sign for "telephone" has evolved to reflect devices used in different eras. In *The Front Page*, written in the 1920s, an old-fashioned candlestick phone would appear on stage; in the 1960s' *Barefoot in the Park*, there is a rotary phone with a receiver; and in the contemporary *Dear Evan Hansen*, characters text on cell phones. Agreements on the appropriate sign for the era would occur early in the team process. The team might also make agreements on cultural matter such as song titles, the Pledge of Allegiance, prayers, and other well-known cultural phrases.

Recently, Candace and Lynnette were members of the interpretation team for The Roundabout Theatre's *Thérèse Raquin.*[18] The team discussed how they would sign "Paris." Would they use the American sign that refers to the Eiffel Tower? Or would they use the French sign for "Paris" that is initialized and has no reference to the Eiffel Tower. The team agreed that they would use the French sign for two reasons. One was to add the flavor of French verité, and the other was for the sake of historical accuracy. The Eiffel Tower was not yet built during the time depicted in the play. Having made that decision, the team incorporated natural ASL discourse for introducing vocabulary into their interpretation by fingerspelling P-A-R-I-S, then introducing the French sign for Paris, an example of an anchoring strategy.

Translating humor would be a book unto itself. It is well understood that translating humor across languages and cultures requires thought and preparation. Puns and jokes often require a collective team approach, and the interpreters may need to make some frozen lexical agreements in order for the punch line to land. Jokes based on sound and wordplay require inventive solutions. Still, humor is often untranslatable, one of the realities of interpretation for all languages. However, the team decides to wrestle with this, agreements need to be developed, and the utterances must make sense in relation to the play and in sign language.

Sign play must always be grounded in the context and the characters' relationships. One tiny moment that exemplifies some of the challenges of humor comes from *The Lion King,* in a jovial exchange between Timon and Pumba as they riff on a pun between "Motto" and "Matta." The joke is that Timon intentionally misuses the word "Motto" as if it were "What's the matter?" This reflects Timon and Pumba's relationship, they engage in playful banter—Timon plays the comic to Pumba's straight man. The interpreting team tried to find a way to express that this was a play on words. The term "motto" led the team to the sign for "belief." The team then explored other signs with the same handshape but a different movement and agreed to use the sign for "marriage." Playing these two signs off each other served the same function of expressing a bad pun while conveying the two characters teasing each other.

Semantic Team Agreements

Since meaning is specified in the context of the play, relying on "go-to" signs for every expression of meaning runs the risk of skewing the interpretation. As an example, the English word "hunt" carries a myriad of meanings. The team has to discover what "hunt" means in each context and sign it accordingly. In a play, "hunt" could mean the Crocodile hunting Captain Hook, characters hunting with guns or bow and arrow, characters going on a scavenger hunt, animals hunting for food, or characters going on a witch hunt. If it is the title of the play, such as *The Hunt* by David Farr, and the concept appears as a theme throughout the play, additional discussions would be necessary. For that show, the team could choose a fingerspelled version as well as the multiple meanings of "hunt" as they appear. While rehearsing for a production of *King Lear*,[19] DOI Noah Buchholz reminded the team that the traditional sign for "hunt" is also an option to consider. It can function as a standard sign—"to hunt"—and as a classifier.

Information often comes from the stage and not from the text. Interpreters would want to know who or what is doing the hunting. What kind of hunt and how are they hunting? The answer to these questions would determine the possible options. The team would want to avoid conceptually inaccurate sign choices that result in the work being in contradiction with the play, the period, and/or the actions on stage. The concept of "hunt" might change throughout the play, so the investigation of meaning is constant.

If during the hunt, one character is shooting a gun and another is using bow and arrows, each interpreter could choose the conceptually accurate sign for their character's action, with no need for a team agreement. However, if all the characters refer to "hunt" in the same way, then this would need a team agreement. They would determine the meaning and corresponding sign(s) by exploring the action and dialogue onstage, as well as from the dramaturgy and research of the period.

Team semantic agreements were made for Tom Stoppard's play, *Travesties.*[20] The characters included historical figures (Vladmir Lenin, James Joyce, and Tristan Tzara) who were all in Zurich just before World War I. DOI Anne Tomasetti's dramaturgy helped the team import the complex political and cultural matter into their interpretations.

One recurring term in the show was "bourgeois," which carried both a specific and a generalized meaning throughout the play. During the rehearsal process, the team explored the nuances of meaning for the concept "bourgeois," thereby building a semantic domain to draw from. This led to a range of signed options that individual interpreters could tailor to their individual characters at specific moments throughout the play. Without that collective conversation, there would have been no assurance that the individual choices would have reflected the concepts. In addition, the characters had a shared understanding of a generalized meaning of "bourgeois" and used it as a disdainful commentary on the privileged class. Therefore, the team needed to come to a shared agreement for the expression of this particular meaning of "bourgeois" as used in this play.

Dialogic Team Agreements

In a discussion of the importance of team dialogic agreements and how they link the interpretation to the play, Anne Tomasetti explained that "Conveying heightened content in ASL is going beyond the mere words of a single interpreter. It includes the team's collective expression of meaning."[21]

The team considers how the characters express themselves when engaged in a conversation or interaction. For example, in Shakespeare's *Othello,* Iago expresses himself in a manner that reveals his duplicity to the audience, while Othello is oblivious to it. In *Mary Poppins,* the children are warm and playful with their new nanny but are formal and reserved when interacting with their father. The relationships, goals, and character's manner of presentation inform translations and the performance of those translations.

The team analyzes character interactions to be able to make agreements on how these interactions will be expressed. They consider the power dynamics, when and where in the course of the play each scene occurs, the stakes, and the context of the interaction in relation to the character arc and narrative arc of the play. The team must have a shared understanding of these character relationships and interactions in order to make dialogic agreements. To convey the intentions and nuances of the interactions, the team draws from natural dialogic features of ASL.

When Anne Tomasetti, the DOI for *Into the Woods*,[22] was asked about the impact of team dialogic translation strategy during the song "Your Fault," she explained,

> The team interaction and translation choices conveyed the energy and meaning of the performance. The cohesion among the team felt different from the conventional delivery of three separate interpreters. In their presentation of the song, I could see the blame being tossed between the characters like a ball in the way they responded to each other. There was a real purpose in that interpretation and interaction that represented what was occurring onstage.[23]

Team Agreements with the Stage

Entering the theatre space with an interpreter's mindset means including the entirety of the experience in the theatre as subject for our interpretation, not merely the dialogue.

Incorporating Stage Visuals in the Translations

Unlike conventional translation in which a translator is working from text to text, the interpreter in the theatre is working with and between two sources simultaneously. The stage picture inherently includes visual information as part of its language.

Visual considerations and stage picture agreements are a consideration for spoken translators as well. The German translators for *Hamilton* discussed their process,

> An unexpected factor was the way that the translation affected choreography . . . as those words changed, there was a risk that the movement would not make sense. For example: Initially the translators proposed to replace "The room where it happens" with a German phrase meaning "behind closed doors," which they thought was a clearer image for the German audience. But the choreography of that song suggests a room-like space, so the choreographer, Andy Blankenbuehler, balked, and the original concept stayed. The song is now called "In diesem Zimmer," meaning "in this room."[24]

By including visual information from the stage in the translations, the team creates a more seamless interface between the stage and the interpreted space. The following are illustrations of visual-to-visual connections to the stage that can be addressed through interpretation.

Sometimes, props can offer visual vocabulary to draw from. "Welcome to the Renaissance," the opening song from *Something Rotten!*,[25] boasts about the latest technological advancements in 1595 (alongside the bubonic plague and the crusades). When singing of new inventions, a line refers to them as the "latest gadgets." The actors' use of props (e.g., a rat trap and a washboard, for example) offers visual specificity to the line. These visual options could be imported into the translation, enhancing the stage-to-interpreter space connection.

At times, choreographic phrases on the stage can be incorporated into the translations. For example, during rehearsals at the theatre for the 2019 interpreted performance of *Be More Chill*,[26] DOI Anne Tomasetti noticed that the audience often left the theatre mimicking several of the gestural phrases that the actors used during the title song. Tomasetti wanted that audience-to-stage connection and incorporated some of the choreographed gestures into the translation. Her decision supported the narrative and flavor of the show and connected the stage, the interpretation, and the audience. Tomasetti notes, "If the gestures are easily understood, you can use them, if not, you interpret them."[27]

Certain genres of shows might inspire interpreters to take on nonnatural signing styles. When interpreting for the character of Captain Hook in *Peter Pan*, there may be a temptation to depict this character by creating signs for the entire show with only the "X" handshape (which resembles a hook). For a signing actor on stage, this choice might be an exciting option. However, as an interpreting choice, this could interfere with clarity of the signing.

Techniques for bridging the visuals on stage to the interpretation can be simple and quick. Many shows incorporate text projections as an integral part of their productions. In a recent production of *Dear Evan Hansen*,[28] the teenagers' texts (e.g., messages, memes, links, photos, etc.) were projected onto the stage and the proscenium. Because texting is already familiar to the audience, the interpreters can choose to use constructed action to depict the act of texting along with the characters' emotional tones. This not only helps identify who is speaking to whom and how, it efficiently links the interpretation to the stage picture.

In *Avenue Q*,[29] monitors placed above and to each side of the stage were used to evoke *Sesame Street*. Imitating the children's TV show, the company (human and puppet) playfully volleyed between stage and screen as they introduced new vocabulary (such as "purpose" or "schadenfreude"). Likewise, the interpreting team had the opportunity to volley between the interpreting space, stage, and screens with the same playful spirit. Once the team identifies, introduces, and frames the necessary information, by pointing to the screen and linking the word to its signed meaning, the team then has a variety of options: point, refer, incorporate, or let the stage picture speak for itself.

Each show has its own visual vocabulary. The team assesses which elements of this vocabulary can be imported into the translation to enhance the interpretation and forge a stronger relationship between the interpretation and the stage. There is not always a literal visual correspondence between the signed utterance and the stage visuals. The team may choose to depict or incorporate iconic choices that represent actions, objects, or people on stage. In the rehearsal process, the team can assess whether these choices are effective by evaluating them in context. The point is to make choices that complement the visual story on stage and not compete with or contradict the visual information.

Incorporating multiple elements of the show into the translation facilitates a more immediate connection between the audience and the play, as well as offers a connection to the stage during the interpretation. This allows more freedom for the audience to surf the stage picture and return to the interpretation because both share a similar visual vocabulary. Inclusion of the stage elements results in an interpretation that has greater fidelity because it honors both the spoken word and the visual expression.

Narration Strategy

Another strategy for creating agreements with the stage is for the interpreter to narrate information. Narrators can briefly step out of the constructed discourse to impart both auditory and visual incidental and environmental information.[30] This strategy is often applied in community interpreting to convey environmental information that is important in the moment. In the theatre, many of these moments are known in advance and planned for.

Narration occurs when reporting auditory information such as gunshots and doorbells or when identifying when dialogue is spoken by actors planted in the audience. The team also interprets spontaneous information such as "oohs" and "ahhs" from the audience when Maria and Tony finally kiss in *West Side Story* or, on a more serious note, if the stage manager asks, "Is there a doctor in the house?" The narrator strategy can also include the reporting of offstage visual information, such as when the majestic puppets enter from the back of the house at the top of *The Lion King* or when the chandelier descends in *The Phantom of the Opera*.

When addressing accents and other auditory information that exist solely in the aural realm, the interpreting team assesses how to effectively impart this information. The team considers whether it can be incorporated into our dialogic interpretation or whether it is best delivered as descriptive narration.

Once it is determined that the narrator function will be used, an additional decision about the role of the narrator needs to be made. Is the narrator conveying this information as an interpreter, an omniscient narrator, or as a character within the play? Each choice necessitates its own grammatical and spatial construction as well as eye gaze agreements.

When importing foreign languages, it is important to think about what is an "equivalent" interpretation? Will simply signing the foreign signed language lead to an "equivalent" audience experience? Will the foreign signed language be readily recognized as a "signed language" or will it create disconnect in the interpretation and thereby with the audience's connection to the narrative?

In a conversation with Carol Padden about interpreted theatre, she commented, "Deaf people don't necessarily know that the interpretation has switched to a foreign signed language. When I'm at the theatre, I can watch someone signing and know right away that it's not ASL, but I can't tell you what it is. . . . I can't detect a specific sign language just from the quality of the signing."[31] However, if the team quickly uses the narrator function to indicate that it is a foreign signed language, then the audience is prepared.

When the team determines that auditory information warrants conveying and that narration is appropriate, that information can be described—rainfall, a train whistle, a character's Brooklyn accent or French accent. Likewise, in music, the team also can describe the quality of music and/or the voice, such as a voice being powerful, a note being held for an exceptionally long time without a breath, or a character singing painfully out of tune, and so on. These textures are part of the content that is conveyed. Narration of this sort would be done selectively.

Of course, narration is not the only way to convey environmental information. Additional options are to return to constructed discourse and distribute meaning among our team. A team member could incorporate information, for example, "I hear the doorbell" or "Who is at the door?" This information may not be uttered by the character onstage but is folded into the dialogue in a natural manner. These are deliberate choices, based on the story and events of the moment.

Conceptual Agreements

Just as the team makes agreements about the semantic domain of the play, they also make agreements for the visual domain used in the interpretation. Visual information that is tacit in English may require visual details when expressed in ASL. This unseen and/or unstated visual information will need to be unpacked in order to transport the cultural matter. This visual vocabulary becomes the foundation to draw from for the translation throughout the play. A shared repertoire of visually accurate descriptors is then available for the team to draw from.

The construction of graphs in *Arcadia,* mentioned earlier, was developed in response to the tacit visual information in the dialogue. By knowing how graphs are plotted and the implications of the trajectory of this specific algorithm, the team was able to develop a visually and conceptually accurate shared translation.

Visual details are grounded in historical, architectural, and other conceptual specifics. Research can help us find the visual references that are not seen on stage but that are necessary to include for an ASL translation to be conceptually accurate. DASL Monique Holt often uses this example: If the room onstage has French windows, and a character mentions "opening the windows," the verb would not be the ASL sign for "opening the windows bottom to top," but rather a classifier showing the action of opening doors outward. By using details such as these, the team anchors the work to the visuals.

Meaning Distribution Strategies

What we call "meaning distribution" is an important tool for dealing with the magnitude of information coming from the play. Teams need to find ways to distribute the content of the play so that the translation can be performed in real time as the play is unfolding, what is commonly called simultaneity and performability. Simultaneity and performability in theatre interpreting address issues of timing—both the timing of information coming from the stage (e.g., dialogue pace, stage action, visuals) and the difference in the time it takes for ideas to be expressed in English and ASL.

The fact that interpreting is a mediated expression, and not a direct expression from the stage, requires the team to explore when, where, and how meaning can be distributed through linguistic and performative means, since the two visual sources (the stage and the signed interpretation) are operating simultaneously. The goal is to always be aligned as much as possible.

Given the different modalities, complexities of input, and our expression of the meaning, the interpretation cannot mirror the production on stage. The interpreting team usually does not have a one-to-one correspondence with the cast. The performed interpretation is taking place simultaneously with the performance, but not on the same stage. Therefore, in order to convey the story with all the inter- and intranarrative cohesions between the two visual spaces, the two visual modalities, and also the character-to-character expressions, the team has to develop ways to make connections to the stage.

When information is so dense that one interpreter cannot manage all of the strands of meaning in the time allotted, the team must look for ways to distribute meanings among its members. The entire team is now responsible for the expression of meaning. Working from a collective framework, rather than an individual framework, opens up new possibilities.

Decisions for how meaning will be distributed among the team are agreed upon during the rehearsal process. Considerations include timing constraints, dialogic communicative norms, responses to the visuals on the stage, and the differences in conventions of expression between spoken and signed languages. Examples are given throughout this book, but here, we introduce the idea that distribution of meaning may take on many forms: delivering the information earlier or later than it is expressed on the stage (i.e., asynchronous delivery), refraining from signing for a moment and allowing the meaning to be expressed by the stage alone, and so on. While performing the translations, the team monitors for meaning expression and if content is missed, other team members can express it.

Simultaneity and Performability

Timing of the performance is an external force that shapes our interpretation. The team is constantly checking the visuals and language to see whether the translatory choices can be accommodated in the time allotted.

During hands-up rehearsals in ASL, because everyone is listening with their eyes and responding to each other's signing and the actions on stage, the team begins to note where the timing of events onstage will affect interpretation choices. Challenges in simultaneity and performability arise most often in response to temporal constraints due to:

- Stage visuals—blackouts or other optics/action on stage
- Stage performance—pace of actors' delivery
- Translation—complexity and amount of cultural matter to be expressed and how much time it takes in each language to express that matter

The team devises meaning distribution strategies to work around to these real-time constraints of interpreting a live performance. Some guiding questions when deciding when and how to distribute meaning include: Is there an important visual onstage or a quick blackout at the end of the scene? Can all the information be included prior to the visual action or blackout, or is it information that can be delayed until afterward? Is the actor's pace or the cultural matter too densely packed to be delivered in the allotted time?

It is during rehearsal that the team realizes where information can get bottlenecked and needs to be distributed because it cannot be handled within the allotted time. Then, the strategies of how, when, and who would be the best conveyors of that information guide the decisions thereafter. Meaning can be distributed synchronously (during the allotted time) or asynchronously (either before or after).

Synchronous translatory strategies include (but not are limited to):

- Bundling—where one interpreter takes on, or incorporates the lines of, several characters for a moment
- Truncating—where a team member takes less time for their responses (such as offering a quick nonmanual reply that sums up the meaning instead of signing an entire line) so that another team member has enough time to express content
- Strategic omission[32]—where a line may be deliberately not interpreted
- Distributing the content among the interpreting team—where one interpreter conveys some of the content from another character's utterance that was not transmitted

Asynchronous translatory strategies include:

- Delivering information earlier or later in the speech or scene—(e.g., holding until after a kiss, finishing early before a blackout)
- Distributing the content among the interpreting team—where there is not enough time to express all of the content when it is uttered on stage, the unexpressed content may be conveyed at another time either by the interpreter assigned to that character or by another member of the team

In Act II, Scene 3 of Shakespeare's *Othello*, Iago expresses his wish to get Cassio drunk to discredit him. Iago urges Cassio to drink and provokes him to start a fight. This scene includes repartee, drinking songs, and speeches. Often, this scene is directed as a raucous party with dancing on the tables. Choosing to foreground the action, the team might choose any of the synchronous strategies above.

An example of an asynchronous strategy occurred when Raúl Juliá starred in *Othello* in the Public Theater's Shakespeare in the Park in 1991. Just prior to the first interpreted show, Mr. Juliá asked how to sign his greeting to his new wife, Desdemona, at the top of Act II. Upon his entrance, he signed his line, "Oh my fair warrior," before he spoke it. The actor's decision to speak directly to the Deaf audience privileged them with the information first. It was important for the team to honor that. Thus, the team allowed time for the audience to watch Raúl Juliá sign his line and for the signing audience to show their appreciation with visual applause. Interpreting began when the Deaf audience's gaze returned to the interpreting team. This affected the amount of time for the delivery of the ensuing lines. The team decided on the fly what could be truncated or moved so that the remaining portion of the scene could continue in a synchronous manner. This was possible because the team knew the play well enough and was accustomed to working in this manner.

Stopping interpreting to watch the stage creates a domino effect; the team must consider how to incorporate the information in less time. This means drawing from resources and shared strategies of asynchronous and synchronous distributions and deciding which information needs to be prioritized at that moment.

One of the additional team responsibilities is to monitor the clarity of content delivery in small moments throughout the interpretation. The team checks to ensure that the important narrative plot points and character points are conveyed. The strategy of meaning distribution is often used in response to timing constraints but is also used to monitor the cohesion of the narrative.

When mistakes happen, as they do, team members can pitch in to help clarify the message to make sure important details for the story come through. This can be accomplished by a team member prompting the interpreter whose character holds the information with questions such as, "Who died? What did you find? How? Why? When?" Or the listening interpreter can include the missing information in their own interpretation (e.g., "Joe died"). These are usually short interventions.

We offer a guide to help navigate meaning distribution (see fig. 4.3).

Once the team recognizes that information needs to be distributed, they then consider what content needs to be foregrounded, when, and by whom. Meaning cannot be arbitrarily distributed. There is a logic to this. Consider which characters have the authority to express certain content. The guiding considerations would be whether the plot allows characters to share such information. The social relationships of characters to the meaning and to each other, character arcs, motivations, plot points, and the way the play is structured also provide cues to recognizing which character can or cannot own content at a particular moment. For example, the interpreter for Othello probably couldn't enter Iago's thought world since Iago is duplicitous and Othello is unaware. Therefore, meaning distribution from Iago

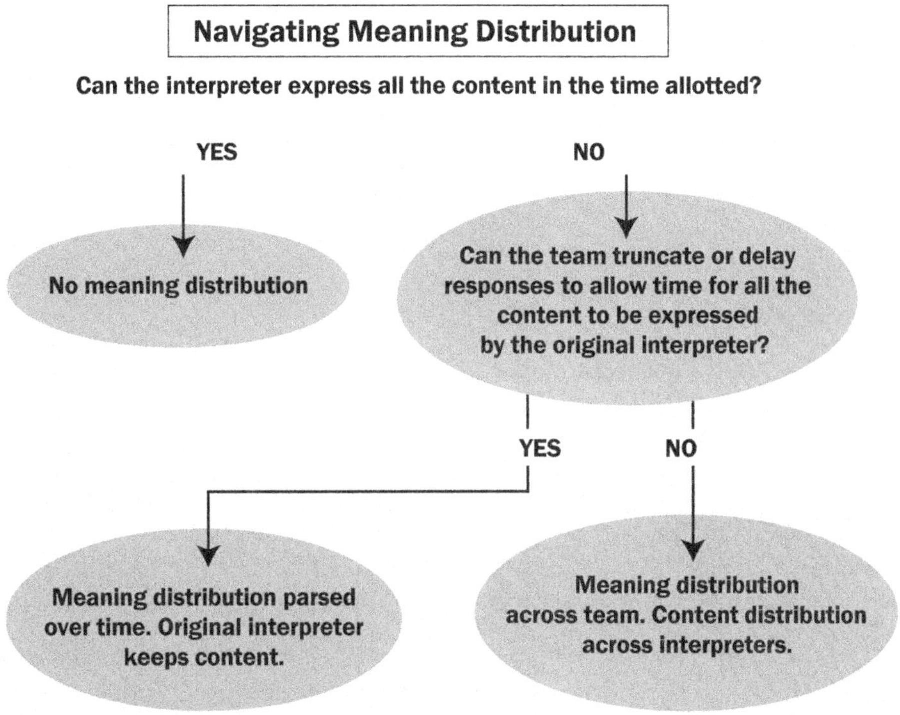

© 2024 Taylor, Feyne, Broecker-Penn

Figure 4.3. Navigating meaning distribution.

would have to be shared with an interpreter who is not assigned to Othello; otherwise, it would be counter to the plot.

The goal of meaning distribution is to clarify information. Interpreters will not be aware of the need to distribute meaning by solely watching the play or reading the script. It is during rehearsals and the live interpreted performance that these issues may arise as a result of the team's timing, an individual interpreter's timing, an actor changing their pacing during performances, or other unanticipated events. It is in these moments that the team recognizes that strategies need to be applied to ensure conveyance of meaning. When distribution is necessary, the team makes agreements to expand or contract interpretation responses to fit within the time constraints, responding to the play, the team, and the moment. This holistic approach to interpretation involves the entire team in the telling of the story.

Exploring Agreements in *Anna Christie*

While the emphasis thus far has been to rely on the live performance as the primary source, the script is also a useful tool. Particularly for touring shows, when there may be limited opportunities to see the show before the interpretation, the script is invaluable. A close reading of the script can help the team identify what kinds of team agreements will need to be made before seeing the production.

Let's do a close read of the opening scene of Eugene O'Neill's *Anna Christie*[33] to illustrate some considerations in making team agreements at the top of a play.

Anna Christie

Act I, Scene 1

It is late afternoon of a day in fall.

As the curtain rises, JOHNNY *is discovered.* "JOHNNY-THE-PRIEST" *deserves his nickname. With his pale, thin, clean-shaven face, mild blue eyes and white hair, a cassock would seem more suited to him than the apron he wears. Neither his voice nor his general manner dispel this illusion which has made him a personage of the waterfront. They are soft and bland. But beneath all his mildness one senses the man behind the mask—cynical, callous, hard as nails. He is lounging at ease behind the bar, a pair of spectacles on his nose, reading an evening paper.*

Two longshoremen enter from the street, wearing their working aprons, the button of the union pinned conspicuously on the caps pulled sideways on their heads at an aggressive angle.

<table>
<tr><td>FIRST LONGSHOREMAN:</td><td>(As they arrange themselves at the bar). Gimme a shock. Number Two. (He tosses a coin on the bar.)</td></tr>
<tr><td>SECOND LONGSHOREMAN:</td><td>Same here. (JOHNNY sets two glasses of barrel whiskey before them.)</td></tr>
<tr><td>FIRST LONGSHOREMAN:</td><td>Here's luck! (The other nods. They gulp down their whiskey.)</td></tr>
<tr><td>SECOND LONGSHOREMAN:</td><td>(Putting money on the bar.) Give us another.</td></tr>
<tr><td>FIRST LONGSHOREMAN:</td><td>Gimme a scoop this time—lager and porter. I'm dry.</td></tr>
<tr><td>SECOND LONGSHOREMAN:</td><td>Same here. (JOHNNY draws the lager and porter and sets the big, foaming schooners before them. They drink down half the contents and start to talk together hurriedly in low tones. The door on the left is swung open and LARRY enters. He is a boyish, red-cheeked, rather good-looking young fellow of twenty or so.)</td></tr>
<tr><td>LARRY:</td><td>(Nodding to Johnny—cheerily.) Hello, boss.</td></tr>
<tr><td>JOHNNY:</td><td>Hello, Larry. (With a glance at his watch.) Just on time. (Larry goes to the right behind the bar, takes off his coat, and puts on an apron.)</td></tr>
<tr><td>FIRST LONGSHOREMAN:</td><td>(Abruptly.) Let's drink up and get back to it. (They finish their drinks and go out left. The Postman</td></tr>
</table>

	enters as they leave. He exchanges nods with Johnny and throws a letter on the bar.)
THE POSTMAN:	Addressed care of you, Johnny. Know him?
JOHNNY:	(*Picks up the letter, adjusting his spectacles.* LARRY *comes and peers over his shoulders.* JOHNNY *reads very slowly.*) Christopher Christopherson.
THE POSTMAN:	(*Helpfully.*) Square-head name.
LARRY:	Old Chris–that's who.
JOHNNY:	Oh, sure. I was forgetting Chris carried a hell of a name like that. Letters come here for him sometimes before, I remember now. Long time ago, though.
THE POSTMAN:	It'll get him all right then?
JOHNNY:	Sure thing. He comes here whenever he's in port.
THE POSTMAN:	(*Turning to go.*) Sailor, eh?
JOHNNY:	(*With a grin.*) Captain of a coal barge.
THE POSTMAN:	(*Laughing.*) Some job! Well, s'long.
JOHNNY:	S'long. I'll see he gets it. (*The Postman goes out.* JOHNNY *scrutinizes the letter.*)

In this opening, the characters in the world of *Anna Christie* and their relationships are being revealed. From the lines, we learn that Larry works for Johnny at the tavern. The Postman enters, delivering a letter that Johnny should hold for Christopher Christopherson, who has not yet appeared. When Johnny doesn't recognize the name on the letter, everyone pitches in, providing clues to help Johnny (and the audience) know to whom the letter is addressed. From these clues, we learn that this character is known variously as "Old Chris" and "Captain" and "Square-head."

As the team begins unpacking the play, some of the considerations that inform the translation are:

- Recognizing the source content and whether it is visual, aural, and/or dialogic
- Weighing and prioritizing the relative importance of the visual referents on the stage and the content in the lines
- Deciding how content will be delivered based on performability of the content (meaning distribution)—whether there is time to focus on the stage or to solely incorporate the content in the interpretation itself
- Deciding how to ensure the cohesion of the performance with the interpreted dialogue, as well as how to establish and maintain connections with our partner, the stage

One kind of agreement that the interpreting team would want to consider is working with the visuals on the stage. In this case, that would entail agreeing when to throw focus to the stage. Is it only at the top when the two men enter? How important is the drinking? How important is the moment when the letter is thrown on the bar? The team begins to weigh and prioritize which visual content will be expressed by throwing focus to the stage and which will be incorporated via lexical (signed) interpretation. Not all onstage visual referents need to have focus or be brought into the token space of the interpretation. For example, unless there is a need to identify which interpreter is which longshoreman, the act of the longshoremen's drinking probably doesn't need depicting in the interpretation. The interpreters often do not need to recreate explicitly what the actors perform so unmistakably. If time allows, focus could be thrown to the stage instead, allowing the audience to be introduced to the onstage world of *Anna Christie.*

From having seen the play, the team knows the importance of the letter in that the remainder of the play turns on its arrival. Therefore, the letter needs to be incorporated into the shared meaning space of the team's interpretation. The team would want to focus on the stage to give the same consideration to the entrance of the letter as to the entrance of a character, since the letter will propel much of the story. They would then anchor the visual referent (by using a classifier to hold up a letter) in the interpretation of the Postman's lines.

The letter is a theatrical device introducing us to the unseen (lead) character of the Captain. There is implicit content in his multiple names, which needs to be included in the interpretation. These names ("Christopher Christopherson," "Square-head," "Old Chris," "Chris," and "Captain") give us insight into this absent character and the nature of his relationships with others in the community.

We learn he's not in port often, he is captain of a coal barge (not as prestigious as other jobs), and he's not known to the community by his legal name. However, the team would need to consider whether his legal name will be important later in the play before agreeing upon ways to express his name. Another question is what does his status as a coal barge captain mean? Once the team understands this implicit content and its function in the narrative, the team can make more specific decisions.

A robust translation can be developed when the team ensures that the specifics (e.g., small moments, subtext, and surface text) align with the larger arcs of the story, thus creating an interpretation that provides the same understanding and tells the same story that's on the stage. If, while rehearsing, the team keeps examining the whole as well as the specific phrases, lines, and moments, then individual utterances will seamlessly fit into the narrative.

In short, a close read of the script can help us prepare for the live interpretation.

Translating Music for the Theatre

Music in a play is contextualized within the narrative framework. Interpreters uncover the meaning in the music, the lyrics, and visuals onstage so that the song is integrated into the show and propels the narrative.

Songs often contain linguistic poetic features (e.g., rhyme, rhythm, alliteration, assonance, repetition), as well as musical, tonal, or sensory qualities (e.g., elevated or emphasized diction, pitch, volume, intensity, melody, background musical instrumentation). All of these elements combine to create the experience of a song.

Songs are normally presented using heightened language, with the lyrics often in poetic form. Options for creating heightened language in ASL include alliteration, spatial referencing, complex spatial mapping, deliberate use of signing space dimensions, inclusion of imagery, and a change in the physical stance of the body and sign production that appears more precise and polished. At times, there is an option of creating fanciful signs that are comprehensible and reflect the style, the mood, the story, or the character. These strategies are used in conjunction with all the other elements of expressing meaning in ASL to create a meaningful interpretation.

Just as interpreters examine the meaning of text, teams must also examine the meaning of the songs in context. In this section, new considerations are added due to the difference between sung and spoken discourse, yet the goal remains the same—to express the meaning of the source in ASL.

CONSIDERATIONS: MUSIC IN CONTEXT

What is the impact of the song on the characters, storyline, and audience, and why?

When interpreting the sung word, the same questions are asked as when approaching the spoken word, with the same goal—to understand the meaning. How will the interpretation signal that it is a song, and not prose? Even though music is a change from the dialogue, it often is used to move the plot along and/or deepen character development. Teams direct their attention to unpacking the meaning for the songs within and apart from the scene. Questions include (but are not limited to):

- Where in the story is the song appearing?
- What is the song's purpose?
- What kind of song is it?
- To whom is the song directed?
- What visuals occur during and around the song?
- Does the song carry sociohistorical content?

There are questions that are specifically about the auditory and poetic information contained in the song. These include:

- What is the impact of the poetic qualities of the song?
- What imagery does the song evoke?
- What is the impact/meaning of the repetition of refrains throughout the show?
- What is the meaning/intent of choral singing?
- What is the auditory information transmitted in the music?
- Is there a melodic motif that recurs in the soundscape in a song or throughout the play? If so, what does it signify?

The meaning of a song is determined by examining where in the play it occurs, who the intended "listener" is, how it affects the characters during and after, what the narrative function of the song is, and what the style (e.g., whimsical, romantic, confrontive) of the song is. The goal is to uncover the meaning of the song so that it can be interpreted in a manner that is congruent with the play and in alignment with the grammatical and prosodic rules of ASL.

The style of the show also affects the interpretation. Is this a play filled with spectacle and show-stopping numbers (e.g., *Hamilton, Wicked, Phantom, The Color Purple*)? Is this a quiet, wistful show with smaller personal moments (e.g., *Waitresses, The Band's Visit*)? Is this a fairy tale or fantasy (e.g., *Beauty and the Beast, Into the Woods, Once on This Island*)? The type of the show lends a palette that teams use to paint their interpretation.

WHERE IN THE STORY IS THE SONG APPEARING?

Consider when a song appears, because the meaning of the song depends on what comes before and after. The song does not exist in a vacuum. Characters, events, and feelings that have been addressed in dialogue are carried forward in songs. Concepts that have already been established may be reinforced in the song, or the song may establish something new that gets carried over into future discussions. Some songs only address the moment in which they occur, but others refer to events beyond that moment.

Some songs are heard only once, while some are reprised (in part or in their entirety) throughout a show. Are the lyrics appearing for the first time and will be repeated? If so, they may need to be marked, or have more emphasis, or the translation may need to anchor it to its context. As information gets embedded in repetition, the interpreting choices can change or allow the stage to speak for itself.

When a song is reprised (whether by the same character or even by a different character), it may carry a new meaning. The performers may have a different spin on the song in its new context, and thus, the interpreters will consider a different approach to the song. Explore the specific meaning each time a song occurs and consider how to express its situated meaning clearly. The same translation does not have to be used every time the lyrics are reprised.

An example of contextual changes in meaning in a reprise is found in "Willkommen" from *Cabaret.* The first occurrence of this song is an exciting introduction to the culture of "decadence" present in the cabaret scene in the Weimar Republic. When it is reprised at the end of the show, the song is performed within the context of the horrors of the Third Reich.

As the understanding of the show deepens from repeated viewings and musings, the team will revisit certain moments to discover whether new depths of meaning can be plumbed.

WHAT IS THE NARRATIVE FUNCTION OF THE SONG?

Identifying the song's purpose is an early step in developing the translation. The function of a song is often reflected in its form: a love song, rallying anthem, hymn, call and response, sing along, or a song of celebration. Here are some examples:

- To propel the story: *Newsies*—"Seize the Day"; *Ragtime*—"Make Them Hear You"
- To reveal the inner life of a character: *Dreamgirls*—"I Am Changing"; *Sweet Charity*—"There's Gotta be Something Better Than This"
- To establish the setting and characters: *Kiss Me Kate*—"Another Op'nin', Another Show"; *Hamilton*—"Alexander Hamilton"
- To contextualize the production: In his 2019 *Much Ado About Nothing,* Kenny Leon's preshow musical selections were Jimi Hendrix's electric guitar version of the "The Star-Spangled Banner" and Marvin Gaye's "What's Going On"

WHY DOES IT MATTER WHO THE CHARACTER IS SINGING TO?

To whom the song is directed makes a difference in how it is interpreted. Is it to one specific person? To oneself? To the audience? To the entire cast? To some, but not all, onstage? Is it sung to someone standing nearby? These questions are relevant because the song has a narrative function in the play. Think about the relational aspect of a song—who is being talked to and why. Theatre is all about relationships—between characters, between the show and the audience, and now between the song and the show.

The actions of the performers onstage reveal a lot of information. Is the character trying to hide from the listener? Is the character singing to themself? Are they addressing one character directly, for example, as Lola tries to seduce Joe Hardy in her song "Whatever Lola Wants" in *Damn Yankees.* On the other hand, in *Dear Evan Hansen,* "You Will Be Found" pivots from addressing each of the characters in the story to breaking the fourth wall and addressing the audience, and assuring them that they are not alone.

Who the character is addressing the song to and why may change during the song. The interpretation needs to identify those shifts in the song, when it is internal, when it is addressing specific characters, and when it is addressing the audience, either real or imagined.

HOW WELL KNOWN IS THE SONG?

In addition, interpreters take into consideration how the culturally embedded meaning of this music will be expressed across cultures. As the team drafts its interpretation, several cross-cultural questions arise. Are the lyrics familiar to the audience? Is the song familiar in its signed English form? What contextual framing needs to be added?

Some songs in shows based on Disney movies are well-known. Many families have seen the movies with captions and know the lyrics and may be signing along with these songs at home, most likely leaning toward a more literal English translation. With this in mind, interpreters consider ways to make songs recognizable to the audience. Sometimes, this is accomplished with a more literal translation of the song title by fingerspelling the title (H-A-K-U-N-A M-A-T-A-TA) before offering the team's ASL translation, as the translations have been developed in the context of the narrative arc of the play. However, if the team chooses to continue with a more transliterated form for the remainder of the song, they will need to consider how effective that transliteration will be in propelling the story.

WHAT VISUALS OCCUR DURING THE SONG?

The visuals onstage always have an impact on interpreting choices. Is this a big number with lots of song and dance behind it? Is there action onstage that should not be missed? For example, does a character raise a pistol to fire at someone else while singing? Or is she kissing her loved one? Just as we ensure that the visuals are honored in the spoken word through meaning distribution strategies, in the case of music, we apply the same strategies.

When *Mary Poppins*[34] was interpreted on Broadway, the song "Supercalifragilisticexpialidocious" was an interesting challenge. It is well-known, even though it is a nonsense word, and the point of the song is that anyone can invent new words. On the Broadway stage, the actors' bodies were posed to depict each letter so that the word was spelled out by their dance. In addition, the word "supercalifragilisticexpialidocious" appeared on the backdrop.

Because we work in a visual modality, interpreters want to make choices that honor as much of the visual information on the stage as possible. When Lynnette interpreted this song, she incorporated many different strategies in her interpretation, throwing focus to the actors, to the stage, and incorporating the playful nature of the word by fingerspelling it with two hands simultaneously. It is a mouthful to say, and two handfuls to spell. The visual-to-visual link was complete. After a few choral repetitions, if no new information is being introduced, the interpreting team can rely on the stage to convey the information, offering space for the audience to take in the staged choreography.

WHAT IS THE TEMPO OF THE SONG?

Another challenge is the tempo of a song, which often is not the same as spoken lines. For example, the rapid pace of many songs in *Hamilton* is the direct antithesis to the slow love songs of Rodgers and Hammerstein, but both have their particular challenges in translation. Recognizing that tempo is content, we then consider how best to convey it. When it came to the German translations for *Hamilton*, Lin Manuel Miranda expressed the importance of balance, "I'm going to feel the internal rhyme, or lack of internal rhyme, . . .so it's important to me whenever that can be maintained without losing comprehensibility."[35]

As we all know, auditory rhythm and rhyme function differently in each language and should be considered when trying to translate them into a song. Signed languages also have their own set of rules around rhythm, rhyme, and meter that need to be factored into a translation. The translator strives for "musicality and rhyme," but not at the cost of comprehensibility.

The goal is to keep the meaning and ASL prosody intact and, if possible, adhere to the timing of the source. If that causes us to lose grammar, sign production, and prosody, then the rules of ASL and comprehensibility must take precedence. Allowing the tempo to influence aspects of a translation is one thing, but prioritizing the tempo of the music, rather than honoring the rhythm and the pace of ASL, is completely another.

In the case of rapid lyrics, the most important advice is to not let the energy of a song overwhelm the clarity of the interpreted message. If signing is so rapid that the meaning is lost, then the song is inscrutable. It's important to maintain clear prosody and phrasing, slow down if needed, and ensure meaning is present.

A song performed extremely slowly is also a challenge in that the temptation is to

s i g n s o s l o w l y

that all meaning is lost. Meaning is only construed when signs are connected to previous and following signs and produced according to ASL prosodic norms (of pace as well as emphasis). There are many creative ways to address the challenge of slow tempo or a sustained word or syllable. Options include repeating signs or phrases, expressing the meaning and pausing to refer to the stage between lines, choosing a sign that can be inflected to indicate duration, narrating that the actor is holding the note for an extended time, and so on. The team relies on the DOI while constructing interpretations to ensure that interpreted songs are meaningful and conform to the natural structure of ASL.

ENSEMBLE SINGING

When approaching ensemble singing, consider the through line of the song, narrative, and characters to help make decisions. If it's a unified message that everyone is participating in on stage (such as "Do You Hear the People Sing" in *Les Misérables*), then one interpreter can express it. However, if there are multiple narratives or a counternarrative running through the song, it is best to assign at least two interpreters to express them. Specific verses can be taken by individual interpreters.

At times, the team may choose to sign in unison, a kind of choral signing. Coordinating unison signing requires time, effort, and preparation. Rather than interpret an entire song in unison, teams may select a limited number of lyrics for simultaneous signing (often the final lines of the refrain). This repetition of choral signing, even though condensed, reflects the collective storytelling seen onstage. An additional way to represent the ensemble experience is to assign various sections of the song to different members of the team, as shown below.

***Ain't We Got Fun*[36]**

(BOUNCY tune)

INTERPRETER A	Every morning, every evening Ain't we got fun?
INTERPRETER B	Not much money, oh, but honey Ain't we got fun?
INTERPRETER C	The rent's unpaid dear We haven't a car But in any way, dear We'll stay as we are

Certain lyrics or refrains can also be assigned to specific interpreters by aligning thought worlds, with one interpreter expressing the worries, and the other responding with lighthearted reassurances.

INTERPRETER A	Every morning, every evening
INTERPRETER B	Ain't we got fun?
INTERPRETER C	Not much money, oh, but honey

INTERPRETER B	Ain't we got fun?
INTERPRETER A	The rent's unpaid, dear
INTERPRETER C	We haven't a car
INTERPRETER B	But in any way, dear
INTERPRETER A, B, and C	We'll stay as we are

The final refrain ends with the three interpreters briefly signing in unison, emphasizing that the characters were all expressing the same sentiment.

When lyrics are repeated, it is also an opportunity for interpreters to explore layers of meaning by deliberately choosing to express different nuances of meaning at different moments. At the end of Act I in *Dear Evan Hansen*, the lead character sings the repeated phrase "You will be found," and the company has their own refrain of "You are not alone." The repetition of these phrases in the song is an opportunity to weave in the different interpretations of meaning imbued in the line, a further example of meaning distribution over time.

Often, in musicals with big dance numbers, when choruses are repeated, the team considers the visual dynamics of balancing the exciting picture onstage with the repeated interpretation of the lyrics. There are many options to choose from, including interpret the chorus continuously, select a point in the chorus where the content has already been expressed and then stop interpreting and turn to the stage, or continue to interpret the chorus but use a smaller signing space and/or a less complex interpretation so the audience focus can go to the stage.

EXPLORING IMAGERY IN "GUN SONG" FROM *ASSASSINS*

The Classic Stage Company described their production of Stephen Sondheim's *Assassins*[37] as a musical exploration of "the lives of nine men and women who either killed (or tried to kill) a President of the United States."[38] In "Gun Song," the voice of the American steelworker, Czolgosz, presents a searing social commentary on the many lives lost in the making of a gun, "long before" it is shot. The song traces the journey of a gun from the mines to the steel mills to the one who pulls the trigger.

When developing a visual domain, an important step in the process is to do visual research to ensure that the specific choices in ASL are accurate. In preparing the translation for "Gun Song," DOI Anne Tomasetti and Lynnette took time to explore the unseen visual vocabulary that the song both references and evokes. What did coal miners look like in this era? What did the steel mills look like? What were the workers doing? What were they wearing? What tools were they using?

Lynnette explained, "We searched images from the late 1800s to early 1900s of workers in the mines and steel mills. We found miners with lanterns, headlamps, and pickaxes, and saw the dirt on their faces and their cramped conditions in the tunnels. We saw steelworkers with aprons and mitts. The details of the working conditions helped to create a sense of their reality: the posture of workers in the mills, the seared arm hair and burn scars for steelworkers, as well as the way they poured molten steel from the vats into the ladles to be carried and poured into the molds. These details, including, of course, the making of the handgun, became the vocabulary of visual references that could be included in the translation. The information gleaned from the research, combined with lexical information from the lyrics as well as sonic information from the song, informed the textures and mood of the interpretation."

Incorporating these details allowed Czolgosz's political views of capitalism and the toll that it extracts from the lives of workers to surface. This toll is at the root of his decision to assassinate President McKinley. It is important that the translation evokes these sentiments to help make his political argument clear.

One translation question Lynnette had was "Can I build a specific and yet general looping timeline of death that will also lead the viewer to think about a system that routinely kills without conscience or consequence?" Just as "Gun Song" traces the many deaths accrued along the way from the mines to the pulling of the trigger, the translation traces these deaths through a visual mapping in space—a timeline that began with the gun's origins from below, in the mines, and followed it upward to the present moment of pulling the trigger. This visual timeline was designed to suggest that this was not a one-time occurrence, but one that had recurred and would recur time and time again.

Another question Lynnette had was "What is the conversation between the finger that pulls the trigger and the gun?" A key translation decision was to use her right and left hands to construct the action of shooting the gun, which was Tomasetti's suggestion. The right hand became the classifier for the gun and the left became the finger which pulled the trigger. Lynnette could then place her left hand over her right to construct the action of shooting the gun. This translation decision opened a conversation between the finger that shoots versus the object, which is inert until the trigger is pulled. This, in turn, allowed Lynnette to actualize the internal conversation as Czolgosz pondered the pulling of the trigger, a simple act that could "change the world."

MUSIC: A CODA

There are many ways to enter a conversation with the translation of a song. The same material can be translated and expressed in a myriad of ways. Many of these nuanced decisions are informed by the specific time, place, and the overall context of the performance, as well as by the cultural and linguistic reservoirs, and sensibilities of the interpreting team.

The importation/exportation of cultural matter is in constant motion, and these exchanges mean that the team examines the cultural significance of content at that moment in time. Considerations include: Is the cultural matter a well-known reference? Is it esoteric? What is its relevance to cross-cultural conversations? Each consideration would guide us to a specific strategy.

The performance aspect of interpreting music is another element to consider. How the auditory, rhythmic expression, and tone will be conveyed is not only translatory but also aesthetic. Just as cultural matter is constantly evolving, what audiences wish to see in terms of interpreted performance is also an ongoing and changing conversation with DOIs, interpreting teams, and the community.

Artistry

Ideally, the artistry of the interpretation is in response to and in conversation with the stage. It is a dialogic dance with the stage events, our interpreting partners, and our audience—the "communicative pas de trois" that Wadensjö mentions.[39]

Artistry goes beyond the skills mentioned thus far. One of our long-time advisors in the Interpreting for the Theatre Seminar, George Garcia, described artistry as "when the interpretation no longer is 2-D, but becomes 3-D." In George's terms, when the work rose to the level of "3-D," it was truly an expression of an embodied living language: alive, clear, and suffused with breath and imagery.

There is a "performative aspect" to the artistry of interpretation as well, which is the ability to depict the characters being interpreted authentically and subtly. This is accomplished through an amalgam of linguistic and translation choices, the interpreter's presence, and depiction of character. When successfully combined, the interpretation appears seamless, as if the interpreter is truly channeling the actor onstage. To accomplish this takes a lot of skill and time spent living, breathing, and being in the language communities to develop one's repertoire. Further, of course, it needs the eye of a DOI to monitor the interpretation/translation and performance choices.

Linguistic features of ASL,[40] such as rhyme, meter, use of space, imagery, elegance of signs, symmetry and balance, metaphor, and more,[41] can combine with character depiction and nonmanuals to create coherent and cohesive utterances that thrill the eyes. These performative aspects of ASL will only make sense if they are connected to the meaning of the lines coming before and after.

Cohesive, cogent utterances are always the goal, whether they rise to the level of artistry or not. Incorporating them requires considerable language fluency, a deep knowledge of discursive possibilities, and the ability to sculpt in space. When interpreters in theatrical venues seek to incorporate these elements in their work, it is always in service of the play. No one wants to privilege the aesthetic over clarity of meaning.

In crafting an interpretation that honors the stage, interpreters need to balance artistry with breath, with spaces between, which allow time and space for the audience to connect the interpretation to the story onstage. If the interpretation is too dense or becomes overly laden with intricate and complex "artistic" elements, it can overwhelm the stage performance.

It is the nature of languages that not everything is translatable. Sometimes, one can produce something in ASL but not in English, and vice versa. Beauty is expressed in different ways in each culture and language. While we strive for performance simultaneity, expressions of beauty may not take the same amount of time in both languages, and thus may not always be synchronous in our performance.

Crafting an artistic translation is a subtle alchemy. Creating a visual translation is akin to shaping a sculpture in space. It entails melding one medium (the source) into the medium of the interpreted language (target) to elevate the translation to a higher aesthetic plane of expression. A successful artistic interpretation is one that incorporates the textures, concepts, nuance, and spirit of the source message into its rendering. As Alberto Giacometti stated, "The object of art is not to reproduce reality, but to create a reality of the same intensity."[42]

Begin with fidelity to the source when delving into artistry, which can be understood in part as a coalescence of all the elements of the architecture of interpreting theatre (e.g., performance, character depiction, dialogic strategies, visual-to-visual connections, as well as linguistic and cultural fluency) with additional features of aesthetic expression (e.g., use of heightened language, choreographed sequencing, and mirrored imagery).

We offer two examples of artistry occurring in the interpretations of the Broadway productions of *Hadestown* and *Cabaret*. In the first, the visual imagery of the show inspired the artistic interpretation. The other was designed around the actors' timing, delivery, and gestural choices.

HADESTOWN

In *Hadestown*, Eurydice is offered a choice between the love of a poor and starving artist, Orpheus, or the comforts of an affluent material life if she agrees to become a mistress to Hades, the ruler of the underworld. The Fates turn up the heat as they sing, "When the Chips Are Down," pressuring Eurydice to choose Hades. How could the interpreter create a visual image that evoked both the meaning (love, money, the chips are down) and visual imagery from the stage picture?

The translation of the song drew from images that were presented earlier in the play—Orpheus "magically" creating a flower that he gave to Eurydice as a token of his love and Hermes offering a coin to Eurydice so she could cross the River Styx to Hadestown. Lynnette, the interpreter for the Fates, incorporated those stage images into her linguistic expression of the song, representing Eurydice's choice as one between true love (the flower) and the material security (the coin). Once imagery has appeared prominently on the stage, it may then be incorporated in the translation at any time.

The choice between "the flower and the coin" could now operate on a metaphoric level. The flower signified magic, love, regeneration, and beauty. The coin signified material survival, the end of the line, earthly needs, eternal life, the desire for power, and greed. In addition, the coin was grounded as an iconic reference to the figurative meaning in the title and lyrics of "When the Chips Are Down"—running out of luck, getting by on hard times. Placing the flower and the coin as counterpoints in space reified the stark choice facing Eurydice. Both Eurydice and the Fates relate to and refer to these elements with different emotions at times. The spatial relationships between the two objects could convey the tensions between these choices and their multiple meanings. Developing the meaning space for this translation required semantic choices (flower and coin), discursive choices (direct and constructed discourse), spatial content, and performative presentation of affective content.

CABARET

For the song, "Tomorrow Belongs to Me" in *Cabaret*, Lynnette brought the lens of art's role in propaganda, as well as an awareness of the sociohistorical moment in time of Germany during the Weimar Republic, right at the cusp of the rise of Nazism and WWII. Germany, having lost WWI, was a country impoverished, disgraced, and desperate to reconstruct a new national identity and reclaim power. This backdrop informed the narrative focus of the translation.

The song, with its beguiling sense of a traditional folk song or anthem, stirs our nostalgic yearning for better times, arouses a love of country, and ignites a sense of patriotism. One might think that this is a cultural treasure, a traditional folk song, but it was written specifically for *Cabaret* to elicit emotions and simultaneously investigate art becoming a dangerous propaganda machine. What begins as a song of idyllic innocence slowly turns into a demonic call for genocide. Lynnette wanted to include the meta-message of "art talking to art" in her translation.

In the Roundabout revival, at the beginning of the scene when the audience first heard the song, they saw an empty stage, save for a gramophone. The Emcee entered in a black leather Gestapo coat and placed a needle on the record. The audience heard a recording of "Tomorrow Belongs to Me." In the final refrain, after

"Tomorrow belongs . . ." the boy's voice cuts out as the Emcee whispers "to me" while simultaneously raising his arm in a "Heil Hitler" salute.

When the song was reprised in Act II, the intention and the impact were different. Drunken revelers wearing Nazi armbands barged in on the engagement party for Herr Schultz (a German Jew) and Fraulein Schneider (a non-Jew). The partygoers were coerced to join in the song. Fraulein Schneider and Herr Schultz watched in horror as the song ended in an enthusiastic Heil Hitler salute, which revealed the human and political fault lines that had ruptured the world of the play.

The sonics the second time around were very different from when the song was first heard. The second time around, the voices and the music were more aggressive and menacing, and the underlying score was performed in a martial manner. It became a rallying anthem that had a chilling impact on the audience as well as the characters onstage.

Translation Considerations

Lynnette's interpretation of "Tomorrow Belongs to Me" was crafted with several considerations. The translation had to include in its design, nonvisual information that was expressed in the vocal quality of the song and its contextual presentation. During the first playing of the song, the sole source image, a record player, did not convey the quality, timbre, or aural experience of the boy's singing.

She chose the narrator function to describe a young boy, sweetly, innocently singing what sounded like a traditional folk song. The vocal qualities of the singing (angelic, innocent, and beautiful with undertones of wistful yearning) were then included as affectual information in her performed interpretation.

The translation needed to pack a lot into its message and be able to morph into different iterations that bore different intentions. It also had to be economic in its delivery, so that later on, it would be easily recognizable. It needed to look like a pastoral German landscape and also transform into a futurist painting with sharp edges—images that could fracture, refract, and emit the layered dimensions that the song's function in the play brought. It had to be able to be performed like a lullaby, shaped as if dancing with air, and later, like a rallying cry, shaped as if slicing the air.

The song's finale was the starting point for the translation. Alan Cumming, as The Emcee, ended the song with the Heil Hitler salute. This was the "given" from which everything else was built. This was the punctuation that ended not only the song but also Act I. Therefore, the timing was a critical consideration (simultaneity). The interpretation had to include the same gesture, the Sieg Heil salute, and be performed synchronously, so that it could be completed before the blackout. The interpretation had to be built in a way that could maintain conceptual and narrative clarity so that the Nazi salute was integrated in a meaningful way, not just as an unanchored performative action.

In thinking about the interpretation in a metaframe, this deliberate double gesture of the interpreter and the performer raising the salute amplified the power of the image, serving as a kind of augury of things to come. This visual-to-visual conversation anchored the ASL interpretation to the stage picture.

Narration Strategy

Initially, the song lulled listeners into a comfortable, familiar place by replicating a beloved folk song. What was so jarring was the unexpected moment in which the audience realized that the song was now calling forth hatred, not love. It became a new kind of anthem, planting the seeds for Hitler's call for racial purity, under the rising fascist ideology. The affirmation of an ideal German identity was embedded in the deep structure of the text, in the text in context, and in the implicit historic meanings that framed the song.

The sociohistorical information was incorporated while mapping the progression of the story—again, looking to the end to find its beginning. This backdrop served as the topography for plotting the shifts in nuance, tempo, intensity, and narrative emphasis. The translation had to build in intensity at the same time as the song, while culling images from the lyrics to arrive at the final Nazi salute, signifying that the war had begun.

Another consideration was the genre of the song and its impact on the listener. It sounded like an anthem. The young boys' voices subliminally stirred the desire to affirm patriotism and rekindle pride in a German identity. The boy's chorus was reminiscent of the Hitler Youth and a powerful reminder of a masterful propaganda machine. The second time the song occurred, the singers on stage wore Nazi armbands and brought a different intention. This song then functioned as a rallying cry, which had a profound effect on the characters and served as a pivotal turning point in the narrative.

The first time the audience heard it, the song evoked the hope that Germany would rise again. The second time they heard it, the future had taken hold. It was no longer an aspiration; it was a declaration. Understanding the sociohistorical import and the narrative function of the song guided the translation choices.

Developing the Translation

The song "Tomorrow Belongs to Me" had a chilling effect, and the goal was for the translation to have the same effect on the audience. Because the lyrics remain the same each time it is sung, the translation also had to have the malleability to express both the utopic and dystopic versions of the song and needed to be shaped in such a way that it would have phrasal recognition with only two viewings. It had to be designed in a way that simulated other classic frozen forms in ASL, such as the National Anthem, Pledge of Allegiance, or prayers like "The Lord is my shepherd." These have collective recognition within the signing community. Lynnette looked for parallel structures that would efficiently signify its genre. This meant using larger gestures, strong enunciation, or markers and also importing literal phrases from the song, such as "Fatherland."

Given that the final gesture of the song was the Nazi salute, the B-handshape became the foundation for the translation. Sign choices were built with deliberate intention and conceptual clarity so they would land in the final salute. The images in the lyrics (e.g., stag, forest, meadow, and river) also lent themselves to sign vocabulary using B-, 4-, and 5-handshapes (see fig. 4.4).

Lynnette looked for lexical choices that would support the two different performative intentions. The images in the lyrics supported alliterative translations, which, through prosody and performance, were inflected differently to depict first the pastoral and then the menacing impact of the song (fig. 4.5).

Lynnette chose to include transliterated details such as linden trees to make it geographically specific and feel more like an "authentic" anthem. The function of that detail was, for Lynnette, akin to the symbol of the American Eagle, a recognizable patriotic American icon. The architecture of the song remained the same; performative strategies and slight changes of lexical choices were utilized to express the darker and lighter overtones heard in the song. For example, the gentle breeze through the linden trees was chiseled into a rigid, barren forest, ominously predicting the future to come.

Figure 4.4. Translation alliteration. Copyright © 2024 Taylor, Feyne, and Broecker Penn.

Figure 4.5. Hopeful alliteration. Copyright © 2024 Taylor, Feyne, and Broecker Penn.

Figure 4.6. Menacing alliteration. Copyright © 2024 Taylor, Feyne, and Broecker Penn.

Final Thoughts on Translation

There are many ways to enter a translation—analysis, visualization, and spontaneous interpretation—to see what arises. Sometimes, overthinking will cause one to miss the mark; likewise, underthinking can also cause one to miss the mark. Sometimes if an interpreter simply lifts their hands and signs the material, they can see where they stumble, where the questions that need to be explored lie. We encourage interpreters to take the time to explore the questions; allow themselves to stumble around in this foreign land and experience it to the fullest extent.

This foreign land can be interpreters' palette, the sources they draw from as they form their interpretations. The stage imagery, aural soundscape, choreography, and gestural movements are source materials they can use to add dimension to their translations/interpretations. There is no roadmap for translating—it is a deeply personal conversation between the material and the translator. The translator must find a way to inhabit the ideas. As much as an artistic translation is a reflection of an individual interpreter's process, it is designed in conversation with the ensemble interpretation in mind and shares the same sensibilities.

Anne Tomasetti discussed the joy of working with fluent interpreters as she worked with the team for *Hadestown*.

> I love when I don't have to fix the grammar, or missing pronouns, or fluency issues. I would rather focus on the artistry and be able to look at the bigger picture to make sure the team is hitting the points that need to be there in the song or that part of the play. This leaves me free to focus on the presentation of character and look to see where there are visual agreements between the stage and the sign choices.[43]

Translations are a reflection not just of the space and time in which they were created, but also of the translator's mind and stage of development as a translator. Translation is, by itself, a very intimate and personal journey, drawing not only from the world of the source message, but also from one's own world, one's own mental map, and one's own language pool. This crosslinguistic, cross-cultural conversation between languages, worlds, and stories can be a very exciting space to enter. It opens up the possibility to discover new aspects of ourselves, challenge our thinking and assumptions, and lead us to deeper understandings of not only the source material, but how we see the world. This endeavor leads to deeply personal connections and discoveries. The collaborative interpreting process has the ability to reshape not only our thoughts and perceptions but ourselves, as art often does.

Notes

1. Damion Searls, *The Philosophy of Translation* (Yale University Press, 2024), 91.
2. Kate Briggs, *This Little Art* (Fitzcarraldo Editions, 2017). Reproduced by permission of Fitzcarraldo Editions.
3. Anne Tomasetti interviewed by Lynnette Taylor and Candace Broecker Penn, June 20, 2020.

4. Tomasetti, interview.
5. *Jordans,* by Ife Olujobi, dir. Whitney White, 2024 Off-Broadway production at the Public Theater. Interpreting team: Kailyn Aaron-Lozano, Candace Broecker Penn, Monique Sarpy, and Lynnette Taylor. DOIs: Andrew Morrill and Kailyn Aaron-Lozano.
6. *Hadestown*, music, lyrics, and book by Anaïs Mitchell, dir. Rachel Chavkin, chor. David Neumann, 2019 Broadway production at the Walter Kerr Theatre. 2019 interpreting team: Alexandria Wailes, Dylan Geil, Justine Rivera, and Lynnette Taylor. DOI: Anne Tomasetti.
7. *The Servant of Two Masters*, by Carlo Goldoni, 1789.
8. *Arcadia*, by Tom Stoppard, dir. Joshua Rosenblum, 1995 Broadway production at Lincoln Center's Beaumont Theater. Interpreting team: Bill Moody, Lynnette Taylor, and Stephanie Feyne.
9. *The Lion King*, book by Roger Allers and Irene Mecchi; adapted from the screenplay by Irene Mecchi, Jonathan Roberts, and Linda Woolverton.
   The Lion King, script courtesy of Disney Theatrical Group.
10. We note that MacDougall also used this example in his 2021 dissertation.
11. The term "cultural matter" is taken from works on translation in linguistic anthropology: Jane E. Goodman, *Encounters in Translation: How Et-Teffeh Became Apples* (Indiana University Press, 2020). Original use from Michael Silverstein, "Translation, Transduction, Transformation: Skating 'Glossando' on Thin Semiotic Ice," in "*Translating Cultures Perspectives on Translation and Anthropology*, ed. Paula G. Rubel and Abraham Rosman (Oxford University Press, 2003), 75–108.
12. *For colored girls who have considered suicide/when the rainbow is enuf*, by Ntozake, dir. Leah C. Gardiner, chor Camille A. Brown, DASL/interpreter dir. Onudeah Nikolarakis. 2019 Off-Broadway revival at the Public Theatre. The sign was also used in the 2022 Broadway run, dir. Camille Brown, DASL/Interpreter Dir. Michelle Banks. Alexandria Wailes performed in both. The interpreting team was also the same for both productions: Jacinda Damas and Kathleen Taylor.
13. Michael Paulson, "They Translated 'Hamilton' Into German. Was It Easy? Nein," *The New York Times*, September 14, 2022, https://www.nytimes.com/2022/09/14/theater/hamilton-germany.html.
14. Paulson, "They Translated 'Hamilton' Into German."
15. Paulson, "They Translated 'Hamilton' Into German."
16. Zavier Sabio interviewed by Lynnette Taylor and Candace Broecker Penn, April 14, 2020.
17. Sabio, interview.
18. *Thérèse Raquin*, adaptation by Helen Edmundson, based upon the novel by Émile Zola. 2015 Roundabout Theatre production at Studio 54. Interpreting team: Candace Broecker Penn, Lynnette Taylor, and Molly Wilson; DOI: Anne Tomasetti.
19. *King Lear*, by William Shakespeare, co-dir. Rob Ashford, Kenneth Brannagh, and Lucy Skilbeck, 2024 Off-Broadway production at The Shed. Interpreting team: Aaron-Lozano Kailyn, Candace Broecker Penn, Stephanie Feyne, Lynnette Taylor, and Miriam Rochford (feed/co-interpreter), DOI: Noah Buchholz.
20. *Travesties,* by Tom Stoppard, dir. Patrick Marber, 2018 Broadway production at the American Airlines Theatre. Interpreting team: Bill Moody, Molly Wilson, and Stephanie Feyne; DOI: Anne Tomasetti.
21. Anne Tomasetti interviewed by Lynnette Taylor, April 18, 2020.

22. *Into the Woods*, music and lyrics by Stephen Sondheim, book by James Lapine, dir. Noah Brody and Ben Steinfeld, Fiasco Theatre adaptation, produced by the Roundabout Theatre 2015. Interpreting team: Bill Moody, Candace Broecker Penn, and Lynnette Taylor. Interpreting director: Anne Tomasetti.
23. *Into the Woods.*
24. Paulson, "They Translated 'Hamilton' Into German."
25. *Something Rotten!* book by John O'Farrell and Karey Kirkpatrick, music and lyrics by Karey and Wayne Kirkpatrick.
26. *Be More Chill*, music and lyrics by Joe Iconis, book by Joe Tracz, Broadway production at the Lyceum Theatre in 2019.
27. Anne Tomasetti interviewed by Lynnette Taylor, May 16, 2020.
28. *Dear Evan Hansen*, music and lyrics by Benj Pasek and Justin Paul, book by Steven Levenson, dir. Michael Greif, chor. Danny Mefford, 2019 Broadway production at the Music Box Theatre. Interpreting team: Candace Broecker Penn, Dylan Geil, and Lynnette Taylor; DOI: Anne Tomasetti.
29. *Avenue Q*, book by Jeff Whitty, music and lyrics by Robert Lopez and Jeff Marx, dir. Jason Moore, chor. Ken Roberson, 2005 Broadway production at the John Golden Theatre. Interpreting team: Alan Champion, Candace Broecker Penn, and Lynnette Taylor; DOI: Manny Hernandez.
30. Our appreciation to Brenda Nicodemus and Paul Harrelson for the terminology. (Brenda Nicodemus, email message to Stephanie Feyne, May 29, 2019.)
31. Carol Padden, email message to Lynnette Taylor, March 15, 2023.
32. Jemina Napier, *Linguistic Coping Strategies in Sign Language Interpreting* (Gallaudet University Press, 2016).
33. *Anna Christie*, by Eugene O'Neill, 1921. 1922 Pulitzer Prize. In public domain.
34. *Mary Poppins, book* by Julian Fellowes, original music and lyrics by Richard M. Sherman and Robert B. Sherman. New songs and additional music and lyrics by George Stiles and Anthony Drewe, dir. Richard Eyre and Matthew Bourne, chor. Matthew Bourne, co-created by Cameron Mackintosh, 2008 Broadway production at the New Amsterdam Theatre. Interpreting team: Alan Champion, Candace Broecker Penn, and Lynnette Taylor; DOI: Anne Tomasetti.
35. Paulson, "They Translated 'Hamilton' Into German."
36. Napier, *Linguistic Coping Strategies.*
37. *Anna Christie*, 1922 Pulitzer Prize.
38. Poppins, new songs and additional music.
39. Cecilia Wadensjö, *Interpreting as Interaction* (Routledge, 1998).
40. Clayton Valli, "Poetics of American Sign Language Poetry" (Unpublished PhD diss., Union Institute Graduate School, 1993).
41. Many of these features are listed in Rachel Sutton-Spence's "Overview of Sign Language Poetry," *European Cultural Heritage Online* (ECHO), accessed December 21, 2020, https://archive.mpi.nl/tla/islandora/object/tla%3A1839_00_0000_0000_0017_DA5A_A/datastream/OBJ/download
42. "Famous Artists' Quotes," *Monet and Chardonnay Events*, accessed August 27, 2024, https://www.monetandchardonnay.events/post/famous-artists-quotes.
43. Anne Tomasetti, interviewed by Lynnette Taylor.

5

Performance of the Dialogic Interpretation

Marinetti, a theatre translation scholar, states:

> The greatest advantage of seeing translation as *performative* is that it allows us to place originals and translations, source and target texts, dramatic texts and performances on the same cline, where what counts is . . . the effect that the reconfigured text (as performance) has on the receiving culture and its networks of transmission and reception.[1]

When we taught the Interpreting for the Theatre Seminar, classes were separated into "Translation" and "Performance" purely for logistical reasons. In our work, however, translation and performance are never separate. Since the translation results in a live performed interpretation of a live performed event, the interpreting team considers their expression of the "performance"-to-"performance" conversation to be equally as important as their "linguistic"-to-"linguistic" expression.

Just as there is a continuum for translation, there is also one for performance of the translation. At one end of the continuum is the expressionless conduit feed, and at the other end of the continuum is the overly expressive interpretation, as explained in chapter 2. Either end of the continuum—underperforming or over-performing (insufficient to overly dramatic)—will lead to an alteration of source meaning. Our aim is to embody the language that expresses the spirit, artistry, intent, and message of the play. Throughout the rehearsal process, directors of interpreters (DOIs) monitor our performed translations, telling us when more or less affective information is needed and when more information is necessary to identify the character(s) being interpreted.

Relationship to the Stage

As interpreters, we are listening to, responding to, and communicating the actor's emotional space, not creating our own, as an actor would. If the intention is to reflect the story on the stage in all its verisimilitude, then the team must find ways to present those onstage moments of fear, vulnerability, love, and the full range of human emotion in our performed interpretations. When interpreters have an intimate knowledge of both languages and are aware of how they are used in interactions, they know how to fully express in American Sign Language (ASL) occurrences such as quarreling with their lover or their mother, keeping a secret, or asserting power over someone. Renowned voice instructor Annie Morrison states, "Embodied words are charged and there are consequences when you speak them; they can be goody bags or grenades . . . Words shape our world and how we interact with it" (Morrison, 2021).[2]

In theatre interpreting, as in community interpreting, the manner and tone of the speaker is content to be delivered. The body and voice of the actor onstage becomes the content that is re-expressed through the interpreter's body. What makes interpreted theatre unique is that the embodied words on the stage (including the "goody bags or grenades") are collaboratively constructed into a signed conversation, revealing the relationships, the conflict, and the intent of the scene as it does on the stage. This requires a deeper analysis of the actor's physical and vocal expression because the essence of the message resides in a corporeal living expression. These forays into the discovery of the other are sometimes surprising because we can find traces of them in ourselves. Literary critic and translator Gayatri Chakravorty Spivak points out, "This, after all, is one of the seductions of translating. It is a simple miming of the responsibility to the trace of the other in the self."[3]

Often, interpreters express concerns about conveying emotion or tone, since that may be perceived as "acting" and not interpreting. What makes the teamed dialogic interactions appear authentic is the incorporation of natural language, active listening, discourse cues, and character responses in the conveyance of the actors' embodied words (character depiction). Depiction of character and conversation is interpreting, not acting, and is a facet of fidelity. Interpreters draw information by studying the actor's portrayal of the character and their mannerisms.

In a 2010 interview for Theatre Development Fund (TDF), Broadway interpreter Alan Champion explained, "There's a difference between a sign language face versus an actor's face. And I think that when we do facial expression and facial grammar, it's very much a part of the language and not part of something we're miming out or trying to act."[4] However, when interpreters imitate an actor's presentation rather than communicating the nuances through language, they have crossed the line between acting and interpreting. For example, if there is a particularly emotional scene, the actor may be crying, but the interpreter is not. Representing a character's emotional truth through ASL grammar and culturally appropriate interaction is not acting.

The aim is to convey the characters' emotional life through language and natural dialogic interactions, not by "performing" the emotional life the way an actor would. It's a delicate balance—and the team relies upon the DOI to ensure that the line is not crossed. Since the team is in close proximity to the stage, the visual-to-visual relationship and the "conversation" between the two spaces need to complement each other.

Body as Instrument

The minute we walk into the interpreters' space in the theatre, we have activated meaning. Each body moves through and inhabits space in its own way, reflecting who we are in our everyday life and what we bring to the world on a daily basis in our interactions with others. We come from different cultures, genders, socioeconomic worlds—and all this information is reflected in our bodies.

When the body is the instrument, as it is in interpreting, our focus needs to include what our bodies are expressing. The body is the medium for our message. The more tools we have, the greater our range of expression. Whether we stand erect, slump over, or sway from side to side when interpreting, these behaviors relay information that may be in support of or obfuscate the intended meaning.

In addition, many interpreters have an ingrained habit of assuming an "interpreter stance" of clasping hands or holding them at the ready, signifying waiting to interpret. This is often assumed to be a "neutral interpreting position" from which a "neutral message" can be transmitted. In the theatre, this traditional interpreter stance ruptures the feeling of natural conversations. When physical habits intrude on interpretations, the audience might wonder whether what they see is indicative of the interpreter or the character.

To help interpreters bring awareness to the habitual ways in which their bodies move through space, our TDF program offered classes in the Alexander Technique, taught by Julliard instructor, Lauren Schiff. She guided participants through exercises to help them learn how to ergonomically support their bodies, recognize where they were holding tension, and practice methods to release body tension. An aligned and supported body allows for cleaner articulation and less stress while interpreting. This leads to an interpretation with fewer distractions of physical tension and mannerisms such as the "interpreter stance."

PRESENCE

The poise, centeredness, and self-control an interpreter brings to the interpreting space—the manner in which interpreters manage their bodies—brings an audience's eye to them without having to act or be effortful is what we call "presence."

Presence is the "it" factor that distinguishes an interpreter who draws an audience's gaze and attention. This "it" factor can be an asset or a distraction from the performance. When successfully applied, presence can lift an entire team's interpretation.

Matthew Penn (a stage, film, and television director) spoke about his understanding of the presence of both performers and interpreters. Although Penn is not fluent in sign, his perception of the presence of interpreters has been developed through years of experience both in front of an audience and observing performances with and without interpreters. We gratefully share his perspective:

> I can always see the presence of an interpreter. I can't absorb the language being expressed but what I see most is the presence and that the interpreter can convey information not just through signing, but through the ability to hold the audience's attention in a more intangible

> fashion. I have seen an interpreter who had a certain degree of presence but wasn't able to make you watch (them). Presence is when it's hard to look away. It allows you to convey information in a way that's interesting beyond its facts. It's how to convey info with your heart and your mind . . .
>
> A good interpreter can inhabit the role and sign it, conveying subtle differences in meaning and hold your attention. Then I'm interested. . . . Sometimes what I see is overacting, which works against presence. I don't want the interpreter to upstage the actor. And I don't want to see the interpreter working so hard on an emotional level so that it is overwhelming. That sort of loss of control creates a disconnect. As an audience member, I need room to breathe. If the interpreter is working too hard, all I see is their effort.[5]

When there is a balance between the presentation of the interpreting team and the stage, then there is a mutuality—a truly shared space.

Presence, when combined with strong interpreting skills, draws the audience in, bringing them closer to the play. It is embodied by a quality of stillness in that extraneous movement, and "noisy signing" is reduced or eliminated. The interpreter can choose deliberately to guide the audience's eye to an exact space at the exact time intended.

Depicting Characters

If we conceive of all interpreting as constructed discourse, character depiction is a way of differentiating between the interactants of the constructed discourse. In theatre, teams have the luxury of repeatedly seeing the show. This allows for a careful observation of the characters to determine which features of the character will be imported and to rehearse "wearing" them before the interpreted performance.

Character depiction helps the audience track who is talking to whom. Deaf audiences report that it is very helpful when the interpreting team identifies who is speaking and which interpreter portrays which characters on stage. Particularly when there is a large cast onstage, knowing who is speaking can be difficult. In community interpreting, the speaker is often identified by pointing, naming, or describing. In interpreted theatre, additional strategies are needed to signal the interpreter-to-character alignment. The depiction choices can include an array of nonlinguistic (such as physical behavior or a quick focus to the stage) as well as linguistic and discursive strategies, which may refer to the character's physical attributes and mannerisms, other characteristics such as manner of speech, tonal quality of the voice, and accents, or a combination of the above. There may be less depicting behavior needed when there is a one-to-one correspondence, but more may be needed in crowd scenes.

The team considers the nature of the characters' interactions. What are the stakes and motivations for each character in the interaction? What are the power dynamics or relative statuses of the conversational partners? How can the sensibilities and intentions of the character be conveyed? These questions help guide us away from acting and toward a meaningful rich interpretation.

The team's dialogic depictions utilize the linguistic and nonlinguistic signals that are carried through our interpreted interactions via subtle physical and discursive choices. The team monitors the interpretations to ensure that the inner life that the actor has imbued into the character is brought to life in the interpreted dialogue.

NONLINGUISTIC SIGNALING STRATEGIES

The goal when using nonlinguistic signaling strategies is to quickly create a "snapshot" of the character so that the audience can more readily identify the character–interpreter connection. The technique we call "touch and let go" is a brief representation of the physicality, mannerism, or trait of a character. Once the interpreter has been connected to the character, this representation is no longer needed. At this point, the physical snapshot can be released, but the essence of the character continues to be conveyed in the translation and interpretation choices throughout.

In nonlinguistic signaling strategies, the stage visuals (e.g., action, props, reference points, and costumes) offer cues for the depiction of characters. It is important to assess which features will enhance the interpreter–character alignment and when they need to be used. These nonlinguistic strategies can be used singly or in concert with each other, as well as in combination with translation choices.

That being said, there are times when the team chooses not to depict every character on the stage. The team assesses the function of a character in the scene to determine if and when that character needs to be brought to the fore. For example, the team may have decided to bundle characters for crowd scenes and chosen to express the thought worlds rather than individualize each utterance. The team may choose not to depict characters when their lines are not propelling the narrative or distinguishable from others at the moment.

Physical Behavior

Throughout the team's interpreted constructed discourses, character attributes are content that the team may incorporate in the interpretation. One option is for the interpreter to portray a mannerism or a way of standing that represents the character.

For example, if the character Tom presents as shy and often hunched over, the interpreter when initially taking on this character, may begin the signed utterance with stooped shoulders. They would hold that posture for a sentence or two, long enough to indicate which character they are interpreting, then include other features such as linguistic choices, more inward-turning signing style and lowered eye gaze to convey the character information. An important caveat is that any depicting choice should not interfere with signing production. This means that the slump shouldered signing for Tom should not restrict the signing space to such an extent that it makes the signs hard to see.

The physical vocabulary would continue if it is a short scene, or if it's needed to quickly differentiate this individual in scenes with multiple characters. Once the physical behavior has been let go, it could be reintroduced if and when the character exits and reappears in another scene or if a new interpreter takes on the character.

In a crowd scene, there may be a need to distinguish a pivotal character (such as Mme. Giry, the ballet mistress in *Phantom of the Opera*). The actor's portrayal gives us information to draw from (her stern voice, imposing demeanor, costume, and props, as well as how the other characters respond to her). She has an imperious posture and holds a staff to count the beats of the dance. An interpreter could select from these features for the depiction. A touch and let go strategy could be to briefly import Giry's action of tapping her staff (utilizing the visual information of her prop) to introduce the character–interpreter alignment. Once the interpretation begins, the interpreter could dispense with the staff and maintain an imperious posture through the scene. It is an opportunity for members of the team to physically contrast the severity and tension of Giry to the gracefulness of Christine in scenes they have together.

Additional Nonlinguistic Strategies

Nonlinguistic strategies include, in addition to physical behaviors, the interpreter's attire and throwing focus to the stage to identify which character is being presented.

Occasionally, attire can reinforce the connection between the interpreter and the main character they are interpreting. Examples of this include Alan Champion wearing a tuxedo interpreting for the title character in *Phantom of the Opera* and the *Biloxi Blues* company giving Jack Jason and Candace Broecker Penn army fatigues to match the 1940s style of the show. For years, The Public Theater brought the Shakespeare in the Park interpreting teams to their costume department to find appropriate attire for the interpreters.

The team can also throw focus to the stage to help identify a new character in the scene. In Neil Simon's *Barefoot in the Park*, the play opens with the Telephone Man entering the stage huffing and puffing after having climbed five flights of stairs. If this show were interpreted, for his entrance, the team would focus on the stage to watch the character's action, in this case, his panting. When the team returns focus to the interpreting space, the interpreter for the Telephone Man could offer a hint of being out of breath, without going overboard and recreating the actor's behavior. That action is the actor's moment for comedy, not the interpreter's.

LINGUISTIC AND DIALOGIC STRATEGIES

During the interpretation, the team is constructing the interactive discourse of the characters onstage. This has an impact on translation choices and performative strategies such as listening behaviors and shared meaning space agreements.

Linguistic Choices

Linguistic translatory choices allow for a more complex representation of character. From interpreters' signed registers and vocabulary choices, audiences can glean information about a character's social identity including generation, education, gender, region, culture, and class. DOIs are an invaluable source of information and guidance for character style development.

Embodiment of the character's delivery is another content strand that must be present in the interpretation; if it is missing, so is fidelity to the performance. If Scar, from *The Lion King*, were interpreted with a flat affect, half of the information about his conniving and ruthless character would be missing. Scar's cunning vocal qualities and physical behaviors help the audience recognize his manipulative character and, therefore, this content needs to be included in the interpretation.

The interpreting team often asks questions such as: If this character were expressing these concepts in a signed language, what would that expression look like? Just like spoken voices can be loud, soft, expressive, or flat, signing can vary in similar ways. Once identified, we consider how this would be physically expressed both in sign choice and in manner and tone of delivery. Would the signing space be placed high or low? Would the signs be larger or smaller? What would the character's signing style be like in terms of pace, pauses, emphasis, facial expression, and grammar?

Lerner and Loewe's *My Fair Lady* offers an opportunity for a team to explore the use of contrasting registers in their interpretation. At the beginning of the play, the interpreters for Eliza and Higgins could begin by using completely different registers. As the play progresses, Eliza's use of language would change under his tutelage, but occasionally, she might revert to her native communication style, as with her line, "Move yer bloomin' arse!"

Gilbert (Gil) C. Eastman, a founding member of the National Theatre of the Deaf (NTD), played with contrasting registers in *Sign Me Alice*[6] (his popular adaptation of *My Fair Lady* and *Pygmalion*), exploring the sociocultural attitudes in the Deaf signing community about the use of ASL. As Joseph Hill reminds us, "The attitudes [toward signing varieties] are tied with the perceptions of social identities related to deafness and signing abilities."[7]

In the Roundabout Theatre's 2019 revival of Sam Shepard's *True West*,[8] informed by the actor's characterization of Lee, Stephanie found it effective to sign with a more cisgendered masculine style. Her signs were more restrained, with a smaller signing space, and were placed lower, near her midbody. When the character had explosive moments, the actor's choices changed and, likewise, her signs became sharper and quicker.

Sometimes, a simple sign choice can bring more depth to a character. During a Hands On/A.R.T./NY theatre-interpreting workshop focused on Christopher Demos-Brown's *American Son*, Zavier Sabio, one of the DOIs advising participants in the workshop, posed a question about the line, "Where's my son?" In the play, this line is uttered by the white father asking the attending officer at the police station where his biracial son is being held. While the participants chose to translate the line using the ASL sign for "son," Sabio offered the loan sign, S-N. He felt it exuded paternal authority and conveyed a sense of the father–son relationship: such a simple choice, and yet so powerful.

Not every interpreter can make the same choices, given our cultural backgrounds. When the team is of mixed cultural backgrounds, the physical gestures or depictions created by one interpreter may or may not be carried over to another interpreter. Alexandria Wailes commented on the appropriate use of culturally embedded gestures. When asked whether a white interpreter could or should use a gesture such as the snap used by a Black actor onstage in their interpretation, her response was, "If it's not in your soul, in your DNA, in your breath, or what you grew up seeing and experiencing on a daily basis, you wouldn't be able to express it. Without that authenticity of life and language and lived experiences to draw from, you can't deliver it in the way that it was intended."[9] As always, the impact of cultural representation of choices must be carefully considered.

Interpreting teams also consider the linguistic details that can help to reveal the salient dimensions of character and sociocultural information. Two examples of importing foreign cultural matter are found in *Cabaret*.[10] Herr Schultz and Fräulein Schneider have an intimate relationship. As an older couple, they respectfully address each other by title and last name, very different from the young American couple, Cliff and Sally.

The interpreting team chose to transliterate the names, "Fräulein Schneider" and "Herr Schultz," rather than using a name sign in their interactions. Their use of Fraulein and Herr convey their shared cultural identity as Germans. The choice to transliterate signals the respect the characters accord each other and serves as a linguistic reminder that the play was set in another time, place, and culture, especially as there was no equivalent for these terms of address in ASL.

Another example from *Cabaret* was the translation choice for the Yiddish word, "mazel," which means luck. The first few times mazel is spoken, both the fingerspelled word and its ASL sign ("luck") were incorporated into the interpretation. Once meaning was established, the transliteration could then stand on its own. This choice conveyed the foreignness of the term, linguistically reminding us of Herr Schultz's status as an outsider, a German Jew at the precipice of World War II. The strategic decision to import the German and Yiddish words avoided the pitfall of "domesticating" the foreignness of the language by keeping the flavor and sensibility of the German life depicted on stage.[11]

Dialogic Constructed Discourse

It is important to identify not only the characters between whom a conversation is taking place but also the nature of the conversation. Is it private or public? Who are the lines directed to? Is the character reading aloud to themselves or is it a shared conversation with others in the room? For example, in *Dear Evan Hansen*, is the actor directing their lines to the device as if they are in conversation with the device, or do they get up and walk away from the computer and then respond to the "imaginary person"? Where in space does the actor refer to this nonexistent character? The team has to track that so that the spatial mapping in the interpretation is cohesive and the dialogic agreements are intact. These actor choices inform our interpretation.

Dialogic Listening in a Scene

Both the actors' presentation of their characters and their interactions with other characters is content that needs to be incorporated into the interpretations. Unless the interpretation is designed to be overlapping dialogue, team interpreters wait for each other to complete their lines before starting their own. In other words, the team responds to their partners' signed utterances rather than the auditory cues of the actor's lines.

In community interpretation, interpreters are usually not working in a dialogic manner. Often, only the spoken interactions are interpreted, not the listening behaviors that thread the conversation together. The act of listening is ripe with meaning that needs to be unpacked and expressed. In the theatre, because the team is interpreting dialogically, that salient interactive content is included.

Listening during an interpreted conversation is a crucial part of team-constructed discourse. How an interpreter depicts listening conveys information both about which character the interpreter represents in the interaction and the manner in which they are listening. Natural signed interaction requires subtle backchannel responses. By following the dialogic norms of ASL, the team conveys the dynamics of the onstage conversation.

How the characters listen (e.g., distractedly, evasively, adoringly) informs our constructed discourse listening behaviors. Some questions that help shape our decisions regarding "listening" behavior include the following: Is the other interpreter's character talking to my character? Is my character listening or not? In what manner is my character listening? What reaction is my character having? Is the character an engaged listener, a passive listener, a covert listener, a bystander hearing information shared publicly, or overhearing information that was not intended for them?

The manner in which interpreters listen to each other and express their lines are powerful signals that help guide the audience in deciphering who a character is talking to or about, whether it is a public or private thought, whether the line is intended to be heard (and if so, by whom) or overheard. A fun example of listening and constructed discourse behaviors for interpreters can be found in Shakespeare's *Twelfth Night* (Act II, Scene 5). As a ruse, Maria has sent Malvolio a letter purportedly from Olivia, expressing love for him. As he reads it aloud, he simultaneously interjects his comments and reactions. Unbeknownst to him, the other characters onstage (Sir Toby Belch, Andrew Aguecheek, and Fabian) are hiding from Malvolio's sight, listening and reacting with laughter to his self-preening responses to the letter.

Since the conceit of this scene is that Malvolio thinks he is alone and is revealing his inner thoughts, the interpreter for Malvolio would not look at or interact with the other interpreters. The remaining members of the team would want to clearly distinguish when they are secretly (yet actively) listening to him from when they are talking to each other and making fun of him. If the interpreters were not seen as actively listening to him, it would undermine the scene.

The photos in figure 5.1 capture a sample interpretation demonstrating character dialogic agreement in a teaching example of *The Lion King*. These agreements include translation, as well as emotive and performative agreements that align with the stage information).

In the top left photo, Lynnette is engaged in active listening in character as Timon. In the top right is an example of a lexical agreement between interpreters. This agreement is the foundation for a joke between them. A pun on the spoken word and a pun on the sign are needed to express the humor in the dialogue that ensues.

In the bottom two photos, the interpreters continue the signed pun as they are listening and responding to each other in a manner that reflects the way in which the characters Timon and Pumba are listening and responding to each other.

Dialogic Constructed Action

The team considers what can be seen and understood on stage without importing the object or including the action, for example, we may hold the phone, but we don't kneel to propose. There are times, however, that even if it is clear onstage, a reference to the object still needs to be included to satisfy the grammatical requirements of ASL, such as a letter being read or a phone being answered. Interpreters selectively choose which objects/props to include based on the objects' narrative functions. When determining what actions will be included in translations, we consider: Is it a prop that is thematic and/or recurring, such as a letter from a loved one? What affective or behavioral information is embedded in the prop (is it being held lovingly, tossed aside dismissively, etc.)?

Sometimes, a character's interactive behavior is briefly demonstrated through constructed action. For example, if a character's line is "I will take down your info" and the

Figure 5.1. Character dialogic agreements. Copyright © 2024 Taylor, Feyne, and Broecker

actor is holding a pencil and pad, ready to take down the message, likewise, the interpreter might briefly imitate holding a pencil and pad (touch and let go) while looking expectantly at the other interpreter, as if waiting to take down the message. This signifies the manner in which the character is actively listening and helps to identify which character is being represented. The interpreter would not continuously mimic the action because that action is visible onstage. Also, when a character makes a telephone call, an interpreter might briefly imitate the action of holding a phone at the top of the call. These instances of constructed action help to reaffirm the interpreter–character alignment and clarify how the character is interacting with others. However, there is no need to recreate the actors' behavior. That is the actor's purview.

Every prop does not need to be imported into the interpretation. The team only depicts those moments and relationships with the objects that foster a connection to the stage or support the narrative. Letters, phone calls, and texts that represent dialogic information from unseen characters may be incorporated into our translation because they carry linguistic information about visible and nonvisible participants in a conversation.

Once the team determines a reference to a prop will be included in the translation, then the considerations move to logistics: Who handles it? How is it handled? How long is it held? Is there time to throw focus to the stage? What is each character's response to the object? If it is an object that several characters use, what will be the team agreements for sharing it? For example, if a character were to hand the phone to another character so they could "talk to Grandma," the "phone" would likely be passed between the interpreters, so that the recipient could be identified as the next interlocutor using this object.

Sometimes, characters respond to letters they read in a dialogic manner with a running commentary while reading, such as Malvolio's responses to the letter he thinks is from Olivia in Act II, Scene 5 of *Twelfth Night*. Malvolio reads aloud, "I may command where I adore." Then, he reacts to her letter by saying, "Why, she may command me; I serve her; she is my lady." He continues his dialogic interaction with the letter throughout his monologue.

In other shows, such as *Mister Roberts*, letters are read aloud, a straightforward reporting of the content.

In both cases, interpreters clarify when the information is from the letter and when the character is responding to the content of the letter. One way to indicate this would be to "hold" a referent for the letter and refer to it while signing its contents. This is a way of indexing the unseen character speaking/writing.

When a prop is passed to another character and is referred to in a conversation, sometimes, the team will then linguistically "pass" the object (such as a letter) to the next interpreter, who "holds" and refers to it. The prop is part of the content of the dialogue. The interpretation would be incomplete without sharing that visual referent.

For example, in *Mary Poppins*,[12] the Banks children have handwritten an advertisement for a new nanny. On Broadway, the choice was for the interpreter to hold an imaginary letter and then refer to it as the children are listing the qualities they want a nanny to possess. Then, onstage, when the children's father took the letter, the imaginary letter was passed to the interpreter for Mr. Banks so that it could be a referent used while he was commenting on and then disposing of the letter. This team agreement was a dialogic tactic, so that the content continued through the "chain of utterances, as a thread in a net of intertwined communicative behavior." (Wadensjö 1998, 43)[13]

Switching Between Depictions of Characters

Theatre interpreters often find themselves interpreting more than one character in a scene. It can be confusing if an interpreter switches to a new character without signaling they are changing character. Often, there is a need to "throw" a character, which means a new teammate will take over interpreting for a character that had primarily been assigned to another team member.

We offer a step-by-step technique for interpreters switching characters midscene:

- Disengage by turning your eye gaze away from your partner.
- Throw focus to the stage (if time allows).
- Take on the new character's linguistic and/or nonlinguistic attributes.
- Return your gaze to your partner as the new character.

This is a subtle change, not one that should distract from the stage or partner's signing. These steps do not take much time when they are deliberate. Both linguistic and nonlinguistic signals can be used when the team "throws" or switches characters. Linguistic cues are often incorporated by team members after a switch.

Interpreters often rapidly switch between multiple characters. It can be complicated enough for the interpreting team to remember who is who when toggling between characters and can be even more complicated for the audience. When shifting to a new character, it can be helpful to include linguistic information in the interpretation to indicate the new character alignment. The following is an example of translatory tactics:

Interpreter A: Son/Mother
Interpreter B: Daughter

Suppose Interpreter A has been assigned to the Son (who has been in conversation with his sister), and now the Mother takes the lead in the conversation. Interpreter A needs to switch to become the Mother. At this point, there is a need to clarify the new interpreter—character alignment. The team would make an agreement about who would indicate that in the signed dialogue.

If next the Daughter has the line, "What do you think?" Interpreter B could make the character switch explicit by signing, "Mother, what do you think?" Another option would be for Interpreter A to respond, "Daughter, I agree." This is a clarification, not "added information." Once the relationships are established, teams don't need to reidentify the characters until there is another switch.

Figure 5.2 is an example of a character switch that could occur in *The Lion King*. These photos are taken from a teaching video designed to demonstrate some of the strategies used when characters onstage outnumber interpreters.

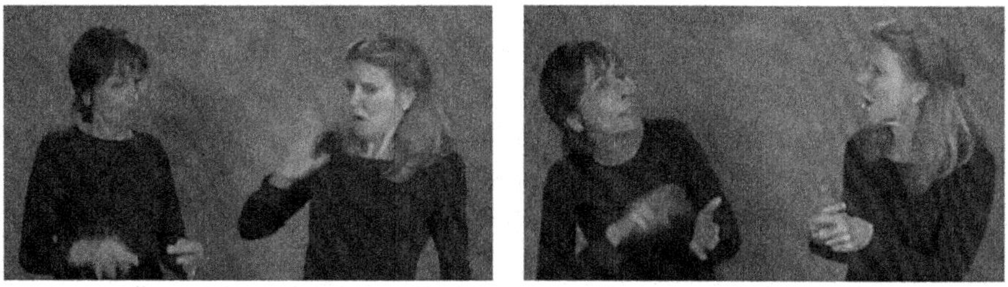

Timon & Pumba addressing Simba   Simba addressing Timon & Pumba

Figure 5.2. Character switching. Copyright © 2024 Taylor, Feyne, and Broecker Penn.

In the staged performance, Simba stands between Timon and Pumba. Though Timon and Pumba have most of the lines in the scene, there are one or two moments when Simba asks questions of them. Lynnette and Candace represent Timon and Pumba, respectively. When Simba speaks, the interpreter for Timon could switch to take on Simba (who is younger and shorter than the other characters). Character-switching strategies include shifts in interpreter stance, eye gaze, positioning, and even body posture.

On the left, you see Timon and Pumba addressing Simba in the conversation. Note that the team has established a shared reference point for Simba (where their eye gaze goes down toward him). On the right is a quick character shift for Simba's question. Note the eye gaze and the physical change for that brief line.

Character depiction is successful when it is integrated into the translation. Primary meaning resides in the discourse with character depiction supporting it, not the other way around.

Strategies for Partnering with the Stage

Ideally, the team looks for as many moments as possible to link the interpretation to the stage performance. DOI Alexandria Wailes explains, "When the story is building to a climactic moment—the anticipated kiss of two main characters—if the interpreting team distracts or pulls my attention away from this pivotal moment onstage, it is disappointing." She cautions, "If the interpreter chooses to interpret the kiss instead of throwing focus to the stage, the audience misses that big moment. I think it's important for the interpreting team to think about when to give it to the stage. The interpreters can and need to honor the action onstage. Especially as an interpreter myself, I would not want to be the one to draw focus away from that big moment. I wouldn't want the blame to fall on me if the audience misses that moment."[14]

THROWING FOCUS TO THE STAGE

Recognizing that the signing audience toggles between the interpreter space and the stage, time is built in to allow the audience to view important onstage action—what is called "throwing focus to the stage." Cueing the audience to look at the stage has become conventionalized over time. The entire team stops signing at an agreed-upon moment. Eye gaze and bodies turn slightly toward the direction of the action on the stage. For example, in Roundabout Theatre's 2019 production of *True West*, Lee (Ethan Hawke) drunkenly peed on the plants in his mother's house. The team threw focus to those onstage moments. (Who would want to miss that?!) When the eye gaze and bodies return to the interpreted space, the interpretation resumes. Figure 5.3 is an example of the 2009 Broadway team for *Mary Poppins* throwing focus.[15]

Sometimes, the team can simply pause, and that will suffice. In an interview, Alan Champion discussed the visual nature of theatre and the audience's acuity, "The audience will look at the show . . . If someone is carrying an umbrella and flying through the roof, we don't have to worry about telling people where to look."[16]

However, there may be small but narratively significant gestures that deserve to be seen. A pivotal moment in *Cabaret* occurs between Sally and Cliff when she insinuates she had an abortion. When Cliff realizes what she did, he slaps her. This crucial visual action occurs between two of her lines. The lines cannot be reordered because the slap is in response to the first thought, and her next line is in response to the slap. The team recognized that Sally's lines that occurred immediately before the slap (regarding the greedy doctor and her fur coat) needed to be completed early enough to allow time for throwing focus to the stage. The interpreter's cue to finish early and the team's cue for the focus were frozen agreements that had to be memorized and rehearsed.

For the sake of timing, to throw focus to the stage, interpreters apply a variety of meaning distribution strategies. These strategies include preloading information by bundling or collapsing lines that overlap with stage action, strategically omitting[17] some of those lines, or holding the interpretation of some of the lines until after the action has been completed.

Figure 5.3. Interpreters throwing focus to the stage during *Mary Poppins*. Left to right: Alan Champion, Lynnette Taylor, and Candace Broecker Penn. Theatre Development Fund, "When Theatre Meets Sign Language."

In addition, when there are theatrical moments in unexpected locations, such as in *Noises Off*, when the director starts speaking from the back of the house, or in *The Phantom of the Opera*, when the chandelier starts shaking above the audience, and when puppets parade in from the back of the house in *The Lion King*, the team may specifically indicate where the information will be coming from. This is an example of partnering with the audience as well as the stage.

Looping in the Stage

The photos in figure 5.4 show a series of moments from *The Lion King* beginning when Pumba is about to sing. You can see the interpreting team focus, incorporate, and then respond to the action on stage.

In the first image above, both interpreters gaze to the stage. Throwing focus to the stage is a signal that the stage action is occurring. This stage action will then be imported into the shared meaning space through constructed action and constructed discourse.

In the second photo, Lynnette guides the audience gaze from the stage back to the interpreted space when she turns to watch Candace representing Pumba. Candace engages in constructed action reflecting Pumba's outlandish singing.

Finally, Lynnette responds dialogically in character to the constructed action.

These hooks and fasteners are means to keep the shared meaning space in conversation with the staged space. Throughout the performance, there is an ongoing interplay between the stage and the shared meaning space.

Figure 5.4. Looping the stage into the shared meaning space. Copyright © 2024 Taylor, Feyne, and Broecker Penn.

CONTENT THAT IS AUDITORY BUT NOT VISUAL

Sometimes, there may be environment-, character-, or other plot-related content that the hearing audience gleans from auditory information that is not present visually (e.g., a scream, a gunshot, a doorbell, or a train whistle). Which sounds are included in the interpretation are often determined by their content information.

In many plays, doorbells have significance. For example, in Noel Coward's *Blithe Spirit,* when the maid's walk to the door is comical, the doorbell serves as a cue not only for someone at the door but also for the audience to watch the maid's action. In Ira Levin's *Deathtrap*, the doorbell is an alarm of impending danger, a warning that the characters' murderous plot might be discovered. In both examples, the auditory information could be incorporated to make the meaning and impact explicit by using the narrator function or adding the information into the interpreted line.

At times, a particular sound is the pivotal information that reveals the climactic moment or provides a crucial piece of information in the narrative. In *Miss Saigon*, Kim goes behind a curtain and the audience hears a gunshot. Chris, the father of their child, runs to open the curtain to find she has killed herself. The narrator function ("I hear a gunshot from behind the curtain") informs the audience what the characters are reacting to and allows the climax to be revealed on the stage.

Thinking through the auditory gunshot moment in *Miss Saigon,* the team is aware that the goal is to maintain the suspense. The audience does not know who is shot. There is a brief window of time for the gunshot to be interpreted because immediately afterward, the character Chris runs to reveal who was shot behind the curtain. Which team member interprets the gunshot and in what manner are both important considerations. Options include an interpreter who is already standing narrating hearing the gunshot, a seated interpreter suddenly standing up to interpret the sound, or a seated interpreter raising their hands from their seat and signing "gunshot" as long as it is visible to the audience. Whoever is selected, it should not be the interpreter for Kim, as the semiotic trace of Kim onto the interpreter could muddy the waters so to speak, spoiling the surprise for the whole audience! The team would choose the least disruptive option.

A different approach for handling auditory information was used for the 2008 production of Patrick Barlow's adaption of *The 39 Steps* at the Roundabout Theatre.[18] The interpreting team chose a strategy that was visually aligned with the energy of the play. Each of the four characters had a corresponding interpreter so the character–interpreter alignment remained stable, thus supporting easier tracking of the actions onstage. A cacophony of sound effects (gun shots, hooves clopping, car sounds, etc.) made by the actors was interspersed throughout the play. As the clown characters playfully popped up on the stage, likewise, the interpreters had free rein to jump up to interpret important sound effects. The interpreting choices reflected the playful mayhem of the show.

NONLINGUISTIC STRATEGIES FOR CONNECTING TO ONSTAGE INFORMATION

There are many options that can be used singly or in concert with each other.

Cheating Out

Just as actors have to project their voice so that the audience can hear them, the interpreting team needs to cheat out so that the audience can see them. The theatrical convention of cheating out entails turning the body outward. "It's a performance technique that helps maintain the illusion that characters are totally committed to the onstage action, but simultaneously reorients their performance so they are playing out towards the audience."[19] For interpreters, this means opening our bodies outward while maintaining eye gaze with our conversational partner. The team is always conscious of the delicate balance of being visible to one another, as in a signing conversation, but not turned in so much that the audience's view is cut off. The conversation needs to be visible to the audience.

Blocking

The interpreted space is viewed as an extension of the stage picture. The mise-en-scène of the interpreting space in relation to the stage also needs to be considered. The team identifies the moments when they must be in position to impart critical content and when they can get out of the way so that the audience can have an unimpeded view of the production, which invites a direct connection with the stage.

Interpreters have borrowed the term "blocking" from the theatre. On the stage, "blocking" is the positioning and movement of the actors during a performance. For the team, "blocking" is the positioning of members of the interpreting team in response to the characters' blocking throughout the play.

Blocking is the interpreters' movement that assists an audience in identifying which interpreter is representing which character. It is a nonlinguistic strategy that establishes and maintains interpreter–character alignment. Blocking is used in conjunction with and in response to the other strategies of character assignment, character depiction, and use of space. As stated earlier, a small team of interpreters is often switching between multiple characters, and blocking serves to clarify who is interpreting for whom in each scene.

Cheating out with active listening.
Partners' eye gaze is on the signer.
Mary Poppins on Broadway.
Left to right: Candace Broecker Penn, Lynnette Taylor, and Alan Champion.
Theatre Development Fund, "When Theatre Meets Sign Language"

Active listening and dialogic interaction.
Winslow Boy on Broadway.[20]
(L-R) Stephanie Feyne, Laurie Nash, and Molly Wilson.

Figure 5.5. Examples of cheating out and eye gaze connections. Photos courtesy of Hands On.

As the team develops the blocking, a good guide is to keep in mind that the interpreting team is highly visible, part of the mise-en-scène, and our approach is to keep blocking to a minimum. Blocking often is guided by either the actors' positions at the beginning of scenes or their positions during most of a scene.

If there is extended action without spoken dialogue, the interpreting team can choose to sit. Conversely, if there is barely a breath between a character's last line and the beginning of their next line, and there is important visual information onstage, it's often preferable to leave the interpreter standing—sometimes with a brief focus, directing the audience's gaze to the action on stage. Through stillness, the interpreting space is almost deactivated, as if our lights have been dimmed.

The goal is to only move when absolutely necessary, such as:

- At the top of a scene, when characters are entering, and the interpreters are establishing who is representing whom
- When a new character enters and an interpreter switches from a previous main character to the new one, and the new character is in a position relative to the other characters that does not match the current placement of the interpreters
- When a character has a long monologue (even if others are silently on the stage, the other interpreters may choose to sit and allow all the visual focus on the one interpreter and the stage, thus supporting the goal of being less visually distracting)

Interpreting team members do not switch positions merely because the stage picture changes. Our goal is to support an audience's understanding of who is interpreting for whom. Once those character–interpreter alignments are established, there is no need for movement on our part, regardless of the stage picture. The goal is to be the least intrusive as possible and to abide by the maxim "less is more."

Blocking decisions depend on timing, placement, familiarity with the play, and events on the stage. The team considers the narrative arc and character relationships. The goal is to create interpreter positioning that more readily reflects the stage picture and narrative intent.

Questions that guide these decisions include: If there is silence or an important visual, how long is it? How can the positioning and movement of interpreters support the narrative on the stage? Will the movement of sitting down or exiting the interpreting space support or distract from the stage moment? These considerations help the team to develop a map of where and when interpreters will enter the interpreting space.

Blocking Chart. Below is the character breakdown with two additional columns for the blocking for the scenes from *Romeo and Juliet*, which correspond to the discussion of character assignment in chapter 3, developed in accordance with the actors' staging. Interpreters often develop their own individual cheat sheets so that they know when and in which direction to enter and exit the interpreting space and list their line cues.

Some interpreters prefer to note their positions from the stage perspective (Stage Left to Stage Right—the interpreter's perspective when they face the audience) and others prefer the audience perspective (House Left to House Right—what the interpreter sees when sitting in the audience). We have included both in figure 5.6.

Please note that while there may be a lot of character movement onstage in each scene, the aim is for the interpreters to keep the blocking changes to a minimum. In most of the scenes, the team remains in the same position. When changing positions, interpreters move between, rather than during lines, as much as possible. Rather than interpreters creating a second stage, this streamlined approach is designed to reinforce the character–interpreter alignment and support the narrative arc of the play.

Character Assignment with Blocking chart for *Romeo and Juliet*

Scene	Page	**Interp A** ROMEO	**Interp B** JULIET/ MERCUTIO	**Interp C** NURSE/ FRIAR	***STAGE Perspective*** *SL to SR*	***AUDIENCE Perspective*** *HL to HR*
Act II Sc 2		Romeo	Juliet		A B	B A
Act II Sc 3		Romeo		Friar	A C	C A
Act II Sc 4		Romeo	Mercutio	Benvolio Nurse	A B C	C B A
Act II Sc 5			Juliet	Nurse	B C	C B
Act II Sc 6		Romeo	Juliet	Friar	A C A B C	C A C B A
Act III Sc 1		Benvolio Romeo	Mercutio *After Mercutio dies:* Benvolio Montague	Tybalt LadyCapulet Prince	A B C A B	B A B A C
Act III Sc 2			Juliet	Nurse	C B	B C

Figure 5.6. Character assignment with blocking. Copyright © 2024 Taylor, Feyne, and Broecker Penn.

PARTNERING WITH ONSTAGE SIGNED CONTENT

There are now more shows in which Deaf performers are "trodding the boards." This occurs not only in plays written for Deaf characters (such as *Children of a Lesser God, Tribes, I Was Most Alive With You, Grey House, Private Jones, Trash, Dark Disabled Stories, Inside/Look, The Signal Season of Dummy Hoy, Sign Me Alice, A Play of Our Own, Language of One, Reflections of a Black Deaf Woman*)[21] but also in bilingual productions (such as *Big River, Spring Awakening, The Music Man, The Laramie Project, A Raisin in the Sun*)[22] and in plays where directors have cast Deaf actors (such as *for colored girls who have considered suicide/when the rainbow is enuf, King*

Lear, Hunchback of Notre Dame, Fiddler on the Roof, To Kill A Mockingbird, and *Richard III*).[23] Around the country, touring companies and regional and repertory theatres such as the Oregon Shakespeare Festival, the Olney Theatre, The Lyric Theatre of Oklahoma, Deaf Austin Theatre, Deaf West Theatre, Deaf Spotlight, Visionaries of the Creative Arts (VOCA), and The Public Theater, among others, are hiring Deaf actors and including signed language in their productions. Some of these plays are interpreted and some are not.

When there is an interpreted performance of any show that includes Deaf performers and/or signed language, there is now additional visual linguistic information on the stage that needs to be considered. The team will need to be attuned to the visual-to-visual interactions, as well as the signed-to-signed interactions, identifying key moments to throw focus to the stage. It is helpful to think of the two signing spaces as a conversation within a conversation.

In keeping with a dialogic approach, interpretations will build cohesive "conversations" with the onstage signing characters. The team considers the following: What information does the interpretation need to import? Which of the signs used onstage will be included in the translations? How much of the signing onstage is visible to the audience? How much spoken dialogue is there between onstage signed utterances? How can the team allow time for the audience to view the signed discourse on the stage as well as the interpreted conversations?

Sometimes, actors want to sign some lines so that they can directly communicate to the Deaf signing audience during an interpreted performance. In New York City, Alan Cumming in Roundabout Theatre's 2014 revival of *Cabaret* and Rául Júlia in The Public Theater's 1991 *Othello* chose to sign a few lines without using their voices. The teams needed to anticipate throwing focus early enough so these moments wouldn't be missed.

Tom Humphries responded to the onstage signing in *Cabaret* in 2014:

> I would like to thank Alan Cumming and the people responsible for the excellent interpreting performance. . . . Alan Cumming's signing and gesturing of the opening lines of the musical were a surprise to those of us in the audience who are Deaf. Whether he knows it or not, he paid homage to the many deaf people who were mistreated or killed in the years leading up to and during World War II at the hands of the Nazis in their purification madness. This personalized for me the sense of desperation, moral abandon and defiance of the *Cabaret*.[24]

When interviewed by Hands On, Alan Cummings shared his thoughts about how signing creates a connection between actor and audience:

> I feel it is important for me as a performer to say, "Hello . . . welcome," and this [signing] is also for the people who are not Deaf in the audience. This [interpreted performance] is what's happening today. *Cabaret* is a great way to do that because it opens by saying "welcome" to everybody. So I signed a little bit of the lyrics of the song to the Deaf people in the audience and I thought it set the whole scene for everybody for that performance, not just the Deaf people, but the whole audience.[25]

Engaging in Responsive Team Practice

During the live interpreted performance, the entire interpreting team is collectively responsible for telling the story. Team members are attentive to what colleagues need—linguistic support (for content and use of meaning space) or nonlinguistic support (for blocking and visibility) and offer what is needed.

The team is constantly monitoring to see whether an interpretation is clear, whether information has been signed too quickly, or whether it needs to be repeated for emphasis. In theatre, there are multiple variables at play and what was planned may not always be what is executed. The same holds true during interpreted performances. If a team member offers a new interpretation, the team responds by incorporating the new vocabulary or reference point, or by offering clarifications. Suppose a character states that Proteus sent a letter, and suppose *who* sent the letter is an important plot point. If a team member feels that that wasn't clear enough in the interpretation, they can build it into their dialogic response, as in, FROM P-R-O-T-E-U-S, a performance corollary to Molly Wilson's "Open Processing."[26]

A responsive team considers all aspects of the interpretation as it unfolds. This may include pitching in when an interpreter misses lines or information, taking a character that was not originally assigned when a member of the team has a coughing fit, or even running to communicate with the house staff that the light for the interpreters needs to be turned on. The standing team may focus more on cohesion of linguistic meaning, while the seated team may often focus more on providing cues for the standing interpreters.

Because teams rarely have the opportunity to rehearse in the actual interpreted space, there may be unforeseen complications that require adjustments during the interpreted performance. Perhaps the interpreters cannot hear the actor's delivery at times or cannot see the visual cues on stage. When this happens, the interpreters who are seated can help the standing team by feeding them the lines, providing the visual information, and/or guiding their gaze. Here are some additional ways support is offered:

- Cueing interpreter entrances and exits
- Guiding eye gaze for reference points
- Cueing blocking moves
- Feeding lines
- Guiding team members to stand in the light or cheat out more

The 2020 interpretation of *Hadestown*[27] on Broadway was illustrative of a collaborative approach to interpreted performance. The team consisted of Alexandria Wailes, Dylan Geil, Justine Rivera, Lynnette Taylor, and DOI Anne Tomasetti. Throughout *Hadestown*, there were so many blocking and focus cues that it was difficult to remember them all. Seated members of the team supported the standing team by discreetly signaling in ways that the interpreting team could see, but the audience could not. Other instances of cueing occurred when interpreters were not in the lit space or when there was difficulty hearing the lines.

None of this was preplanned. Every instance of support was spontaneous. These cues were offered (and gratefully accepted) because of the team's mutually held belief that each member has a shared responsibility for the whole of the story. This collaborative engagement honors cueing as a part of the interpreting process.

Even in a show with only one performer, there still can be teaming. In 2000, Alan Champion interpreted the title character in *Dame Edna: The Royal Tour*,[28] a two-hour monologue. The actor on stage delivered lines toward imaginary conversational partners. Alan relied on his team member, Candace, who was seated and could see the stage, to direct his eye gaze and reference points, ensuring that his interpretation matched the actor's choices.

LIFE HAPPENS . . . STEPPING IN AS NEEDED

Sometimes, unforeseen circumstances, such as slow traffic or a family emergency, can prevent an interpreter from making it to the theatre on time. In those cases, the other team members need to move forward and interpret the roles originally assigned to the missing team member(s) until they arrive. The benefit of working collaboratively and the team knowing the whole play—and not just the characters that were assigned to each—is that when life gets in the way, the team is adaptable. By having watched each other during the team's rehearsal process, the play is now living within the team in ASL.

An interpreted performance is the result of translation, rehearsals with the team, and presentation of the play. Another benefit of the collaborative approach is that it cultivates a community that cares for each other, the work we do, and the audiences we serve. In the words of DOI Anne Tomasetti,

> It feels like a gift when both the show and the interpreting team are in sync. When their translations are spot on, the pacing is spot on, their interactions are spot on, and the energy on the stage is present in the team's energy, it feels like everything is in harmony, like a visual concert. And when that happens, the full story comes alive. I know how each character is feeling, how they're saying their lines, and I am completely transported into that world. I feel 100% present in the experience of the show, and that gives me such joy.[29]

Notes

1. Cristina Marinetti, "Translation and Theatre: From Performance to Performativity," *Target International Journal of Translation Studies* 25, no. 3 (2013): 307–20.
2. Annie Morrison, *The Moment of Speech: Creative Articulation for Actors* (Methuen Drama, November 2, 2021, accessed January 30, 2022, https://actorsandperformers.com/the-moment-of-speech/.
3. Gayatri Chakravaorty Spivak, *Living Translation*, ed. Emily Apter, Avishek Ganguly, Mauro Pala, and Surya Parekh (Seagull Books, 2022), 37.

4. Theatre Development Fund, "When Theatre Meets Sign Language," Theatre Development Fund YouTube, September 27, 2010, https://www.youtube.com/watch?v=wUK_OUxN-1Q.
5. Matthew Penn interviewed by Lynnette Taylor, Stephanie Feyne, and Candace Broecker Penn, February 19, 2014.
6. Gilbert Eastman discusses *"Sign Me Alice,"* The HeART of Deaf Culture, accessed December 1, 2023, https://www.youtube.com/watch?v=U4FOLRBu3OI.
7. Joseph Christopher Hill, *Language Attitudes in the American Deaf Community* (Gallaudet University Press, 2012).
8. *True West*, by Sam Shepard, dir. James Macdonald, produced by the Roundabout Theatre Company in 2019 at the American Airlines Theatre. Interpreting team: Laurie Nash, Sandra Romero-Cañas, and Stephanie Feyne. DOI: Anne Tomasetti.
9. Alexandria Wailes interviewed by Lynnette Taylor and Candace Broecker Penn, June 20, 2020.
10. *Cabaret*, music by John Kander, lyrics by Fred Ebb, book by Joseph Masteroff, dir. Sam Mendes, co-dir. Rob Marshall, chor. Rob Marshall, produced by the Roundabout Theatre Company in 1998 at the Kit Kat Club. Interpreting team: Lynnette Taylor and Stephanie Feyne; DOI: Anne Tomasetti.
11. Lawrence Venuti, *The Translator's Invisibility* (Routledge, 1995).
12. *Mary Poppins*, music and lyrics by Richard M. Sherman and Robert B. Sherman, additional music and lyrics by George Stiles and Anthony Drewe, book by Julian Fellowes, dir. Richard Eyre and Matthew Bourne, chor. Matthew Bourne, 2006 Broadway production at the New Amsterdam Theatre. Interpreting team: Alan Champion, Candace Broecker Penn, and Lynnette Taylor; DOI: Anne Tomasetti.
13. Cecilia Wadensjö, *Interpreting as Interaction* (Routledge, 1998), 43.
14. Alexandria Wailes interviewed by Lynnette Taylor and Candace Broecker Penn, June 20, 2020.
15. Screenshot from "When Theatre Meets Sign Language," Theatre Development Fund, September 27, 2010, https://www.youtube.com/watch?v=wUK_OUxN-1Q.
16. Screenshot.
17. Jemina Napier, "Interpreting Omissions: A New Perspective," *Interpreting* 6, no. 2 (2004): 117–42, https://doi.org/10.1075/intp.6.2.02nap.
18. *39 Steps*, by Patrick Barlow, adapted from the 1915 novel by John Buchan and the 1935 film by Alfred Hitchcock, dir. Eileen Atkins, 2008 Broadway production produced by the Roundabout Theatre at the American Airlines Theatre. Interpreting team: Stephanie Feyne, Bill Moody, Keith Wann, and Molly Wilson; DOI: Anne Tomasetti.
19. "Cheating Out," TDF Dictonary. Accessed April 10, 2025. https://www.tdf.org/on-stage/theatre-dictionary/search-by-letter/cheating-out/.
20. A.R.T./NY, ART New York, accessed April 22, 2022, https://artny.memberclicks.net/assets/images/Roundabout_ASL.jpg.
21. *Children of a Lesser God* by Mark Medoff, *The Signal Season of Dummy Hoy* by Allen Meyer and Michael Nowak, *Tribes* by Nina Raine, *I Was Most Alive With You* by Craig Lucas, *Grey House* by Levi Holloway, *Private Jones* by Marshall Pailet, *Trash* by James Caverly and Andrew Morrill, *Sign Me Alice* by Gil Eastman, *A Play of Our Own* by Dorothy Miles, *Language of One* by Lewis Merkin and Doug Emery, and *Reflections of a Black Deaf Woman* by Michelle A. Banks.

For more, see Willy Conley, 2023, "*Plays of Our Own: An Anthology of Scripts by Deaf and Hard-of-Hearing Writers*," London: (Routledge Press, 2023).

22. *Big River*, music and lyrics by Roger Miller, book by William Hauptman, Deaf West production, dir. and chor. Jeff Calhoun, with multiple Deaf performers; *Spring Awakening*, book by Steven Sater, score by Duncan Sheik, adapted from the nineteenth-century German play by Frank Wedekind, Deaf West production, dir. Michael Arden, chor. Spencer Lieff, with multiple Deaf performers; *The Music Man*, music, book, and lyrics by Meredith Wilson, co-dir. Sandra Mae Frank and Michael Baron, produced at the Olney Theatre in 2022, with multiple Deaf performers including James Caverly, who won the Helen Hayes Award for Outstanding Lead Actor in a Musical; *The Laramie Project* by Moisés Kaufman and the members of the Tectonic Theatre Company, dir. Jules Dameron, Deaf Austin Theatre production, with multiple Deaf performers; *Raisin in the Sun*, by Lorraine Hansberry, co-dir. Michelle Banks and Nayte Paxton, VOCA production at the Atlas Performing Arts Center, with multiple Deaf performers.
23. *For colored girls who have considered suicide/when the rainbow is enuf*, by Ntozake Shange, 2019 Public Theater production, dir. Leah C. Gardiner, chor. Camille A. Brown, 2022 Broadway revival, dir. and chor. Camille A. Brown, at the Booth Theatre, with Alexandria Wailes (understudy [u/s] Treshelle Edmond on Broadway; *King Lear*, by William Shakespeare, dir. Sam Gold, 2019 Broadway production at the Cort Theatre, with Russell Harvard (u/s John McGinty); *Hunchback of Notre Dame*, music and lyrics by Alan Menken and Stephen Schwartz, dir. Glen Casale, chor. Dana Solimando, 2016 Sacramento production at the Music Circus, with John McGinty; *Fiddler on the Roof*, music by Jerry Bock, lyrics by Sheldon Harnick, book by Joseph Stein, dir. Michael Baron, chor. Brain J. Marcum, 2016 production at the Lyric Theatre of Oklahoma, with Sandra Mae Frank and Christopher Tester; *To Kill A Mockingbird*, by Aaron Sorkin, based on the book by Lee Harper, dir. Bartlett Sher, Broadway production at the Shubert Theatre, with Russell Harvard; *Richard III*, by William Shakespeare, dir. Robert O'Hara, 2022 Public Theater production at the Delacorte Theatre, with Monique Holt (u/s Maleni Chaitoo).
24. Roundabout Theatre, "Cabaret Sign Interpreted Performance," BroadwayWorld.com. accessed April 17, 2025. https://www.broadwayworld.com/article/Cabaret-Sign-Interpreted-Performance-20140620.
25. Alan Cummings, email with Hands On, personal communication, 2014.
26. Molly Wilson and Stephanie Clark, "The Open Process Interpreting Mode: The Power of Language," StreetLeverage 2018, accessed July 15, 2024, https://streetleverage.com/live_presentations/the-open-process-interpreting-model-the-power-of-language/
27. *Hadestown*, music, lyrics, and book by Anaïs Mitchell, dir. Rachel Chavkin, chor. David Neumann. Produced on Broadway at the Walter Kerr Theatre. Hands On interpretation, January 10, 2020. Interpreting team: Alexandria Wailes, Dylan Geil, Justine Rivera, and Lynnette Taylor; DOI: Anne Tomasetti.
28. *Dame Edna: The Royal Tour*, written and performed by Barry Humphries. Produced on Broadway at the Booth Theatre. 2000. Interpreting team: Alan Champion and Candace Broecker Penn.
29. Anne Tomasetti interviewed by Lynnette Taylor and Candace Broecker Penn, June 20, 2020.

6

Interpreting for Young Audiences

"It is crucial that Deaf children have access to the arts. Young audiences today are the artists of tomorrow."

—DJ Kurs, artistic director, Deaf West Theatre[1]

"I love theater. Children should just be able to walk in and feel they belong. When they don't feel that they are of worth, it is heartbreaking to see."

—Alexandria Wailes[2]

All the strategies used for theatre are applicable in children's theatre, but theatre for younger audiences entails additional translation considerations. For many children, this may be their first theatre-going experience or the first time they are seeing an interpreted performance. There is a lot to absorb and, in addition, young audience members will have to navigate when to look at the interpreter and when to look at the stage. Recognizing this, when inviting young audiences into the world of interpreted theatre, teams incorporate age-appropriate strategies, such as language choice and engagement techniques, and cues to guide focus to the stage.

When interpreting children's theatre, the goal is to welcome young audiences by creating an inviting atmosphere and making the space feel comfortable. Before the show, the team meets with the audience, introducing themselves and getting an idea of their language use, their theatre experience, their familiarity with interpreters, and more. Not only are these social interactions pleasurable, but the audience also has time to become familiar with the interpreters, their signing style, and placement during the show.

A friendly conversation with school groups is a rich opportunity for the interpreters to learn from the students, teachers, teaching artists, and classroom interpreters about their preparation for the play. Everyone is included in building the framework for this interpreted theatre experience. Interpreters can engage in an impromptu crowdsourcing strategy by asking the students what signs they use for certain characters or references in the play. These signs can then be incorporated into the interpretations, giving the students agency and involving them in the co-construction of the interpretation. This can make the interpreted space feel more familiar both linguistically and socially.

All the complex interactions that occur in theatre (performer-to-performer, performer-to-audience, audience-to-audience, audience-to-stage, interpreter-to-audience) are heightened and clarified in children's theatre. Since children's theatre is highly participatory, the interpreting team needs to include supports that will encourage audience participation. Perhaps more in this genre than others, honoring the integrity of the play calls for the team to infuse the interpretation with the same playfulness that the actors bring to the stage.

Strategies include:

- Interactive Language
  Children often respond excitedly when performers elicit responses from the audience, such as, "Where are my shoes? Can you help me find them?" In these moments, the interpreters intentionally use dialogic strategies of American Sign Language (ASL), incorporating direct eye contact with the audience, while actively encouraging the signing audience to participate and help the actor find their shoes.
- Narrative Function
  Depending on the age and experience of the audience, the interpreting team may utilize more directive storytelling features, such as guiding their gaze to the stage before continuing with the dialogue. For young children, the interpreters may make statements such as, "Look! There is the Hungry Caterpillar," referring to the stage as if it were a picture book. When many characters are on stage, they may also identify which character is speaking (e.g., "The Queen is saying . . .") before interpreting her actual line. In addition, the narrator function may be effective to describe the actions or feelings occurring onstage, such as, "The Queen feels sad." Especially in children's theatre, the narrator function directly connects the audience to the storytelling.
- Character Depiction
  As a performative translation consideration in children's shows, interpreters may animate the character depiction more than with other audiences.

Of course, every strategy is in response to the age range of the audience as well as the content and style of the show.

One of the magical moments for young Deaf audiences is when they see themselves reflected in the interpreting team. This is true for any underrepresented cultural group. In *Transgressive Bodies*, Niall Richardson writes, "Most people with disabilities do not share their identity with the other members of their family (like, say ethnicity or class) nor with their friends or neighbours."[3] Alexandria Wailes interpreted the title role for the Broadway production of *Cinderella.* In an interview, she shared how elated the Deaf students were when they realized she was a Deaf interpreter. She stated, "My presence sends the message, 'I'm Deaf like you. You can do this too.'"[4]

The more opportunities young Deaf audiences have to see theatre, the more the world opens in a myriad of ways. Paramount is the experience a Deaf young audience has when, in this shared space, they see themselves. As Wailes conveyed, "It opens up a world of possibilities . . . While it is wonderful, [it is also] a bittersweet moment . . . because . . . many Deaf children don't have a lot of exposure to rich sign language models, or to ways of being Deaf in the world. Interactions with Deaf interpreters offer validation, recognition, and affirmation that say 'I belong. I deserve to be here.'"[5]

It is quite thrilling to see the development of young audiences' theatre literacy. There is nothing more rewarding than when they tell the interpreters, "I remember you!" and then watching the flurry of conversation as they share their mini-reviews, starstruck crushes, and wish list for the upcoming season.

There is a growing body of ASL translations of children's literature. These performances by Deaf interpreters and actors offer stellar interpretations geared toward young audiences in many countries and in multiple signed languages. Many of these translations are designed with bilingual literacy in mind, using signed language storytelling techniques in innovative ways to guide young viewers/readers between the signed and the written language. Some examples of early forays into the recording of signed children's literature include Sign Media, Inc.'s *Four for You* and *High 5* series, Linda Bove's series *Sign Me A Story,* and the DawnSignPress's *Once Upon a Time* series with Nathie Marbury and Ben Bahan, to name a few.

More recently, Motion Light Lab at Gallaudet University has been producing translated works and original stories in both signed and written languages with the aim to provide literacy tools for young readers.[6] One of these projects, *Evon Discovers Black Pride,*[7] is a bilingual ASL/English storybook app that invites readers to join Evon as she "explores her family roots and learns about Black Pride." Motion Light Lab founder Melissa Malzkuhn says, "What excites me today is the potential of bringing talented storytellers to young deaf children, no matter where they are in the world. . . . To do this, we need to get the tools and resources out to talented deaf teams and work together to develop more literacy resources."[8]

The entertainment industry has also begun to provide signed translations of movies geared to families such as *Barbie, Finding Nemo, Frozen, Inside Out,* and *Moana,* often with Deaf actors as the interpreters. These frozen translations are additional resources when developing interpretations for young audiences. It is a gift to be able to see these extraordinary language models.

With a growing body of children's literature in signed language, these resources become invaluable for anyone stepping into interpreting for children's theatre.

Notes

1. DJ Kurs, interview with Lynnette Taylor, June 15, 2018.
2. Alexandria Wailes, interview with Lynnette Taylor and Candace Broecker Penn, June 18, 2020.
3. Niall Richardson, *Transgressive Bodies* (Routledge Press, 2016).
4. Wailes, interview.
5. Wailes, interview.
6. Motion Light Lab is part of the Science of Learning Center on Visual Language and Visual Learning (VL2); the storybook apps are designed based on VL2 research to provide an optimal literacy experience for young Deaf/HH children.
7. "Evon Discovers Black Pride," *VL2 Storybook Apps*, accessed January 8, 2025, https://vl2storybookapps.com/evon-discovers-black-pride.
8. Global Book Alliance, "Gallaudet University Envisions a Digital Sign Languages Library for Every Deaf Child," August 22, 2019, https://www.globalbookalliance.org/news-views/gallaudet-university-envisions-a-digital-sign-languages-library-for-every-deaf-child.

7

Considerations for Virtual and Recorded Performances

"How does the emergence of new technologies, such as the central role of digital media in late modernity, shape cultural understandings of the relationship between language and the body, and vice versa?"

—Mary Bucholtz and Kira Hall[1]

"This is new territory for all of us to explore. What we say in five years might be very different from what we say now because technology, as well as culture, changes all the time."

—John McGinty (actor, director of interpreters, and technical advisor)[2]

During the Covid pandemic in 2020, New York City was in lockdown, forcing theatres to close. Artists and theatres sought new ways to invite audiences back by offering online performances. Some of these were new works performed live and recorded on site but without an audience, some were designed specifically for the recorded medium, some were archived footage being offered online, and some were experimental and live-streamed performances. While audiences are returning to live theatre, these online performances and technology are still being integrated and explored in works today.

As these online and streamed performance events increased, so too did the requests for signed interpretation. Interpreters were stepping into this nascent digital performance environment. While many had experience with technology and had worked in virtual settings, strategies specifically designed for the online delivery of artistic content (for both the story and the aesthetic presentation) needed to be developed.

In the words of Christine Marinetti, "Live performance . . . is now profoundly intertwined with technology in ways that will have serious consequences for our understanding of how culture is communicated. As Canning cogently put it,[3] 'theatre is no longer constituted through the physical boundaries of the live.

Instead, it can be tweeted, texted, posted on YouTube, simulcast, and delivered through a host of other electronic means. Local spectators can be transformed into a global audience.'"[4]

Language and Performance Considerations

What works on the stage doesn't always work on the screen, and vice versa. Practices that work in a theatre space, such as larger signing for projecting to audience members several rows back, may overwhelm the visual space in a small digital frame. The medium of film and the compression of a three-dimensional language into a two-dimensional screen, as well as the new spatial relationships (of interpreter to the camera, to the stage, and to their team), generate a new set of questions for the interpreting team. Working with a camera has an impact on language choices and the relationship to the shared interpreting space and to the audience. Bucholtz and Hall share that linguistic anthropologist "Elizabeth Keating (2005) illustrates how Deaf signers innovate new forms of communication and participation, and hence subjectivity, as they adapt their bodies to the constraints and affordances of online webcams."[5]

To be effective, interpreters need to become familiar with the constraints of working in a digital medium and discover what linguistic and performance adjustments are necessary to create signed utterances that look natural in a digital format. The camera becomes a new conversational partner, raising the question of how to interact with it. Even when the camera is a passive observer, the team intermittently connects with the audience by looking to the camera. This helps the audience at home to feel more engaged with the performance. Director of Interpreters (DOI) John McGinty cautions that when an interpreter's eye gaze breaks from the camera for too long, there is a potential disconnect from the audience.

Due to the two-dimensional nature of the medium, teams need to explore sign choices and delivery to ensure clarity by considering: Does the interpretation fit within the frame? How much of the body is visible in the camera shot? Is it best to deliver signs directly to or slightly away from the camera and at what angle (three-fourths, full frontal, etc.)? Is there a need to produce signs differently (e.g., open the hand, change placement, slow down)? How does speed of delivery affect clarity?

John McGinty reminds us to be cognizant of how the camera affects the interpretation, "Using a large signing space or overly animated facial expressions can be distracting or interfere with the performance on the screen."[6] The goal is to strike a balance between the visual action of the performance and visual delivery of the interpretation. McGinty continues, "This allows the Deaf audience the freedom to take in both visual sources without needing to be glued to the interpreter and miss what's happening on the screen."[7]

SHARING MEANING SPACE ON A VIRTUAL PLATFORM

In live theatre, the physical space is shared by the audience and the interpreting team, and everyone sees the same stage picture. In the virtual world, however, the source space (the stage) is separate from the interpreters' space, in which they are constructing an imaginary shared space for an imagined audience. Establishing virtual reference points and identifying the characters in conversation requires more preplanning in this context because the physical references are existing in a different space.

For cohesion of the interpretation, the interpreting team needs to make explicit spatial agreements so that the linguistic references in the signed conversations align with the virtual "stage" space. To do that, the team needs to map and agree upon the virtual referents (where characters and events on the screen are located). For example, if the actor in the recorded sequence reaches for a box to their right, but the interpreter reaches for it to their left, it would be incongruous. The more spatial details that are incorporated into a virtual interpretation, the more the imaginary space becomes integrated, and the more cohesion there is in the translation.

The team also needs to consider their screen placement in relation to each other and the stage source, and this becomes even more critical when interpreters are filmed while in separate locations. The team needs to know where the interpreters' placement will be vis-à-vis the performance area onscreen (to our left or our right, or above or below our signing frame). It will also be necessary to know where the individual interpreters will be placed on the screen in relation to each other (which interpreter is to the left or right, or above or below each interpreter's signing frame). Mapping and discursive considerations are different for each configuration.

DIALOGIC USE OF CAMERA

Virtual interpretations are developed with the premise of the camera as an additional team member. This requires camera-friendly strategies. When deciding to use a direct address to the camera, there are several factors to consider.

The camera can take on multiple imaginary roles: the virtual audience, the virtual character, the virtual stage, and virtual interpreter team. The moment-to-moment relationship to the camera needs to be understood in relation to the narrative so that decisions can be made about how to interact with the camera throughout the performance. The director's and actors' choices inform the interpreters' relationship to the camera.

Knowing who the camera is affects the interpretation. Questions that guide the team's interaction with the camera include: How can the camera help to clarify discursive relationships? What is the impact of looking directly into the camera? Is the camera a communicative partner? If so, who is it at that moment? Is it the audience, a character being addressed, the inner world of the character during a monologue, or our interpreting team? For example, if an actor engages an (imaginary) audience member, saying, "You sir, were in my dream last night dressed as a gorilla," the interpreter would directly address the camera as well. The interpreter might also choose to sign directly to the camera during a character's monologue, as the narrator, or if a character is making an aside to the audience.

Does this dialogic partner respond back? If so, how can these responses be incorporated in an interactive way? Natural discourse features are utilized to guide our dialogic use of the camera. Since our goal is to create interpretations that look natural and conversational, we must remember to interact with the camera as we would in a signed conversation with someone and include the natural signed nuances that would occur in an ASL conversation.

It is helpful to imagine the camera as another person in the room *with you* and let that imaginary presence guide your turn-taking, interaction, and gaze accordingly. Think about your signed face-to-face interactions. When do you look to and when do you look away from someone? Why do you do that? The same factors apply in the virtual world as in the physical world.

It is worth exploring the dialogic use of the camera ahead of time. We recommend recording the team in rehearsal, then evaluating the language to see if it looks natural in the framing and if the work complements the play's action on the screen.

Teaming in the Virtual Realm

The onscreen positions of the interpreters in relation to each other and the performers add additional demands on navigating timing and focus. The team makes agreements about how to indicate which characters are talking to whom, so as to clarify the communicative relationship between the interpreters on screen. The team needs to know their physical placement on screen in order to make dialogic agreements. Eye gaze, indexing, or other strategies need to be carefully considered to make clear who is interacting with whom. The signed dialogue must support the corresponding onscreen sight lines (between the interpreters and also their screen relationship to the performers and the performance). Teams will need to agree in advance how to designate their conversational partner (e.g., mother, boss, Santa Claus, name sign) as well as specific agreements for handling backchanneling and other dialogic norms.

John McGinty worked with The New Victory Theater as they designed signed interpretations for their online content. He shared, "I always recommend that the interpreters be in the same room while filming whenever possible because it is easier for dialogue to maintain the same rhythm, tone, expression and natural turn-taking when they are together."[8]

If the interpreters are being filmed together in the same location, many of the same strategies used in live interpretation can be applied. When interpreters are filmed in separate locations and/or will be shown in separate windows, more questions have to be answered. What is their relative position (Interpreter A to the right, the left, above, or below Interpreter B)? And what their position will be relative to the actors (again—to the right, the left, above, or below) because their positions will affect the spatial referents being developed.

In the virtual world, it becomes even more critical for timing to be precise. There is not the same latitude with lag time in the digital medium as there is in live theatre. The editing of scenes constrains the timing even more. In order to ensure that interpreted utterances are complete, there needs to be clear communication with the technical crew about when the interpreters will be taken off-screen.

In the digital realm, some of the nonlexical signaling strategies used for the camera may need to be adjusted. In fact, "interactional researchers are able to show in fine detail how minute movements such as the flash of an eyebrow, the twist of a torso, or the lifting of a finger are consequential for ongoing talk and other activities."[9] In this medium, eye gaze will go a long way accompanied by, if needed, a slight tilt of the head or a slight body shift toward the action if needed. The camera will pick up these subtle cues, so this can be used to its full advantage.

Technical Considerations

The following are some of the technical considerations that will help the team be prepared to work in the virtual setting.

The interpreting team will need copies of the script and access to the recorded performance with captions. A determination needs to be made about who is responsible for the recording and where the filming will take place. If the interpreter is recording the interpretation off-site and with their own equipment, what kind of technical support will be offered?

The team will need access to a technical package that includes lighting, a recording device (phone, tablet, or camera), a tripod and/or stand for the device, a solid color background, and a separate monitor or device to view the source performance. Prior to the recording, directorial and technical issues need to be addressed:

- Will the interpretation be recorded in a continuous take or shot in segments? The team makes agreements about the duration of each shot.
- Will the DOI or Deaf technical advisor work with the screen manager to choreograph placement of the interpreter's windows, or when the interpreters are visible or not visible on screen?
- It is helpful to have a discussion of the background for the interpreters. Aesthetic considerations will influence the choice of color and style.
- It is always advisable to do a test run before the final shoot and check the background, lighting, interpreter's framing, and internet connectivity (if needed).
- Will there be captions on the final product?
    - If so, will some of the auditory information (e.g., sound effects) be presented only using captions or will the interpretation include that information? Who makes that decision?
    - Who determines placement of the captions to ensure that the signed interpretation and the captions are both visible?

If interpreting team members are recording from separate locations, additional questions include:

- Background—Will the interpreting team have the same background? If so, who will provide that?
- Video file sharing—How will the video files be shared (Dropbox, Google Drive, WeTransfer, etc.)?
- Who is responsible for recording the interpretation?
- An assistant to help with the production needs (such as starting and stopping playback of the source material, turning the recording device on and off, setting the appropriate height of the tripod, lighting, and general troubleshooting) would be a plus.

Considerations for when the interpretation is live-streamed:

- Will there be a screen manager monitoring the interpreters' placement on the screen?
- Will the interpreters be on camera the entire time? If so, be mindful of your onscreen presence even when not interpreting.

COMPOSITION ON THE SCREEN

Screen composition is an important relationship to consider. Where will the interpreters be placed on the screen in relation to the action and to each other?

Examples of interpreter placement:

- In a frame that is separate and distinct from the performance space (e.g., side by side, above or below, in a corner, etc.) as shown in figure 7.1.

2022, Patrick Ferreri and P. Tyler Britt
Interpreters: Monique Sarpy and Jeniece Frasier

2021, Patrick Ferreri and Melle Phillips
Interpreters: Justine Rivera and Monique Sarpy

New Victory ® Dance with sign language interpreters.

Figure 7.1. Two examples of virtual interpreter placement. Video stills courtesy of New 42/ New Victory Theater.

Zack Ramadan, assistant director of Creative Content at the New Victory Theater, collaborated with Candace Broecker Penn from Hands On in changing the design of interpreters on the screen after seeing pieces directed by Jules Dameron for Sesame Street's YouTube channel and a signed infomercial from Apple. Zack noted, "They place the interpreter in a square right next to the main video, which results in eyelines being more parallel with the onscreen speaker. Instead of having to look up-left and down-right, I'm just looking left and right. The result feels like neither is subordinate—the visual parity between the two reinforces that the interpretation is just as important as the sourcematerial."[10]

- Interpreters alongside actors in a gallery view (figure 7.2)

  In 2021, the Actor's Theatre of Louisville incorporated interpreters in their live Zoom performance of *Block Association Project*. This interactive play simulated a town hall meeting, with Deaf actor John McGinty leading some of the discussions in the breakout rooms. The technical directors customized the Zoom view to keep the interpreters and actors in their assigned locations onscreen. The design and delivery of this interpreted performance was overseen by Alexandria Wailes, the DOI for this project.

- Another option is for the theatre to provide two links, one for viewing the performance and a separate one for viewing the interpreters. The National Football League, The National Association of the Deaf, and LOVESIGN have provided streamed performances by Deaf artists during the Super Bowl on a separate link since 1992.

Figure 7.2. Block Association Project. Top left to bottom right: Interpreter Amber Marince, Lauren Lane, Interpreter Cathleen Riddley, Jane Park, Anne-Marie Trabolsi, Myra Lucretia Taylor, Ceci Fernández, Nathan Darrow, and John McGinty. Image provided by Actors Theatre of Louisville.

It is important for the team to know what the final product will look like when viewed by the audience because each configuration will affect translation choices. Decisions for optimal interpreter placement should include considerations of what makes the narrative the most clear and supports the vision of the performance.

Examples of Virtual Interpretations

While many theatres around the country were shutting down due to Covid in 2020, The New Victory Theater in New York City posted a series of recorded performances and made them more accessible by including audio description, captioning, and interpreting. Since The New Victory and Hands On had a long and successful history of providing interpretations of live performances, their collaboration continued for the interpreted recordings. They experimented with the placement and size of the interpreters' screens to find the optimal configuration for each show and shared those decisions with each team prior to filming the interpretations.

The New Victory Theater provides administrative and technical support, including space and crew for filming and editing. Hands On selects the interpreting team, which includes a DOI as well as a Deaf technical advisor who collaborates with the theatre's technical director throughout the process. John McGinty has functioned in both capacities and discusses the benefits of separating the roles of DOI and technical advisor:

> Keeping these roles distinct makes the collaboration more effective because as the technical advisor, I can focus on the timing and all the technical aspects while the DOI focuses on the translation process. It is also beneficial to have more than one pair of Deaf eyes on the interpretation. This allows us an opportunity to discuss different interpreting strategies for the camera, such as spatial referents, the use of role shifting and direct address, and the effectiveness of each in front of the camera.[11]

The theatre supplies the Deaf technical advisor with a script and a time-coded captioned video. The Deaf technical advisor and the theater's tech person then work on breaking the script down into smaller segments, making it easier for the interpreters to both shoot and reshoot segments, as necessary. They also design the aesthetic presentation, which includes the appropriate background color and wardrobe attire to complement the backdrop. It is important to schedule ample time for takes and retakes.

John McGinty works with the information provided by the theatre to prepare the shooting timeline, "I appreciate when the company adds the time code into the script. This helps me know the timing of when scenes start and stop so that I can create a schedule for recording segments."[12] In his capacity as technical advisor, he organized the shooting of each scene by time code, interpreter, the character being represented, and their placement on the screen, and he also noted questions for the technical crew. He generously shared a sample of his work:

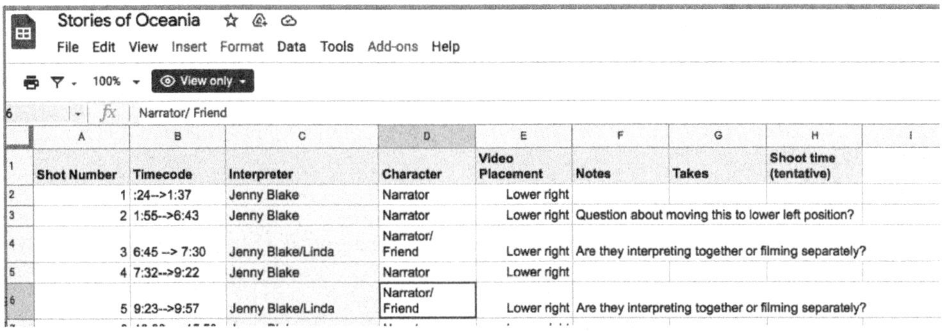

Shot Number	Timecode	Interpreter	Character	Video Placement	Notes	Takes	Shoot time (tentative)
1	:24-->1:37	Jenny Blake	Narrator	Lower right			
2	1:55-->6:43	Jenny Blake	Narrator	Lower right	Question about moving this to lower left position?		
3	6:45 --> 7:30	Jenny Blake/Linda	Narrator/ Friend	Lower right	Are they interpreting together or filming separately?		
4	7:32-->9:22	Jenny Blake	Narrator	Lower right			
5	9:23-->9:57	Jenny Blake/Linda	Narrator/ Friend	Lower right	Are they interpreting together or filming separately?		

Figure 7.3. Shooting breakdown for *Stories of Oceania*.[13] Photo courtesy of John McGinty.

While filming, the DOI and Deaf technical advisor consider choices that work well with the camera. They monitor the interpreters' spatial references to ensure that team eye gaze agreements and references are aligned and that signs are within the screen space, and offer direction as needed. The theatre's tech director and the Deaf technical advisor keep track of the best takes for editing. In the example shown in figure 7.4, Bill Moody is being filmed while interpreting from his source material, a digital performance of *The Snail and The Whale*.[14]

Figure 7.4. John McGinty, ASL technical director, and Zack Ramadan, assistant director of Creative Content, monitor two screens—the live recording of the interpretation and the prerecorded performance. Photo courtesy of Candace Broecker Penn. *The Snail and the Whale*, The New Victory Theater, 2021.

Another early foray into the interpreted digital performance realm was The Public Theater's production of *The Line*. In 2020, Jessica Blank and Erik Jensen developed a documentary-style online performance about the physical, emotional, and spiritual toll on frontline workers during the early stages of Covid as the pandemic swept across New York City. Eight actors portrayed the workers sharing their experiences in this powerful piece.

Anne Tomasetti, the DOI for the project, working with Hands On and with the support of The Public Theater, hired eight Deaf actors to interpret the series of monologues. She directed the Deaf actors and guided their performance and translation considerations. She also worked closely with The Public Theater's technical crew, advising the editor on the timing of the exits and entrances of the Deaf interpreters, as well as the overall aesthetic design of their screen placement. She set the bar for the kind of collaboration needed to make a quality product. Such a collaboration requires willingness and expertise on both ends—the theatre and the interpreting team.

Tomasetti wanted to give primacy to both forms of delivery—the spoken word and the signed word—and looked for creative ways to support the narrative structure and intent of the scene. This included exploring the distinctions between acting and interpreting. This early foray into a collaborative production of interpreted performance in the digital realm addressed many of the foundational questions of this genre. Tomasetti described her process, "Initially, I dramaturged the play and outlined the arc of each character as well as how each monologue fit into the play's increasing intensity as the crisis worsened. I then shared this with the ASL team and asked them to develop their translations with this in mind, building a throughline for their character and the play."[15]

To document the DOI/interpreter/theatre collaboration that occurred with *The Line*, The Alliance of Resident Theatres/New York (A.R.T./ New York) hosted a webinar, "Zoom In: Best Practices for ASL Interpretation in Virtual Theatre," with Rich Denney, director of audience services at The Public Theater; Beth Prevor, executive director of Hands On Sign Interpreted Performances; and Anne Tomasetti, the DOI and technical advisor for the interpreted production. This video can be viewed on the A.R.T./ New York YouTube page at bit.ly/3DKazDL.[16]

Beginning in 2020, Deaf Broadway (Garrett Zuercher, James Caverly, Miriam Rochford, and Kimberly Hale) began to experiment with using the Zoom platform for a full Deaf cast rendition of musicals.[17] They played the recorded video of a Broadway production on a portion of the screen, and the Deaf signing cast appeared in individual windows positioned to the right. Their screen entrances and exits were coordinated by a screen manager. The creative use of screen choreography, along with their exciting performances, introduced new vocabulary in the repertoire of signed digital performance. They continue to experiment with these forms in their live productions.

An additional bonus of these online forays is having access to a virtual library of interpreting models by interpreters, Deaf interpreters, and Deaf talent. This gives us the means to reflect and assess the possibilities of technical and translatory choices, as well as allowing us to explore new ways to work in this digital realm.

One exciting prospect of working digitally is that members of teams no longer need to be in the same location to rehearse and interpret for a virtual show. There is the option to team with colleagues from across the country. This allows for a shared conversation and the opportunity to collectively develop practices and approaches to the work. To illustrate this, during the 2021–22 season, the New Victory Theater planned to present the digital version of *Stories of Oceania* by the Honolulu Theatre for Youth. Because it was virtual, Hands On was able to hire a Deaf and hearing interpreting team based in Hawaii. An extra boon was that the team was familiar with The Honolulu Theatre for Youth.

In addition, audiences are no longer restricted by geography. These recorded interpreted performances are shared online and available for periods of time to the entire ASL community.

In the words of Bucholtz and Hall, "More openness is needed to meet the challenges posed by the new contexts surrounding translation today. For instance, we have only just begun to map the effects that technology is having on the way we think, communicate and relate with one another (Cronin 2013), all activities that are central to translation."[18]

Regardless of how technology changes, the dialogic and interactive interpreting strategies are always guided by the intention to engage in conversation with our audience, the production, and our team.

Notes

1. Mary Bucholtz and Kira Hall, "Embodied Sociolinguistics," in *Sociolinguistics: Theoretical Debates*, ed. Nikolas Coupland (Cambridge University Press, 2016): 173–97.
2. John McGinty, interview with Candace Broecker Penn, January 4, 2022.
3. Charlotte Canning, "Editorial: Looking Ahead," in *Theatre Research International* 38, no. 1 (2013): 1–4
4. Cristina Marinetti, "Translation and Theatre: From Performance to Performativity," in *Target International Journal of Translation Studies* 25, no. 3 (2013): 317.
5. Bucholtz and Hall, "Embodied Sociolinguistics."
6. McGinty, interview.
7. McGinty, interview.
8. McGinty, interview.
9. Bucholtz and Hall, "Embodied Sociolinguistics."
10. Zack Ramadan, email to Candace Broecker Penn, July 15, 2022. Reprinted with permission.
11. McGinty, interview.
12. McGinty, interview.
13. *Stories of Oceania*, written and performed by the Honolulu Theatre for Youth Ensemble, 2022, digitally available via New Victory Theater. Interpreting team: Jenny Blake and Linda Lambrecht; ASL tech. dir. John McGinty.

14. *The Snail and The Whale*, by the Tall Stories Theatre Company, adapt. Julia Donaldson and Axel Scheffler, dir. Toby Mitchell, interp. Candace Broecker Penn and Bill Mood, DOI and ASL tech. dir. John McGinty, The New Victory Theater, New York, NY, November 17, 2021–June 30, 2022.
15. Anne Tomasetti, interview with Lynnette Taylor and Candace Broecker Penn, June 20, 2020.
16. A.R.T./New York, "Zoom In: Best Practices for ASL Interpretation in Virtual Theatre." YouTube, June 1, 2021, 1:28:16, https://www.youtube.com/watch?v=SVND3xjhXSI.
17. "Deaf Broadway," accessed May 7, 2025. https://www.deafbroadway.com/.
18. Bucholtz and Hall, "Embodied Sociolinguistics."

8

Building an Ecosystem

> "Access to theater is very important for me as a Deaf person because of equity . . . I'm a part of this world, a member of humanity, a citizen of the world, and I want to be included. Art has the power to bring about change and the ability to change the world. I, too, want to change the world through art. But if we keep our worlds separate, that won't be possible. Without access, I can't keep up with the current social issues and political trends. Access to this knowledge empowers me. As an empowered person I can change the world with you."
>
> —Frank Dattolo, actor, educator, translator, and theatregoer[1]

An interpreted show is not just another "ordinary" day at the theatre. Bringing signed languages and Deaf audiences into the theatre invites audiences to consider that there are many ways to tell a story, many stories to be told, many ways to live a life, and that diversity is the heart of humanity. Interpreting for the theatre performed in a public space invites the potential for all kinds of connections, relations, and understandings to occur. It is a reminder, in the words of Sonia Nieto, that "affirming language diversity is at the heart of democratic and civic life."[2]

When these public spaces are open, unexpected encounters can happen. It was pure serendipity that the great grandnephew of Thomas Hopkins Gallaudet had a Roundabout Theatre subscription series that fell on the same schedule as the sign interpreted performances. On these occasions, he would come over and introduce himself to the interpreters and the Deaf audience and proudly share his lineage. He was always greeted warmly and "fussed over." The interpreters ensured that there was easy communication between the audience members and this gentleman—a brush with history.

Exposure to interpreted theatre can also bring an awareness of new possibilities to audience members. During the intermission of a Broadway show, a woman approached the interpreting team and told them she had a Deaf granddaughter. She never thought she could share her love of theatre with her granddaughter and couldn't wait to bring her to the next interpreted show.

Interpreted theatre is a rare opportunity for families who are both Deaf and hearing to come together and share an experience. Roy Stelzer, a Deaf teacher who attends interpreted family theatre, said, "I see some of my deaf and Deaf-parented students with their families. It's wonderful to see the whole family enjoying theatre together."[3]

Often, Deaf students from multiple schools and programs attend interpreted performances on the same day. Zavier Sabio reflecting on the experience of Deaf students says,

> Theatre is a perfect hub for communities to come together and find each other and themselves. They see that sign is an important part of the Deaf community, a language that brings a sense of pride, and that they too can feel a sense of pride in being Deaf . . . Kids begin to dream of themselves as artists.[4]

Sometimes, we interpreters do not realize the influence that our presence in the theatre has on an audience. Lynnette recalls one instance when an audiologist approached the interpreting team after a show and explained that his entire view of Deafness and American Sign Language (ASL) had been upended after watching the performance. His training had led him to believe that sign language was an obstacle to learning to speak, a rudimentary form of gestures, and that learning sign language would be detrimental to a child's language development. By observing the Deaf community interaction as well as the interpreted performance, he realized not only that sign language could express complex concepts (for him a recognition of its status as a language) but also that the community shared a language and a culture. He said he would now encourage his clients to learn sign language.

Lynnette states, "It was then that I realized, the space in front of the house is not only for interpreting theatre, but also functions as a kind of political real estate, a site with the potential to awaken minds, change attitudes about language diversity and Deaf culture. And as every New Yorker knows, one of the most precious commodities is real estate, so we do not want to give up that political real estate, that site of potential."[5]

Part of stepping into a public space as an interpreter is to recognize that we are stepping into a social, historical, and complex political narrative derived from the power dynamics of a colonized past defined by who has been at the center of the narrative; who has been telling the stories; who makes the decisions about language use; who is representing the stories; which languages, cultures, and bodies have been invited in and which have not; how and by whom are these decisions being made. Sharing public space is a key to affording historically separate communities an opportunity to engage with each other, offering potential for greater social change.

Over time, we have seen the power of this engagement seep into the theatre and the field of entertainment in many ways. It isn't unusual to see cast members use the visual hand wave for applause or the "I Love You" sign "ILY" or "Thank you" during the curtain calls for interpreted shows. On national television, Chuck Cooper, winner of the 2022 Tony Awards Best Featured Actor for *Trouble in Mind*, signed ILY to the camera as it zoomed in on him during the nominee announcement. A testament to the strides that the community has made!

Stepping into the mainstream, Deaf actors have become a familiar presence in theatre, television, and films. Deaf West Theatre brought two shows to Broadway to great acclaim, *Big River* and *Spring Awakening*. Several recent television series such as *The Walking Dead, New Amsterdam, This Close, The Last of Us, Echo*, and *Switched at Birth* bring Deaf talent into people's living rooms. Newer films such as *CODA* (Oscar for Best Actor, Best Film), *Eternals, A Quiet Place 1* and *2, Sound of Metal, Baby Driver*, and *Wonderstruck* feature Deaf actors on the big screen.

Around the country, works are being presented by Deaf playwrights and directors with Deaf actors. In New York City, Deaf performers have trod the boards on Broadway with Kenny Leon's production of *Our Town* with John McGinty, *Grey House* with Millicent Simmonds, *for colored girls . . .* with Alexandria Wailes, and *King Lear* with Russell Harvard; and Off Broadway with The Public Theater's *Dark Disabled Stories* with Dickie Hearts (Obie winner Best New American Play), The Public Theater's *Richard III* with Monique Holt and Maleni Chaitoo, Playwrights Horizons' *I Was Most Alive with You* starring Russell Harvard and Tad Cooley (including lighting designer Annie Weigand and seven Deaf actors interpreting the show), and Lincoln Center's presentations of Deaf Broadway productions. Currently, ASL translations of Shakespeare plays are underway with Directors of Artistic Sign Language (DASLs) working in collaboration with The Public Theater and the Apothetae, as well as Fiasco Theater and Deaf West Theatre. Deaf playwrights Joey Caverly and Andrew Morill had their work *Trash* performed as part of Jack's "Radical Acts" festival, and Garret Zuercher's *Inside/Look* was presented as part of the Shed's Open Call program.

Extending beyond the stage into New York City cultural institutions, works by Deaf artists (such as Christine Sun Kim and Chella Man), Deaf poets, and ASL Slam events (founded by Douglas Ridloff) have been presented at various museums, including the Museum of Modern Art, the Whitney Museum, the Jewish Museum, and the Guggenheim Museum. Noah Buchholz, one of the Deaf poets showcased at the Guggenheim Museum's Sound/Off, an event organized by Meg Day, their 2024 poet-in-residence, stated, "Now that society has largely acknowledged the existence of Deaf culture and sign language, it is time to delve deeper into Deaf culture and learn more about the contributions it can make to mainstream society."[6]

Seeing interpreted theatre as part of a more complex ecosystem can be a countermeasure to the "tick box" practice of access, which views an interpreted performance as a one-off work-for-hire process, separate from the art and life of the theatre community and its audiences. If an interpreted event has relevance only for the duration of the occasional show, it becomes a more transactional relationship among the interpreter, signing community, and the institutions that hire them. These "tick box" approaches, as Ahmed (2012) refers to them, include "when institutions can 'show' that they are following procedures but are not really 'behind' them (showing can be a way of not committing),"[7] as a way of gaining institutional benefit but offering no reciprocal community benefits.

An antidote to these transactional approaches is to extend the collaborative practices into the larger ecosystem in which interpreted theatre lives. It's an ideological shift for everyone to see interpreted theatre as more than access, indeed, as part of a larger, more complex ecosystem. When seen within a larger arts and community system, it no longer feels so insular and separate, but rather interconnected, laying at our fingers a wider swath of thinkers and doers, with the capacity to enact social change. Dattolo states, "You, as access providers, have no idea how powerful you are. You have the ability to change the world."[8] In case this feels a bit daunting, Chef Bryant Terry reassures us, "All hands lifting makes the load lighter."[9]

A collaborative approach intentionally explores ways to increase community interactions and build more networks to invite more people in. The aim is to bring communities together, elevate the art, create systems that support each other, and turn interpreted performances into vibrant multicommunity experiences. The aspiration is for cultural spaces to become welcoming "third spaces," which, again, in Corinna Hill's words are "crucial for fostering social interactions, creating a sense of belonging, and enhancing overall well-being"[10] for all the communities sharing that space.

It Begins with the Deaf Community

The National Association for the Deaf, along with many disabled activists, take the following stance: "Nothing about us without us." Only those from within the community can know what really serves the community.

For many years, the Theatre Development Fund (TDF) Interpreting for the Theatre Seminar invited Deaf individuals to discuss their contributions to the development of programs for signing audiences at local theatres. Panelists Sue Decker, Eileen Forrestal, Lewis Merkin, among others shared how they convinced theatres to provide interpreted performances. All of them pointed out the importance of having Deaf people involved from the get-go. This fostered relationships between the theatre and the community, thus gaining credibility among future signing audiences.

A single request from a patron asking to see a specific show interpreted could be the spark that later leads to more robust programming. Eileen Forestal recalls that in the early 1980s, New Jersey had no interpreted theatre and she reached out to Papermill Playhouse in Millburn, New Jersey. She explained, "After inviting their executive director to see an interpreted show in New York, it was a complete buy-in . . . Through connections with the Deaf community, we got support from a variety of sources including the NJ Division of the Deaf and Hard of Hearing and also NJRID (New Jersey Registry of Interpreters for the Deaf)."[11] Forestal, along with members of the Deaf and interpreting community, helped them vet interpreters and advised on the best placement for the interpreters and the optimal seating for the signing audience.[12] Since theatres are often searching for ways to invite in new audiences, these initial contacts can lead to long-lasting relationships between the theatre and the signing audience.

Community resources are invaluable as they can offer theatres information about how to find qualified interpreters and Directors of Interpreters (DOIs), provide outreach to the ASL community, and offer optimal interpreted performance date suggestions that won't conflict with other ASL community events.

Responsibilities of the Theatre

Theatres need to recognize theatre interpreting teams as "vital collaborators in the storytelling process," like all staff in the theatre. Zachary Stewart, chief critic for TheaterMania, points out that, "Producers and directors should absolutely treat house and security staff as vital collaborators in the storytelling process, rather than just crowd control. They are the people who set the tone in the lobby and the line outside, and that makes them part of the performance."[13]

While this book addresses a more traditional proscenium presentation of a play with the interpreters abutting the stage, there is room for creativity in the design of the interpreted performance so that it responds to the theatre's unique space and the creative team's sensibilities and vision for the production. There are multiple options for placement of the interpreters onstage—shadow, zoned, integrated, projected—each incorporating the interpreter(s) in a different way. Theatres can be creative in the forms of delivery as long as it resonates with the Deaf audience. Some artists may want interpreters dressed in attire that corresponds to the play (as in interpreted shows at Dance Theatre Workshop). Regardless of the way in which the interpretation is integrated into the theatre space and the performance, there are still requisite preparatory steps that must happen for the program to be successful.

In order for interpreted theatre to be effective, there first has to be a commitment from the theatre to the signing audience. This means institutional support for the interpreting teams. The first level of institutional support is to include interpreting services in their budget.

The second level is hiring a skilled interpreting team, including the Deaf DOI. Working with a local organization that has expertise in the field of interpreted theatre can establish connections with high-caliber interpreting teams. In addition, these organizations can also serve as a valuable resource for audience development within the Deaf community.

While an interpreted event has many components, these are the bare necessities for an interpreted performance. Once an interpreting team is hired, the theatre is responsible for providing the following:

- Copies of the script for each team member
- Audio or video recordings of the show when possible
- Access to the theatre to see the performances (ideally as many times as possible before the event)
- Arrangements for rehearsal locations on-site

- Placement of the interpreting team with good visibility for the ASL audience members
- Seating for the ASL signing audience in close proximity to the interpreting team
- Lighting for the interpreters

Theatres in New York City, as well as regional and local theatres across the country, are increasingly providing access to audio and/or video recordings of performances for rehearsal purposes. However, nothing is as beneficial as having access to the live performance.

The DOI works with the interpreting team and the theatre staff to determine the optimal placement and lighting in front of the stage that can accommodate a team of three or four interpreters. DOIs also can provide guidance for seating that ensures optimal viewing of the interpreted show.

The theatre often arranges an opportunity for the cast and interpreting team to be introduced and logistics discussed, such as curtain call, interpreters' entrances and exits into the interpreting space, and any questions that arise. Actors sometimes initiate conversations with the interpreting team (e.g., "How do you sign my line?," "Which of you is interpreting for my character?," and "How do we sign 'thank you' to the audience?").

Everything works more smoothly when there is a dedicated point person from the theatre working with the team to coordinate all logistics. During the interpreted performance, it's crucial that the theatre has designated individual(s) to address unanticipated glitches, such as when the light on the interpreters goes out, when a patron in the interpreted section needs a seat reassignment, or any other needs.

Theatres, theatre interpreting organizations, and DOIs have approached events in creative ways working with house, box office, and audience development staff to enhance the theatre experience.

As Zachary Stewart reminds us, storytelling begins in the house. Ushers have learned basic signs to communicate directly with audience members—guiding them to their seats, restrooms and other simple interactions. Some ushers have had their mobile device at the ready with preprogrammed large font texts "WELCOME TO THE THEATRE. CAN I HELP YOU FIND YOUR SEAT?" These casual interactions create a more welcoming theatre experience for Deaf and signing audiences.

The inclusion of the interpreting team in the program book, a common practice in New York City theatre, makes public the theatre's institutional support of interpreting and recognizes their work. They include photos and bios of the team, as well as a brief description of the sponsoring organization working with the theatre. Sometimes, illustrations or photos of the character name signs are also included.

Many theatres hire Deaf community liaisons or work with the DOI to engage in outreach, by posting signed videos that inform the audience about the upcoming interpreted performance on social media platforms and/or email these informational videos to their signing audiences.

Some have created special events in conjunction with the interpreted shows specifically for the signing patrons. When *Tribes* was performed at Berkeley Repertory Theatre, the theatre hired a Deaf liaison to coordinate community outreach, video advertisements in ASL, bathroom signage with historical factual info regarding sign language, and Deaf culture trivia as a way to infuse the theatre with cultural information. The Oregon Shakespeare Festival offered preshow sessions hosted by the team's DOI to introduce the audience to the play and to specific signs be used in the interpretation. Several theatres have offered discounted individual tickets and subscriptions to their season of interpreted performances to develop new audiences from the signing community. One of these, the Roundabout Theatre subscription series, came about through conversations between Beth Prevor from Hands On and Julia Levy, their development director. Levy reasoned that offering a season subscription developed deeper ties between the theatre and its audience. It was an agreement with mutual benefits—a commitment from the theatre to provide ongoing services and a commitment from the community to support the theatre by becoming subscribers.

Pre- and postshow talkback sessions with the cast and audience are often part of a theatre's regular programming, providing additional background information for the performance. These events are an extension of the interpreted performance. As mentioned in chapter 2, some DOIs will give a brief introduction before the show.

In addition to interpreting the regularly scheduled audience talkbacks, Hands On has been offering DOI-moderated postshow conversations in ASL between the signing audience and the interpreting team at the theatre. These ASL community talkbacks provide an opportunity for the audience to share their experience of the play and have an open conversation about the interpreting process.

At a recent ASL community talkback after Robert O'Hara's powerful revival of *Raisin in the Sun* at The Public Theater, Patrice Joyner-Creamer, the DOI, addressed the power of representation in the interpreting team for conveying the story. Among the topics raised by Deaf audience members were translation choices that the team made about provocative triggering language in the play, such as the "N-word."' Music was another question the audience raised. Everyone had a different relationship to music, and they discussed whether, when, and how interpreting the music would be meaningful to their experience as an audience member.

When there is the opportunity to have these postshow discussions—to come together as a community to talk about art, interpreting, the choices made for translations, and the way the interpretation is performed or delivered, it opens the door to the community engaging in a broader, deeper level of inquiry into the nature of meaning itself. In addition, the willingness of the theatres to grant the space is a reflection of their commitment to the signing audience and these community conversations. These are all examples of interpreted theatre as part of a larger ecosystem, which has tendrils that extend to the interpreting, Deaf audience, and theatre communities.

Strategies for connecting with a signing audience in interpreted theatre change over time in response to the audience. When interpreted theatre began in New York City in the early 1980s, interpreting teams tried to identify salient aspects of the theatre-going experience that could be incorporated. Initially, interpreters aligned with theatre conventions. One of the early decisions was that the interpreters would not enter the interpreting space until moments before the show began, emulating the actors entering onstage. The thought was that by honoring the protocols of the theatre, we expressed fidelity to the theatre experience—but it was not as effective as we had hoped; replicating the mainstream theatre experience kept us too aloof from the audience.

We feel aligning with interpreter-Deaf community norms and behaviors was more beneficial to the transmission of the overall message than aligning with the theatre protocols. In our opinion, the most effective way to do that is by creating a welcoming environment that embraces community interactions and social norms (e.g., greeting, hugging, and catching up) in the "hybrid space." These preshow interactions not only strengthen community relations but also offer an opportunity for audience members to adjust to or get a sense of the interpreter's language style. As Beth Prevor says, "It's a community event. It's a different kind of experience than going to the theatre alone. I see people that I know, people hug you . . . ask how you're doing . . . it's a welcoming environment."[14]

The relationship between the theatre, the audiences, and the interpretation is not stagnant. In this chapter, we offer current best practices. Who knows what the future constellation of interpreted theatre will look like?! What we do know is if the service delivery is rooted in the desire to welcome communities into the storytelling, then however the services manifest, they will resonate well with the audience. Creating a welcoming climate that can respond and evolve, as theatres and communities evolve, will maintain community connections and support interpreted performances that reflect the artistry on the stage.

FRAGILITY OF ECOSYSTEMS

Mounting an interpreted performance requires coordination across many departments and community resources and requires specialized knowledge about the field of theatre interpreting. Beth Prevor, executive director of Hands On, explains, "Originally, we developed a timeline for the workflow to produce an interpreted show and shared it with the theatre. We thought that would be enough, and they would simply follow the steps. But when they saw it, they were overwhelmed and didn't know how to or have the resources to do this work, and asked us to do it. So, over the years our work has been both producing the interpreted performances and guiding theatres as they plan for them."[15]

Service systems are fragile, and theatres often rely upon a single individual to make them work. Prevor recognizes that, "Over time, the greatest risk in the continuity of interpreted services is staff turnover, which results in the loss of institutional memory and the loss of connections to both service providers (DOIs, interpreters, and consultants) and the signing audience."[16] Once an individual leaves, the risk is that this coordinating knowledge leaves with them, leaving the theatre in a place of "re-learning" or reinventing the wheel. However, if a theatre has an established relationship with a trusted theatre interpreting organization, it will still be able to continue programs during times of change and maintain the level of quality of their interpreted performances.

What has become evident over the years is that the services, when not baked into the institutions, are more reliant on current trends, budgets, and politics of the time.

Theatre interpreted performances, when coming from an institutional position of simply "ticking the box" or virtue signaling, can result in merely the illusion of access with the dominant culture determining what constitutes access, which may or may not be effective. This system will always be fragile and depend upon the whims of those in power.

Thinking of interpreted theatre as part of a larger ecosystem that is built on a network of ongoing relationships leads to programming that incorporates these services into their practice. This doesn't just happen. It takes intention and attention to develop the relationships that will sustain the services. Dylan Geil, theatre interpreter and Hands On director of programming, advises that "Cultivating a robust network of relationships with artists, directors, producers, and general managers has proven to be the most effective strategy for increasing the number of ASL-interpreted performances on and off Broadway. Much like a family, productions, theaters, and theater companies operate within close-knit circles—gaining access becomes significantly more attainable when an insider advocates on your behalf and invites you in."[17]

INTERPRETER RELATIONSHIPS AND RESPONSIBILITIES

One of the joys of this work is the collaborative nature of working as a team of interpreters. These dynamic interactions keep the work from becoming stagnant and static. In Martine Sainvil's 2022 interview with theatre translators, she noted that they all agreed "the best part of translation for the theater is the collaborative nature of it. They all point to theater translation as being special because it's done in community."[18]

We agree! Our approach entails a kind of reset mindset—away from thinking of this as individual practice, a shifting from the "me" to the "we."

It is a gift to be able to gather in this way and take the time to reflect on our human experience. The stories we are unpacking are the stories of lives, and each of us brings our unique lens to the experience of life. The team's ongoing exploration of what is "culturally universal" and what is "specific" in the play guide our translation decisions. These intersectional, interlingual, and intercultural conversations offer us an even deeper reservoir from which to understand the story and allow us to bond more deeply as a team and as members of a community of practice.

Joy of the work alone, of course, won't pay the rent or feed our bellies, but it will give us the motivation to keep coming back to this work. It would be remiss not to recognize the economic realities of keeping this work and this access alive. There need to be structures in place and an economic commitment from society to support these endeavors. We are grateful to the theatres, organizations, and individuals that sustain this work.

Scheduling—Teaming with Colleagues

The building of community begins with something as simple (never—as freelancers know) as scheduling. Starting the process with a gathering of the team in person or via Zoom offers a space to get to know each other, become familiar with each other's signing style, explore expectations and questions, and schedule rehearsal times. Choosing one member of the team to be the point person to coordinate the schedule and be the liaison with the theatre is beneficial for both the theatre and the interpreting team in that it streamlines communication.

These conversations form the foundation of the team relationship. Agreeing to spend time together is the first step in building a creative community, a space in which everyone feels able and willing to offer perspectives, find moments to play, and collaboratively contribute to the work.

Interpreting theatre is a creative process that is both an individual and a collective undertaking. Even the English-to-German translators for *Hamilton*, (Finale and Shroeder) recognized that the power of co-creating was more successful. They "tried divvying up the songs and writing separately, but didn't like the results, so instead they spent a half year sitting across from one another at the kitchen table in Finale's Berlin apartment, debating ideas until both were satisfied."[19]

While we may not have the luxury of sitting across the table for half a year, regardless of how seasoned an interpreter you are, team co-construction of signed discourse takes longer than just a few meetings or two or three hands-up rehearsals. The team needs time to acclimate to the process, to see the show, to discover the show's inner connections, to listen to each other, and to offer ideas as they collectively create the interpretation, not to mention the time needed for individual translation. And this process will take more time than one thinks—so we have to plan for that. Interpreting for the theatre requires a commitment to the artistry—it is not just a transactional interpreting event.

Patrice Joyner-Creamer, one of the first Deaf interpreters on Broadway and a DOI, emphasized that "one of the most important things for the team to do is to schedule enough time for rehearsals. The team needs to be together to practice cueing, looking at each other, looking at the stage . . ."[20] She also mentioned that when she is an interpreter on the team, "scheduling includes not only the performing team's work, but also time for the Deaf interpreter and the designated co-interpreter to develop and rehearse their agreements."[21]

At times, the team may only have access to a show a week before the interpreted performance (e.g., touring shows). When faced with a tight timeline, the collaborative process is even more beneficial. A lot of the groundwork can be laid before seeing the show. The team can get accustomed to each other, unpack the play, assign characters, and develop individual and team dialogic translations. This doesn't mean that the translations will be fixed in stone, as an integral part of our approach is responsiveness to source, but it gives the team a leg up before walking into the theatre for the first time. Having done the preparatory work of unpacking the play, as well as understanding the story and the character relationships, the team can then readily respond to the live performance.

Responsibility as a Theatre Community Member

Just as in any specialized field, the interpreters need to master not only the practice of interpretation but also be knowledgeable about the world of theatre. The American Association of Community Theatre (AACT) offers a free online dictionary with more than 1,000 definitions of theatrical terms at https://aact.org/terms.[22] The interpreting team interacts with a variety of people who work in the theatre: including the house managers, stage managers, box office, ushers, and performers. These individuals are also liaisons to the signing audience. Interactions with theatre staff leave an impression with the theatre, and as "guests" in the house, interpreters want to make a good impression and be invited back. This means taking the time to recognize the theatre's rules of etiquette. Theatre interpreter Cathy Markland often reminds colleagues that one of the important skills that an interpreter needs to possess is the ability to "play well with others," and this includes everyone in the theatre.

Responsibility to the Artistic Signing Community

Part of the ethical responsibility of being a theatre interpreter is supporting the health and well-being of the artistic communities in which we work. This means in attending Deaf theatre (local, on tour, or online), supporting Deaf artists, and attending interpreted theatre to support as well as learn from our colleagues. Theatre interpreters' repertoires (cultural, linguistic, and sociopolitical) are enriched when they are actively engaged in multiple communities.

Collegial Responsibility

Theatres across the country have been working to address "deeply ingrained systems of White supremacy and racism"[23] in response to "We See You White American Theater." During his 2021 Tony awards acceptance speech for *A Soldier's Play*, Director

Kenny Leon said, "No diss to Shakespeare, no diss to Ibsen, to Chekhov, to Shaw. They're all at the table. But the table got to be bigger."[24]

Theatre interpreters also need to make the interpreting table bigger. Historically, interpreting for theatre has been a homogenous, elite, and closed system. Interpreters, theatres, and the Deaf community together can find ways to welcome everyone to the interpreting table—one that reflects the spectrum of the human experience (cultural, linguistic, racial, religious, gender, disability, and socioeconomic). Moving away from the traditional gatekeeper system and bringing communities together will create new pathways and new partnerships, which can lead to new expressions of interpreted theatre.

The goal is to expand our network of relationships within and among the interpreting, Deaf, and theatre communities. Each community will have its own resources to offer, as will each person. The more the social, cultural, political, economic, and institutional resources are shared, the greater the capacity for change. Through actively supporting each other and the work, interpreters and the signing community are cultivating an ecosystem of joy and justice.

If the greater community thinks of this practice as a means to engage in deeper social transformations, broader ideological and social questions about the future of the field arise: What is interpreted theatre? What should it be? Why do we do it? Moving forward, how can we support positive growth in response to a dynamically changing social world?

As traditional spaces for gathering have dwindled in the ASL community and society at large, the opportunities for these conversations have also dwindled. We cannot go back in time and recreate the systems of the past, nor would we want to, since much of that history is embedded in segregation. With a little planning, conversations with the signing audience can occur not only among a few friends in a coffee shop or bar after the show, but also in a more formalized way in the theatre space.

Building a Vibrant Ecosystem

Actress Laura Linney speaks about the importance of the stage and what motivates her to do the work. "I . . . strongly believe that it [theater] is a part of public good. Theater provides a nourishment, intellectually and emotionally and spiritually, to audiences."[25]

The move from the "me" to the "we" is in seeing ourselves as part of a larger community. We need to be thinking forward, as well as in the moment, and recognize that our individual actions can have consequences that may be harmful to the Deaf and signing community. Our intentions when stepping into these spaces should be guided by what will contribute to the well-being of the community. We must be mindful not to participate in the cultural dislocation of Deaf bodies by appropriating the language and closing the doors to Deaf signing bodies.[26]

Languages and communities are always evolving. Interpreted theatre emerged from a kinship between the two communities, and it should continue that way, guided by a belief that everyone has a right to be a part of the social narrative. As interpreters, our responsibility is to be responsive to the needs and desires of the Deaf community. Even the founders of the Registry of Interpreters for the Deaf recognized that professional interpreters have an obligation to keep these social ties vibrant and alive by staying current with the changes in the language and the community. An original Code of Ethics tenet stated: "The interpreter shall seek to uphold the dignity and purity of the language of signs. He shall also maintain a readiness to learn and accept new signs, if these are necessary to understanding."[27]

What actions can create generative positive growth going forward? What will make the ecosystem healthier? How can we create spaces to engage in courageous conversations that challenge our assumptions and our prior knowledge and allow room for new ways of seeing and sharing space? How can we foster, initiate, and support the systemic and attitudinal changes that create a more diverse interpreting community? Others in the arts community are recognizing the need to build networks across communities and generations, to ensure that the strides made keep moving forward. Antwaun Sargent, a director at the Gagosian Gallery in New York, praises artist Kehinde Wiley "for serving as a bridge between scenes, continents, and generations. 'The job isn't just for one of us to make it,' [Sargent] concluded. 'The job is to create a network.'"[28]

A team interpreting approach offers us a means to develop deeper conversations within and among fellow practitioners, diverse signing communities, and artists. By engaging in this practice and examining our work, and by engaging with the community, there is the potential to deepen our practice, expand our thinking and worldview, and develop stronger bonds. This ongoing engagement offers ways to participate in a larger community of Deaf artists and the arts. Through ongoing interactions, lived and shared experiences, what is often seen as a unidirectional interaction now becomes a more reciprocal exchange. This sense of belonging to a greater community becomes a pathway to living our lives more fully—more consciously—allowing ourselves to be transformed along the way, creating a restorative, inclusive, and hopefully nurturing practice.

In Closing

Jenny Toutant, chief of engagement and education officer at the Milwaukee Repertory Theater, states, "There's a dynamic and an ephemeral experience that is happening between the performers on stage and the audience members . . . There's some way that you're really connecting with people on a human level."[29]

Interpreted theatre provides opportunities for this human connection. Jane Moran Breiter, a self-professed "avid theatergoer," shared with us:

> My mother introduced me to an interpreted Broadway play when I was fifteen. It was *The Elephant Man*, and from that moment I was hooked. For the first time I was able to experience and enjoy a show and understand what was happening. I had been to shows before, but until *The*

> *Elephant Man*, I had not had the "whole" package! That night moved me then and still moves me to this day.
>
> Interpreted plays give Deaf audiences access to theater culture that we never had access to before. I love to go to the city and get lost in a play and put work and home to the side for a few hours. ASL interpreters have made that possible![30]

We hope that this book serves as a helpful guide to the art and practice of interpreting for the theatre. We have infused it with our love for the community, our love for the arts, and our beliefs that guide our way. Our wish is that you find as much love, joy, and inspiration, and support from the communities you are engaged with as we have.

Lynnette, Stephanie, and Candace

Notes

1. Excerpt from Hands On Testimonials page, accessed October 1, 2022, https://www.handson.org/media/.
2. Sonia Nieto, *Affirming Diversity: The Sociopolitical Context of Multicultural Education* (Pearson, 2017).
3. Roy Stelzer, interview with Candace Broecker Penn, November 21, 2014.
4. Zavier Sabo, interview with Lynnette Taylor, February 8, 2023.
5. Sabo, interview.
6. Ilaria Parogni and Chad Unger, "Guggenheim Offers the Poetry of Motion: Sign Language Verses," *The New York Times*, December 14, 2024, www.nytimes.com/2024/12/14/arts/design/sign-language-poems-guggenheim.html.
7. S. Ahmed, *On Being Included: Racism and Diversity in Institutional Life* (Duke University Press, 2012); Sarah Mayorga-Gallo, "The White-Centering Logic of Diversity Ideology," *American Behavioral Scientist* 63, no. 13 (April 18, 2019): 1789–809. https://doi.org/10.1177/0002764219842619.
8. Excerpt from Hands On Testimonials.
9. "Mindful Cooking with Chef Bryant Terry," *Lion's Roar*, January 19, 2025, https://www.lionsroar.com/good-food-a-qa-with-chef-bryant-terry/.
10. Corinna Sara Hill, "Without Our Deaf Clubs, Where Will We Go?" (Paper presented at American Historical Association 138th Annual Meeting, New York City, January 5, 2025).
11. Eileen Forestal, interview with Stephanie Feyne, August 21, 2022.
12. Forestal, interview.
13. Zachary Stewart, "Story of the Week: Is Theater Etiquette Dead?" *TheaterMania.com*, April 14, 2023, https://www.theatermania.com/news/story-of-the-week-is-theater-etiquette-dead_1697971/?smclient=cbdfe9cf-7115-11ed-bcae-18cf24ce3548&utm_source=salesmanago&utm_medium=email&utm_campaign=Weekly-April20th.
14. "Hear the World's Sounds," *SoundCloud*, accessed January 15, 2025, https://soundcloud.com/new-york-theatre-workshop/march-community-spotlight-an-interview-w.
15. Beth Prevor, interview with Lynnette Taylor, Candace Broecker Penn, and Stephanie Feyne, August 13, 2022.

16. Prevor, interview.
17. Dylan Geil, personal communication with Candace Broecker Penn, January 14, 2025.
18. Marie Sainvil, "Finding Meaning—The Art of Translation," *Women in Theatre Journal Online* (2022), https://witonline.org/2022/08/08/finding-meaning-in-translating-words-and-culture/.
19. Michael Paulson, "They Translated 'Hamilton' Into German. Was It Easy? Nein," *The New York Times*, September 14, 2022, https://www.nytimes.com/2022/09/14/theater/hamilton-germany.html.
20. Patrice Joyner-Creamer, interview with Candace Broecker Penn, September 9, 2022.
21. Joyner-Creamer, interview.
22. American Association of Community Theatre (AACT) offers a free online dictionary with over 1,000 definitions of theatrical terms, https://aact.org/terms.
23. A.R.T./New York "Dismantling Oppression," accessed October 10, 2022, https://www.art-newyork.org/dismantling-oppression-in-the-theatre.
24. Kenny Leon, 2021 Tony Awards Speech. As reported in the *New York Daily News*, September 27, 2021, https://www.nydailynews.com/entertainment/broadway/ny-a-soldiers-play-kenn-leon-best-revial-20210927-zahk4fdys5erfjlde47nabyg2i-story.html.
25. Alexis Soloski, "'Like a Romance': Laura Linney and Jessica Hecht's Spring Fling Onstage," *The New York Times*, April 17, 2023, https://www.nytimes.com/2023/04/17/theater/laura-linney-and-jessica-hecht-summer-1976.html.
26. Amanda Morris, "Fake Sign Language Is Spreading on TikTok. Deaf People Are Worried," *The Washington Post*, May 8, 2023, https://www.washingtonpost.com/wellness/2023/05/08/fake-sign-language-asl-tiktok/.
27. Code of Ethics, *Registry of Interpreters for the Deaf* (RID Press, 1964).
28. Julian Lucas, "How the Artist Kehinde Wiley Went from Picturing Power to Building It," *The New Yorker*, December 26, 2022, https://www.newyorker.com/magazine/2023/01/02/how-the-artist-kehinde-wiley-went-from-picturing-power-to-building-it.
29. Laura Bengs, "Research Links Increased Empathy with Live Theater Experience," *Discover Magazine*, July 8, 2022, https://www.discovermagazine.com/mind/research-links-increased-empathy-with-live-theater-experience.
30. Jane Moran Breiter, email to Candace Broecker Penn, December 19, 2022. Reprinted with permission.

ACKNOWLEDGMENTS

We are so inspired by and grateful for the many hours of conversations about this work with our friends and colleagues, who have become extended family. Over wine and coffee, in true New York fashion, we kvetched and kvelled about what performing arts interpreting is and why we do it when it takes hours of our time and pays a pittance. What we found is that the pay is in the heart, in sharing art, time, lives, and ideas—engaging in "breaking spiritual bread together" in the social fabric of our communities. Art is the place where we share our human connections. These conversations led us to write a book that celebrates the inquiry, discoveries, and path of the performance interpreting field. We do it because we cannot imagine life without art and people to share it with. The talent and heart in the community has grown over the years. We thank the ASL community of New York that has welcomed us, challenged us, supported us, shared feedback openly, and contributed to us finding a home in this world.

Special thanks to our dear friend and trailblazer, Beth Prevor, executive director of Hands On Sign Interpreted Theatre, for her dedicated and innovative leadership, for so many hours of conversations about the future of interpreted theatre, for educating theatres about authentic access and disability rights, her unwavering commitment and advocacy work to ensure that theatres are spaces that welcome everyone, and her ongoing commitment to the training of future interpreters for the theatre; Anne Tomasetti for her collaborations as an interpreter director/dramaturg/colleague extraordinaire, whose contributions over years of shows and late night discussions of craft and art cannot be underestimated; and Alexandria Wailes for sharing her artistry, passion, dramaturgical expertise, and commitment to the integrity of the work. They keep raising the bar, pushing us to explore the myriad possibilities of interpreted theatre, not only what it is, but also what it can become.

We are also very grateful to our colleagues and friends who graciously shared their time and wisdom in our interviews, enriching our practice, and offering gems for us and our readers: Jane Moran Breiter, Lisa Carling, Janis Cole, Frank Dattolo, Andrew Fisher, Craig Fogel, Eileen Forestal, Dana Fuller, Dylan Geil, Joyce Hom, Tom Humphries, Patrice Joyner-Creamer, DJ Kurs, Melissa Malzkuhn, John McGinty, Andrew Morrill, Carol Padden, Matthew Penn, Frenchetta Perez Kilpatrick, Beth Prevor, Justine Rivera, Zavier Sabio, Anne Tomasetti, and Alexandria Wailes.

There are many companies and organizations that have committed to signing audiences and supported interpreted theatre in our community for years, allowing us to continue honing our craft. We wish to acknowledge The Public Theater, Roundabout Theatre, The New Victory Theatre, Dance Theatre Workshop, Manhattan Theatre Club, and organizations including Theatre Development Fund, Hands On, and The Alliance of Resident Theatres/New York (A.R.T./NY). We offer a special thanks to A.R.T./NY for partnering with Hands On to continue offering local training for interpreting in the theatre.

We also have so much love, respect, and gratitude for our cherished New York City colleagues who along with us shared the early discoveries and developed the practice of interpreting for Broadway and Off-Broadway theatre: Alan Barwiolek, Alan Champion, Alexandria Wailes, Ann Silver, Anne Tomasetti, Beth Prevor, Bill Moody, Bruce Hlibok, Cathy Markland, Christina Trunzo Mosleh, Claude Shirts, Dana Fuller, Debbie Matthews, Eileen Forrestal, Frank Dattolo, George Garcia, George Pehlgrim, Jack Jason, Jackie Roth, Janet Harris, Janis Cole, Kathleen Taylor, Kathy Diamond, Laura Murphy, Laurie Nash, Lewis Merkin, Linda Lamitola, Margaret Ransom, Marie Tacogna, Mark Morrison, Mary Beth Miller, Mary Darragh MacLean, Michelle Banks, Molly Wilson, Nancy Frishberg, Patrice Joyner-Creamer, Phil Giambarisi, Priscilla Cooper Jones, Rick Rubin, Tavoria Kellam, Wolfe Nelson, and Vivian Berry.

New York City is fortunate to have a vibrant and growing community of theatre interpreters joining in these conversations, including, Aisha Simpson, Alaina Drake Mitchell, Alberto Medero, Alonso Rivera, Amber Martin, Amelia Hensley, Amy Meckler, Andrew Fisher, Andrew Morrill, April Cheng, Carllee James, Cheritha Saulsby, Christopher Tester, Craig Fogel, Darren (Dax) Fudenske, David Bowell, David Cañas, Dylan Geil, Diana Abeyeva, Felice Shays, Frenchetta Perez-Kilpatrick, Gabriel Silva, Gloria Vargas, Jacinda Damas, James Caverly, Janna Sweeney, Jared Lopahtin, Jason Norman, Jeniece Frazier, Jess Ames, Jillian Deaton, Jina Porter, John McGinty, Jose Gomez Jr., Josh Castille, Joyce Hom, Justine Rivera, Kailyn Aaron-Lozano, Kellie Shanahorn, Lusanne Massaro, Mark Weissglass, Miriam Rochford, Monique Sarpy, Noah Buchholz, Onudeah Nicolarakis, Saadia Kahn, Sandra Cañas, Susanne Morgan Morrow, Tolly Tollenburg, and Zavier Sabio.

We owe a debt of gratitude to Katie Lee of Gallaudet University Press for believing in our book and supporting us through the process of writing during a pandemic. We also wish to thank the readers and staff of Gallaudet University Press, whose invaluable feedback helped us to improve this book. Nods to graphic illustrator Amane Kaneko for his digital artistry and patience and to Vicky Everhardt for her close read. Kudos to entertainment attorney Noel Silverman for tilting at windmills to help us get script rights. A special heartfelt thanks for his persistence and belief in the importance of this work.

Special thanks to Christine Sun Kim and the Institute of Contemporary Art, Los Angeles (ICA LA) for generously allowing us to use her 2023 image "Bounce Back," commissioned for ICA LA, for our cover art. Her image "Bounce Back" captures the playful dynamism and responsiveness that we feel is the essence of a collaborative approach to interpreting.

While it is pro forma to thank family and friends, this book has been in the making for a long time, so we owe years of thank yous to our dear ones for hanging in there through our process as we talked about our frustrations, discoveries, and celebrations. For cleaning the house, making the dinners, doing the dishes, offering hugs and encouragement (even the many emojis) when we needed them, picking up in all the places we couldn't during this time. For our distractions, "Wait—I have to jot this thought down, be right back." All of those moments are the pulse of this book. Finally, there will no longer be the question, "Is it done yet?" And to Dennis Cokely who for years said, "FINISH THE BOOK!"—Dennis, WE DID!

INTERPRETING FOR THE THEATRE SEMINAR RECOGNITIONS

The annual Interpreting for the Theatre Seminar would not have existed without the generous support of the Theatre Development Fund (TDF). Lisa Carling (director of the TDF Theatre Accessibility Programs [TAP]) had the vision for an interpreter training program in 1991. Her support throughout the program's development into a national seminar cannot be underestimated. Running this seminar for over a decade gave us a rare opportunity to collectively explore the craft.

We cannot thank TAP Director Lisa Carling and TDF staff Laura Klein, Sarah Aziz, and Fran Polino enough for the countless hours they spent, ensuring all the details were in place for us, our staff, and participants: an Alexander Technique instructor, Lauren Schiff, twenty Deaf advisors, and up to twenty participants annually. From 1998 to 2009, the TAP administration and staff in collaboration with the Juilliard Evening Division coordinated access to two interpreted Broadway productions, housing for participants, audition materials, participant acceptance, and funding for the week-long program. We also extend our gratitude to Alan Barwiolek and Mary Beth Miller for their passionate and invaluable contributions to what became the Interpreting for the theatre seminar. None of this would have been possible without the support from the National Endowment for the Arts.

We wish to thank the Evening Division at the Juilliard School: Director Katherine Gertson, her successor Daniella La Senna, and Romel Jarin, the administrative coordinator, for their generosity in allowing us to occupy their space. Using their facilities was a privilege.

Our Deaf partners in the TDF Interpreting for the Theatre Seminar were a vital and defining part of our program. Annually, Deaf advisors worked in a variety of capacities—as screeners for entry into the program, evaluators assigned to individual students, in-class advisors, performance project advisors, panelists, one-on-one advisors, and occasional special guests. We offer gratitude to all the Deaf individuals who were involved with our program for more than twelve years and list many of them here:

Abby and Marvin Lambert, Adrian Blue, Alaina Drake Mitchell, Ann Marie "Jade" Bryant, Anne Tomasetti, Bernard Bragg, Camille Jeter-Lorello, Carole Lazorisak, Carole Moskowitz, Christopher Tester, Darlene Sarnouski, Darren (Dax) Fudenske, David Rivera, David Thacker-Bowell, Debra Cole, Dennis Smith, Eileen

Forestal, Emmanuel von Schack, Emmy Azodeh, Frank Dattolo, George Garcia, George Pehlgrim, Guthrie Nutter, Jackie Roth, Janna Sweeney, Jane Moran Breiter, Jason Norman, Joel Goldfarb, Joyce Houghton, Lalita Chaitoo, Larry Cohen, Lauren Ridloff, Lewis Merkin, Linda Bove, Liza Offreda, Maleni Chaitoo, Manny Hernandez, Maureen Woods, Michael Kaufer, Michael Lamitola, Monique Holt, Patrice Joyner-Creamer, Rachel Naiman, Regan Thibodeau, Robert DeMayo, Robin Resnick, Samuel Caraballo, Sandra Rivera, Stephanie Sforza, Sue Decker, Tom Samuels, Warren King, and students Idy Fass, Jeremy Black, Nicole Perkins, and Yanni Cema. And so many more.

We also thank the producers, companies, and theatre staff of the shows who offered opportunities to our students: *Les Misérables* (1998), *Miss Saigon* (1999), *Jekyll and Hyde* (2000), *Rent* (2001), *42nd Street* (2002), *Thoroughly Modern Millie* (2003), *Phantom of the Opera* (2004), *La Cage Aux Folles* (2005), *The Producers* (2006), *Company* (2007), *Hairspray* (2008), and *The Lion King* (2009). Each year participants also attended an additional interpreted Broadway show, which demonstrated our approach. We appreciate all the companies that allowed our presence in the theatre.

Last and most certainly not least, we thank the extremely talented pool of NYC interpreters who graciously teamed with selected seminar participants for these Broadway productions. We are grateful for their kindness and support.

REFERENCES

Abenchuchan, Alex. "Interview with Wild Zappers Founding Members." *Daily Moth.* February 24, 2021. https://www.dailymoth.com/blog/interview-with-wild-zappers-founding-members.

Ahmed, S. *On Being Included: Racism and Diversity in Institutional Life.* Duke University Press, 2012.

Alter, Alexandra. "Shining a Spotlight on the Art of Translation." *The New York Times*, February 11, 2022. https://www.nytimes.com/2022/02/11/books/literary-translation-translators-jennifer-croft.html.

American Association of Community Theatre. "Terms." https://aact.org/terms.

Anderson, Brittany. "Gallaudet University Envisions a Digital Sign Languages Library for Every Deaf Child." *Global Book Alliance.* August 22, 2019. https://www.globalbookalliance.org/news-views/gallaudet-university-envisions-a-digital-sign-languages-library-for-every-deaf-child.

The Allen Ginsberg Project. "The Heart of the Hydrogen Jukebox—ASL." February 5, 2020. https://allenginsberg.org/2013/10/the-heart-of-the-hydrogen-jukebox-asl/.

A.R.T./New York. "Dismantling Oppression." Accessed April 10, 2025. https://www.art-newyork.org/dismantling-oppression-in-the-theatre.

A.R.T./New York. "Images." Accessed April 15, 2025. https://www.art-newyork.org/.

A.R.T./New York. "Spotlight on DASLs: The Role of Directors of Artistic Sign Language." June 2, 2021. Youtube. 1:21:19. https://www.youtube.com/watch?v=pGDPLpEvcY4&t=1241s.

A.R.T./New York. "Zoom In: Best Practices for ASL Interpretation in Virtual Theatre." YouTube. June 1, 2021. 1:28/16. https://www.youtube.com/watch?v=SVND3xjhXSI.

"ASL Shakespeare." Accessed January 1, 2025. http://aslshakespeare.org.

Doyle, John, dir. *Assassins, Journey Through the Dark Side of the American Dream.* Classic Stage Company. https://www.classicstage.org/show-archive/assassins.

Bahan, Ben, and Sam Supalla. *ASL Literature Series: Bird of a Different Feather and For a Decent Living.* DawnSignPress, 1994.

Bailey, Janet. "Special Certificate: Performing Arts, An RID History Lesson." *RID Views*, May 1998.

Baldwin, Stephen C. *Pictures in the Air: The Story of the National Theatre of the Deaf.* Gallaudet University Press, 1993.

Balk, Tim. "Kenny Leon 2021 Tony Award Speech." *New York Daily News*, September 27, 2021. https://www.nydailynews.com/entertainment/broadway/ny-a-soldiers-play-kenn-leon-best-revial-20210927-zahk4fdys5erfjlde47nabyg2i-story.html.

Beaufort, John. "Theater in Sign Language—The Drama Is Still There." *Christian Science Monitor*, August 12, 1981. https://www.csmonitor.com/1981/0812/081201.html.

Beethoven's Nightmare. http://www.beethovensnightmare.com.

Bell, Sharon Masingale. "In the Shadow of the Father Tongue: On Translating the Masks in J.-S. Alexis." In *Between Languages and Cultures: Translation and Cross-Cultural Texts*, ed. Anuradha Dingwaney and Carol Maier, 66–89. University of Pittsburgh Press, 1995.

Bengs, Laura. "Research Links Increased Empathy with Live Theater Experience." *Discover Magazine*, July 8, 2022. https://www.discovermagazine.com/mind/research-links-increased-empathy-with-live-theater-experience.

Berklee. "Dramaturg." Accessed April 10, 2025. https:/www.berklee.edu/careers/roles/dramaturg/.

Briggs, Kate. *This Little Art*. Fitzcarraldo Editions, 2017.

Britannica. "National Theatre of the Deaf." https://www.britannica.com/topic/National-Theatre-of-the-Deaf/.

Bucholtz, Mary, and Kira Hall. "Embodied Sociolinguistics." In *Sociolinguistics: Theoretical Debates*, ed. Nikolas Coupland, 173–97. Cambridge University Press, 2016.

Butler, Judith. *Who's Afraid of Gender*. Farrar, Straus and Giroux, 2024.

Butler, Judith, and Stephanie Berbec. "We Are Worldless Without One Another: An Interview with Judith Butler." *The Other Journal*, 27 (2017). https://theotherjournal.com/2017/06/worldless-without-one-another-interview-judith-butler/.

Canning, Charlotte. "Editorial: Looking Ahead." *Theatre Research International* 38, no. 1 (2013): 1–4.

Chester, Mark. "In My Mind's Eye—Deaf Awareness." *Falmouth Wicked*. https://www.wickedlocal.com/story/archive/2010/10/18/in-my-mind-s-eye/39517458007/.

Cohen, Susan. "Spotlight: Hands On's Beth Prevor Connects the Deaf and Theater Communities in NYC." *6stf.com*. November 13, 2015. https://www.6sqft.com/spotlight-hands-ons-beth-prevor-connects-the-deaf-and-theater-communities-in-nyc/.

Cole, Janis. "Deaf Translators: What Are They Thinking?" *Journal of Interpretation* 28, no. 1 (2020): 3.

"Community Integration." ADA.gov. Accessed April 10, 2025. https://www.ada.gov/topics/community-integration/.

Cone, Kitty. "Short History of the 504 Sit-In." *Disability Rights Education and Defense Fund*. April 4, 2013. http://dredf.org/504-sit-in-20th-anniversary/short-history-of-the-504-sit-in/.

Course Hero. "Titus Andronicus | Character Map." March 22, 2018. https://www.coursehero.com/lit/Titus-Andronicus/character-map/.

Dameron, Jules. "Jules Dameron Directed On Sesame Street." YouTube playlist. https://www.youtube.com/playlist?list=PLx1wHz1f-8J8Mk6C-bK76YaRdl26daKvU.

"David Henry Hwang Discusses His Play *Yellow Face*, Now on Broadway." *Columbia News*, December 6, 2024. https://news.columbia.edu/news/david-henry-hwang-discusses-his-play-yellow-face-now-broadway.

Deaf History. "Deaf History—Europe—1880: The Milan Conference." Accessed April 10, 2025. https://deafhistory.eu/index.php/component/zoo/item/1880/.

Deaf Media. "Deaf Media Programs." Accessed April 10, 2025. http://www.Deafmedia.org/programs/programs.htm.

Deaf Theatre. "Shanny Mow." https://deaf-theatre.com/profiles/shanny-mow/.

"Deaf Women United 'Empowerment Is Contagious—When We Light Each Other's Path, We Create a Brighter Future for All." *Deaf Women United*, Facebook, November 25, 2024. www.facebook.com/story.php?story_fbid=971985191727473&id=100067480027433&_rdr.

Dunning, Jennifer. "Dance Musign Group." *The New York Times*. August 28, 1983. http://www.nytimes.com/1983/08/28/arts/dance-musign-group.html.

Dunning, Jennifer. "Out-of-Town Dancers Welcomed Anew." *The New York Times*, August 21, 1983. https://www.nytimes.com/1983/08/21/arts/out-of-town-dancers-welcomed-anew.html.

Ehrlich, Susan, and Tanya Romaniuk. "Discourse Analysis." In *Research Methods in Linguistics*, ed. Rovert J. Podesva and Sharma Devyani, 466–99. Cambridge University Press, 2013.

Encyclopedia. "Michelle Banks." https://www.encyclopedia.com/education/news-wires-white-papers-and-books/banks-michelle.

Evans, Greg. "'Purlie Victorious' Broadway Review: Leslie Odom Jr. Keeps Ossie Davis' Groundbreaking Comedy True to Its Title." *Deadline*. September 27, 2023. https://deadline.com/2023/09/purlie-victorious-broadway-review-1235555904/.

Forestal, Eileen, and Janis Cole. "Translation: Socio-Cultural Space." Workshop at the 2019 RID Biennial Conference, Providence, RI, July 7–11, 2019.

Frishberg, Nancy. *Interpreting: An Introduction*. Rev. ed. Registry of Interpreters for the Deaf, 2015.

Goodman, Jane E. *Encounters in Translation: How Et-Teffeh Became Apples*. Indiana University Press, 2020.

Grim, Andrew. "Sitting-In for Disability Rights: The Section 504 Protests of the 1970s." National Museum of American History. July 8, 2015. https://americanhistory.si.edu/blog/sitting-disability-rights-section-504-protests-1970s.

Hall, Stuart. *Cultural Studies 1983: A Theoretical History*. Duke University Press, 2016.

Hands On. "Videos." Accessed October 1, 2022. https://www.handson.org/media/.

Hatim, Basil, and Ian Mason. *The Translator as Communicator*. Routledge, 1997.

The HeART of Deaf Culture. "Gilbert Eastman Discusses 'Sign Me Alice.'" Youtube. 2:12. https://www.youtube.com/watch?v=U4FOLRBu3OI.

The HeART of Deaf Culture. "Overview." Accessed April 15, 2025. https://heartdeaf.com/overview/.

Heumann, Judy. *Being Heumann: An Unrepentant Memoir of a Disability Rights Activist*. Beacon Press, 2020.

Hill, Corinna Sara. "Without Our Deaf Clubs, Where Will We Go?" Paper presented at American Historical Association 138th Annual Meeting, New York, NY, January 5, 2025.

Hill, Joseph Christopher. *Language Attitudes in the American Deaf Community*. Gallaudet University Press, 2012.

Holcomb, Thomas K. *Introduction to American Deaf Culture*. Oxford University Press, 2012.

Horowitz, Simi. "The Rest Is Silence: How Mute Moments Move Audiences." *Backstage*. November 4, 2019. https://www.backstage.com/magazine/article/rest-silence-mute-moments-move-audiences-20453/.

Humphries, Thomas K. "Communicating Across Cultures (Deaf-Hearing) and Language Learning." PhD diss., Union Institute and University, 1977.

Internet Broadway Database. "*Children of a Lesser God* Broadway Awards." Accessed April 10, 2025. https://www.ibdb.com/broadway-production/children-of-a-lesser-god-3694#Awards.

Johnston, David, ed. *Stages of Translation: Essays and Interviews*. Oberon Books, 1994.

"Juilliard Interpreter Training." Dave Boles Blog, November 2, 2002. https://bolesblogs.com/2002/11/02/juilliard-interpreter-training/.

Kaufman, Jane. "Bridging the Sound Barrier." *Canvas*. http://canvascle.com/signstage/.

Kennedy Center. "Deaf Enlightenment and Arts Festival | Kennedy Center." Accessed April 10, 2025. https://www.kennedy-center.org/whats-on/millennium-stage/2021/september/deaf-culture-arts-festival/.

Kolb, Rachel, and Timothy Y. Loh. "How Deaf and Hearing Friends Co-Navigate the World." In *Sapiens*, August 17, 2022. https://www.sapiens.org/language/friendterpreting/.

Lane, Harlan. *The Mask of Benevolence: Disabling the Deaf Community*. DawnSignPress, 1999.

Lang, Brent. "Despite Success of 'CODA,' Study Finds Deaf Community 'Rarely' or 'Never' Sees Itself Reflected on Screen." *Variety*, November 22, 2022. https://variety.com/2022/film/news/coda-study-nrg-deaf-representation-movies-tv-1235439108/.

Larson, Mildred. *Meaning-Based Translation: A Guide to Cross-Language Equivalence*. University Press of America, 1998.

Lucas, Julian. "How the Artist Kehinde Wiley Went From Picturing Power to Building It." *The New Yorker*, December 26, 2022. https://www.newyorker.com/magazine/2023/01/02/how-the-artist-kehinde-wiley-went-from-picturing-power-to-building-it.

Lundy, Katia. "TDF-TAPS Broadway Shows." *Playbill*, August 29, 1996. https://playbill.com/article/tdf-taps-broadway-shows-com-68283.

"Malz-Velez Jabberwocky." Facebook. https://www.facebook.com/watch/?v=1737130106316087.

Marinetti, Cristina. "Translation and Theatre: From Performance to Performativity." *Target International Journal of Translation Studies* 25, no. 3 (2013): 307–20.

Mayorga-Gallo, Sarah. "The White-Centering Logic of Diversity Ideology." *American Behavioral Scientist* 63, no. 13 (April 18, 2019): 1789–1809. https://doi.org/10.1177/0002764219842619.

Meisner, Sanford, and Dennis Longwell. *Sanford Meisner on Acting*. Vintage Books, 1987.

The Meisner Technique Studio. "Meisner Technique | the Meisner Technique Studio," January 9, 2019. https://themeisnertechniquestudio.com/meisner-technique/.

Merriam-Webster Dictionary. "Audism." https://www.merriam-webster.com/dictionary/audism.

Metzger, Melanie. *Sign Language Interpreting: Deconstructing the Myth of Neutrality*. Gallaudet University Press, 1999.

Miller, Betty. "If My Hands Could Speak. Betty Miller Art Pioneer." September 6, 2011. https://ifmyhandscouldspeak.wordpress.com/2011/09/06/betty-g-miller-art-pioneer/.

Monet and Chardonnay. "Famous Artist Quotes." Accessed April 10, 2025. https://www.monetandchardonnay.events/post/famous-artists-quotes.

Morris, Amanda. "Fake Sign Language Is Spreading on TikTok. Deaf People Are Worried." *Washington Post*, May 8, 2023. https://www.washingtonpost.com/wellness/2023/05/08/fake-sign-language-asl-tiktok/.

Morris, Bonnie J. "How Should We Archive the Soundtrack to 1970s Feminism?" *Smithsonian Magazine*, March 30, 2018. https://www.smithsonianmag.com/arts-culture/how-should-we-archive-soundtrack-1970s-feminism-180968637/.

Morrison, Annie. *The Moment of Speech: Creative Articulation for Actors*. Methuen Drama, 2021.

"Moving Pictures, Moving Hands: The Story of Ernest Marshall." April 17, 2020. Gallaudet University. https://media.gallaudet.edu/media/Moving+Pictures%2C+Moving+HandsA++The+Sotry+of+Ernest+Marshall/1_9enr1u7k.

Museum of Deaf. "DE'VIA: Deaf View/Image Art." Accessed April 10, 2025. https://www.museumofdeaf.org/de-via.

Napier, Jemina. "Interpreting Omissions: A New Perspective." *Interpreting* 6, no. 2 (2004): 117–142. https://doi.org/10.1075/intp.6.2.02nap.

Napier, Jemina. *Linguistic Coping Strategies in Sign Language Interpreting*. Gallaudet University Press, 2016.

The National Academy for Television Arts and Sciences. "1978/1979 San Francisco/Northern California Awards." News release. https://emmysf.tv/files/2015/11/Emmy79PressRelease.pdf.

"National Association of the Deaf—NAD." December 28, 2010. https://www.nad.org/2010/12/28/historic-nad-film-selected-for-preservation-by-library-of-congress/.

National Association of the Deaf. "NBDA, NAD, RID Statement on Culturally Appropriate Interpreters." News release. November 22, 2022. https://www.nad.org/2022/11/22/nbda-nad-rid-statement-on-culturally-appropriate-interpreters/

National Research Group and Deaf West Theatre. "Deaf Representation." November 2022. https://downloads.ctfassets.net/4ivt4uy3jinr/6TDIhMpZdL9iILN2CcNnbn/3e601d88e31a0c00c7c3487d2e72497c/Deaf_Representation_Report.pdf.

National Research Group and Deaf West Theatre. "Spotlight on Deaf Representation: A Roundtable Discussion." YouTube. April 14, 2023. https://www.youtube.com/watch?v=bjN4salwtUM.

National Theatre of the Deaf. "National Theatre of the Deaf History." 2014. https://old.ntd.org/ntd_history.html.

Neisser, Arden. *The Other Side of Silence: Sign Language and the Deaf Community in America*. Gallaudet University Press, 1983.

New York Deaf Theatre. "Who We Are." https://newyorkdeaftheatre.org/about.

New York Theatre Workshop. "Hear the World's Sounds." SoundCloud. Accessed January 15, 2025. https://soundcloud.com/new-york-theatre-workshop/march-community-spotlight-an-interview-w.

Nieto, Sonia. *Affirming Diversity: The Sociopolitical Context of Multicultural Education*. Pearson, 2017.

Padden, Carol, and Tom Humphries. *Deaf in America: Voices from a Culture*. Harvard University Press, 1990.

Parachuk, Tara. "The Lion King Live Action Cast – Diversity in Voice Over. *Voices*, August 27, 2019. https://www.voices.com/blog/the-lion-king-diversity-in-voice-over/.

Parogni, Ilaria. "How These Sign Language Experts Are Bringing More Diversity to Theater." *The New York Times*, January 7, 2023. Sec. Arts. https://www.nytimes.com/2023/01/07/arts/sign-language-experts-diversity-theater.html.

Parogni, Ilaria. "What Matters in a Name Sign?" *The New York Times*, July 16, 2021. https://www.nytimes.com/interactive/2021/07/16/arts/kamala-harris-name-sign-language.html.

Paulson, Michael. "They Translated 'Hamilton' Into German. Was It Easy? Nein." *The New York Times*, September 14, 2022. https://www.nytimes.com/2022/09/14/theater/hamilton-germany.html.

Pennycook, Alastair. "Performativity and Language Studies." *Critical Inquiry in Language Studies* 1, no. 1 (2004): 1–19, P. 7. https://doi.org/10.1207/s15427595cils0101_1.

Project for Public Spaces. "Ray Oldenburg." December 31, 2008. https://www.pps.org/article/roldenburg.

Registry of Interpreters for the Deaf. *RID Code of Ethics*. RID Press, 1964.

Rich, Adrienne. "The Burning of Paper Instead of Children." Poetry Society. https://poetrysociety.org/poems/the-burning-of-paper-instead-of-children.

Richards, I. A. *Towards a Theory of Translation*. American Anthropological Association, University of Chicago Press, 1953.

Roundabout Theatre Company. "Cabaret Sign Interpreted Performance." BroadwayWorld.com. https://www.broadwayworld.com/article/Cabaret-Sign-Interpreted-Performance-20140620.

Rocks, Siobhán. "The Theatre Sign Language Interpreter and the Competing Visual Narrative: The Translation and Interpretation of Theatrical Texts to British Sign Language." In *Staging and Performing Translation: Text and Theatre Practice*, ed. Roger Baines, Cristina Marinetti, and Manuela Perteghella, 72–86. Palgrave Macmillan, 2011.

Roundabout Theatre. "A Soldier's Play: An Interview with Director Kenny Leon." January 15, 2020. https://www.roundabouttheatre.org/about/our-blog/an-interview-with-director-kenny-leon/.

Roy, Cynthia. *Interpreting as a Discourse Process*. Oxford University Press, 1999.

Sainvil, Marie. "Finding Meaning—The Art of Translation." *Women in Theatre Journal Online*. https://witonline.org/2022/08/08/finding-meaning-in-translating-words-and-culture/.

San Francisco Public Library. "Deaf Theatre." Accessed April 10, 2025. https://sfpl.org/locations/main-library/deaf-services/deaf-theatre.

San Francisco State University. "Virtual Tour | Patient No More," n.d. Accessed December 8, 2024. https://longmoreinstitute.sfsu.edu/patient-no-more/virtual-tour.

Schiffrin, Deborah. *Approaches to Discourse*. Blackwell, 1994.

Searls, Damion. *The Philosophy of Translation*. Yale University Press, 2024.

Seleskovitch, Danika. *Interpreting for International Conferences*, 2nd rev. ed. Pen and Booth, 1994.

SemDom. "Semantic Domain." https://semdom.org/description.

Shapiro, Samantha M. "Shirley Childress Johnson." *The New York Times*, December 18, 2017. https://www.nytimes.com/interactive/2017/12/28/magazine/the-lives-they-lived-shirley-childress.html.

Simmons, Paul. "Spotlight On: Dr. Frank Bowe—The Father of 504." Rocky Mountain ADA, September 29, 2020. https://rockymountainada.org/news/blog/spotlight-dr-frank-bowe-father-504.

Soloski, Alexis. "Like a Romance: Laura Linney and Jessica Hecht's Spring Fling Onstage." *The New York Times*, April 17, 2023.

Spivak, Gayatri Chakravaorty. 2022. *Living Translation*. Edited by Emily Apter, Avishek Ganguly, Mauro Pala, and Surya Parekh. Seagull Books.

Stein, Ken. 20th Anniversary Victorious 504 Sit-In for Disability Civil Rights Celebration Commemoration Committee. 1997.

Stewart, Mariah. "Deaf and Hard of Hearing Community Suffers from Dearth of Diverse Interpreters." *Insight into Diversity*, October 16, 2020. https://insightintoacademia.com/deaf-and-hard-of-hearing-community-suffers-from-dearth-of-diverse-interpreters/

Stewart, Zachary. "Story of the Week: Is Theater Etiquette Dead?", TheaterMania.com, April 14, 2023. https://www.theatermania.com/news/story-of-the-week-is-theater-etiquette-dead_1697971/?smclient=cbdfe9cf-7115-11ed-bcae-18cf24ce3548&utm_source=salesmanago&utm_medium=email&utm_campaign=Weekly-April20th.

Suggs, Trudy. "Deaf Disempowerment and Today's Interpreter." StreetLeverage, 2012. https://streetleverage.com/live_presentations/deaf-disempowerment-and-todays-interpreter/.

Sunpride Foundation. "Catherine Opie | The Community of Difference." November 30, 2021. https://sunpride.hk/catherine-opie-community-difference/.

Sutton-Spence, Rachel. "Overview of Sign Language Poetry." European Cultural Heritage Online (ECHO). https://variety.com/2023/film/news/deaf-representation-hollywood-animation-video-games-kids-tv-1235582543/.

Swarthmore College. "Commencement 2016: Carol Padden." YouTube, May 30, 2016. https://www.youtube.com/watch?v=gJQJDlfs1YI.

Tangcay, Jazz. "Deaf Representation Is Improving in Film and TV, but Falls Short in Video Games, Animation and Kids TV." *Variety*, April 14, 2023. https://variety.com/2023/film/news/deaf-representation-hollywood-animation-video-games-kids-tv-1235582543/.

Taylor, Lynnette, dir. *The Treasure: Poems by Ella Mae Lentz*. DVD. DawnSignPress, 1997.

TDF Dictionary. "Cheating Out." Accessed April 10, 2025. https://www.tdf.org/on-stage/theatre-dictionary/search-by-letter/cheating-out/.

Terry, Bryant. "Mindful Cooking with Chef Bryant Terry." *Lion's Roar*, January 7, 2025. https://www.lionsroar.com/good-food-a-qa-with-chef-bryant-terry/.

"Theatre Development Fund." http://www.tdf.org/TDF_Landingpage.aspx?id=109.

Theatre Development Fund. "When Theatre Meets Sign Language" YouTube, September 27, 2010. https://www.youtube.com/watch?v=wUK_OUxN-1Q.

Tracy, Marc. "Who Can Play the King? Questions of Representation Fuel Casting Debates." *The New York Times*, July 28, 2022. https://www.nytimes.com/2022/07/28/theater/richard-iii-casting-debates.html.

Valli, Clayton. "Poetics of American Sign Language Poetry." PhD diss., Union Institute, 1993.

Venuti, Lawrence. *The Translator's Invisibility*. Routledge, 1995.

Visionaries of the Creative Arts. "Play Production Spring 2024." *A Not So Quiet Nocturne*, VOCARTS.Org. https://www.vocarts.org/production2023-2024/anotsoquietnocturne.

"Visual Vernacular A Global Phenomenon." *Connecticut Deaf Theatre* (blog), September 23, 2022. https://www.conndeaftheatre.org/posts/visual-vernacular-a-global-phenomenon.

VL2 Storybook Apps. "Evon Discovers Black Pride." Accessed April 10, 2025. https://vl2storybookapps.com/evon-discovers-black-pride.

Voyage Chicago. "Meet Levi Holloway of Neverbird Project." April 3, 2018. http://voyagechicago.com/interview/meet-levi-holloway-neverbird-project-na/.

Wadensjö, Cecilia. *Interpreting as Interaction*. Routledge, 1998.

We See You White American Theatre. "Principles for Building Anti-Racist Theatre Systems." https://www.weseeyouwat.com/.

West Oyedele, Erica. "Persistence of African-American/Black Signed Language Interpreters in the United States: The Importance of Culture and Capital." Thesis, Western Oregon University, 2015.

Williams, Janaya. "Deaf Actors Demand Equal Stage Time." *WYNC*, November 7, 2009. https://www.wnyc.org/story/1382-deaf-actors-demand-equal-stage-time/.

Wilson, Molly, and Stephanie Clark. "The Open Process Interpreting Mode: The Power of Language," StreetLeverage, 2018. https://streetleverage.com/live_presentations/the-open-process-interpreting-model-the-power-of-language/.

Previous Works on Theatre Interpretation

Ganz Horwitz, Miriam. "Demands and Strategies of Interpreting a Theatrical Performance into American Sign Language." *Journal of Interpretation* 23, no. 1 (2014): Article 4.

Gebron, Julie. *Sign the Speech: An Introduction to Theatrical Interpreting.* Butte Publications, 1996.

Llewellyn-Jones, Peter. "Interpreting Shakespeare's Plays into British Sign Language." In *Shakespeare and the Language of Translation*, ed. Ton Hoenselaars, 199–216. Arden Shakespeare, 2004.

MacDougall, Danny. "Sign Language Interpreter Space: A Phenomenological Case Study of Interpreted Theatre." PhD diss. Heriot-Watt University, 2021.

Mielke, Kaitlyn. "The Song That Goes Like This: The Art of Theatrical Sign Language." MAThesis. University of Minnesota, 2014.

Richardson, Michael. "To Be or Not to Be? Towards a Performance Model of Interpreting." In *Solving the Riddle of Interpreting Quality: Dimensions and Challenges*, ed. Rafael Barranco-Droege, 59–86. Editorial Comares, 2020.

"Performing Arts Interpreting." *RID Views.* Special Issue.

Rocks, Siobhán. "The Theatre Sign Language Interpreter and the Competing Visual Narrative: The Translation and Interpretation of Theatrical Texts to British Sign Language." In *Staging and Performing Translation: Text and Theatre Practice*, ed. R. Baines, C. Marinetti, and M. Perteghella, 72–86. Palgrave Macmillan, 2011.

Snyder, Lyndsey D. "Sawing the Air Thus: American Sign Language Translations of Shakespeare and the Echoes of Rhetorical Gesture." PhD diss., University of Maryland, 2009.

"Terptheatre." *TerpTheatre.* https://terptheatre.org/.

504 Sit-In Personal Recollections

Disability History. "Disability Social History Project: The 504 Protests and the Black Panther Party." December 19, 2021. https://disabilityhistory.org/2021/12/19/the-504-protests-and-the-black-panther-party/.

Hicks, Ashley J., and Lynnette Taylor. "Warrior Love." Produced by David E. Shane. *What's Off,* July 18, 2023. Podcast, MP3 audio. 57:47. https://www.art-newyork.org/.

Landes, David. "Political Organizer for Disability Rights, 1970s–1990s and Strategist for Section 504 Demonstrations, 1977: An Interview with Kitty Cone." *Online Archive of California.* https://oac.cdlib.org/ark:/13030/kt1w1001mt/.

McCormick, Erin. "'Disability Is Not a Tragedy': The Remarkable Life of Activist and Rebel Hale Zukas." *The Guardian.* January 8, 2023. https://www.theguardian.com/society/2023/jan/08/disability-rights-warrior-hale-zukas-life.

San Francisco State University. "Disability Activist Joanne Juarigi on the 504 Protests and the Unique Implications on the Deaf Community." Paul K. Longmore Institute on Disability Collection. https://diva.sfsu.edu/collections/longmoreinstitute/bundles/230604.

San Francisco State University. "Disability Activist Judy Heumann on Being One of the Key Leaders of the Section 504 Protest." Paul K. Longmore Institute on Disability Collection. https://diva.sfsu.edu/collections/longmoreinstitute/bundles/230641.

San Francisco State University. "Disability Activists and Activism." Paul K. Longmore Institute on Disability Collection. https://diva.sfsu.edu/collections/longmoreinstitute.

San Francisco State University. "Disability Rights Activist Eddie Jauregui Recalls His Involvement in the 1977 Section 504 Occupation as a Deaf Protester." Paul K. Longmore Institute on Disability Collection. https://diva.sfsu.edu/collections/longmoreinstitute/bundles/230609.

San Francisco State University. "Joe Quinn on His Experience at the 504 Sit-In as a Deaf Interpreter and Protester." Paul K. Longmore Institute on Disability Collection. https://diva.sfsu.edu/collections/longmoreinstitute/bundles/230603.

San Francisco State University. "Lynnette Taylor on Her Experience as an Interpreter at the Section 504 Protests." Paul K. Longmore Institute on Disability Collection. https://diva.sfsu.edu/collections/longmoreinstitute/bundles/231044

Shoot, Britta. "The 1977 Disability Rights Protest That Broke Records and Changed Laws." *Atlas Obscura*. November 9, 2017. https://www.atlasobscura.com/articles/504-sit-in-san-francisco-1977-disability-rights-advocacy.

INDEX

Page numbers in italics *refer to figures.*